The Middle Ages

**Recent Titles in
Historical Facts and Fictions**

The Middle Ages

Facts and Fictions

Winston Black

Historical Facts and Fictions

ABC-CLIO®

An Imprint of ABC-CLIO, LLC

Santa Barbara, California • Denver, Colorado

Library of Congress Cataloging-in-Publication Data

Names: Black, Winston E., 1977– author.
Title: The Middle Ages : facts and fictions / Winston Black.
Description: Santa Barbara, California : ABC-CLIO, 2019. | Series: Historical facts and fictions | Includes bibliographical references and index.
Identifiers: LCCN 2019011697 (print) | LCCN 2019013002 (ebook) | ISBN 9781440862328 (eBook) | ISBN 9781440862311 (hardcopy : alk. paper)
Subjects: LCSH: Middle Ages. | Civilization, Medieval. | History—Errors, inventions, etc.
Classification: LCC D117 (ebook) | LCC D117 .B49 2019 (print) | DDC 940.1—dc23
LC record available at https://lccn.loc.gov/2019011697

ISBN: 978-1-4408-6231-1 (print)
       978-1-4408-6232-8 (ebook)

23 22 21 20 19 1 2 3 4 5

This book is also available as an eBook.

ABC-CLIO
An Imprint of ABC-CLIO, LLC

ABC-CLIO, LLC
147 Castilian Drive
Santa Barbara, California 93117
www.abc-clio.com

This book is printed on acid-free paper ∞

Manufactured in the United States of America

Every reasonable effort has been made to trace the owners of copyright materials in this book, but in some instances this has proven impossible. The editors and publishers will be glad to receive information leading to more complete acknowledgments in subsequent printings of the book and in the meantime extend their apologies for any omissions.

Contents

Preface

People invent fictions about every period of history as they reshape the past to their own liking. Perhaps no other historical era has been misunderstood and reinvented as much as the Middle Ages. In the millennium between the fall of the Western Roman Empire in 476 and the first Atlantic voyage of Columbus in 1492 (or you can choose other events around 500 and 1500 CE), you can find a vast range of cultures, ideas, individuals, or events that have been used to represent the essence of the "Middle Ages." Attila the Hun, Joan of Arc, Charlemagne, or Dante: each of these people has been used to define "medieval." Likewise, barbarians or knights in shining armor, filthy hovels or towering cathedrals, brutal tyrants or parliamentary governments, and the violence of the Crusades or the pacifism of St. Francis can legitimately evoke key aspects of the Middle Ages. The historical problems begin and fictions are created when authors, teachers, journalists, and scholars choose just one of these medieval images to represent the entire medieval millennium.

This book introduces eleven fictions about the European Middle Ages that have developed and persisted throughout the last two centuries or more. Others could have been included, especially if we expanded "medieval" to include the premodern Islamic world and other cultures contemporary with medieval Europe. Entire books have been written to challenge errors about the history of the Crusades or the place of women in the Middle Ages, issues that are covered here in specific cases. The eleven fictions were chosen to cover the entire Middle Ages and to touch on issues big and small, from specific myths about individuals to broad fictions about the very meaning of "medieval." Most of these fictions are extensions of the "big myth" introduced in the first chapter—namely, that the Middle Ages were nothing but the "Dark Ages." Imagining the medieval era as a prolonged "Dark Age" helps preserve a sense of continual progress in history: the Renaissance improved on the Dark Ages, the Enlightenment on the Renaissance, the modern era on the Enlightenment, and so on. Acknowledging that some parts of the Middle Ages might have been "better" than periods that came afterward can be difficult for many people to accept. What does that say about our own twenty-first century? Could later historians see it as a step backward from the twentieth?

Each chapter addresses a commonly held misconception about the Middle Ages, first summarizing the core elements of the fiction. After that are two longer sections: first, on how the fiction developed, became popular, and spread; and second, on how we can correct the misconceptions. Both sections are accompanied by primary sources, documents, and images from the past, which provide evidence for the fiction and the fact. Some of these sources are medieval, many of them are from the nineteenth century (a period that produced many of our medieval myths), and some even come from books and websites of the twentieth and twenty-first centuries as we trace the authors who perpetuate these fictions and the scholars who try to correct them.

I would like to thank George Butler of ABC-CLIO, who invited me to write this book, Cindy Crumrine for her careful copyediting, and my medieval history students at Clark University, who have been eager to share their own preconceptions about the Middle Ages, both fictional and factual.

Winston Black
Worcester, Massachusetts
December 2018

Introduction

The fact is that everyone has his own ideas, usually corrupt, of the
Middle Ages.
Umberto Eco, *Reflections on "The Name of the Rose"* (1985)

The Middle Ages are all around us in the modern world, once you start
looking: not the historical Middle Ages but "medieval" as a metaphor for
a time and a culture that is related to ours but is clearly not now. This
metaphorical Middle Ages is partly shaped by genuine medieval history,
but it shapes, in turn, how we study the medieval past. It provides a style,
a look, or a setting in books, movies, television shows, and video games
that is readily understood. *The Lord of the Rings, The Chronicles of Nar-
nia, Dungeons & Dragons, Game of Thrones, Harry Potter, Assassin's Creed,
The Legend of Zelda, Warcraft*, and even *Star Wars* draw on stereotypically
"medieval" ideas and imagery and frequently encourage people to learn
more about the real Middle Ages.

Long before these modern creations, popular views of the Middle Ages
were shaped in the eighteenth and nineteenth centuries by stories of Robin
Hood and King Arthur, the chivalric novels of Walter Scott, and the art
and literature of the Gothic Revival and Pre-Raphaelites. Their fanciful
creations continue to shape our expectations of a properly "medieval"
story or history: castles, kings and queens, knights on horseback, feudalism, downtrodden peasants, primitive technology, widespread disease
and plague, magic and superstition. A typical medieval setting is usually a

fantasy vision of Western Europe (and usually just England and France), including only white people as central and good, only men as the leaders and women as helpless and in need of rescue, and the central religion reflecting Christianity or a pre-Christian northern polytheism (such as Thor, Odin, and company). In the last few decades, the Middle Ages in popular culture have become synonymous with graphic violence, including brutal warfare, rape, torture, widespread censorship, and the slaughter of non-European or non-Christian groups. Viewers know what to expect when they see that Mel Gibson's *Braveheart* (1995) received an "R" rating "for brutal medieval warfare." More recently, the *Game of Thrones* novels and series, although taking place in a fictional and fantastical land, reinforce most of these negative stereotypes about a "medieval" past.

The depiction of the Middle Ages in popular culture, and the study of that depiction, is known as "medievalism." It is a culturally constructed "medieval," which shapes our understanding of the real Middle Ages, even for serious students of history. Modern medievalism is frequently dated to the year 1816, when Thomas Malory's *Le Morte d'Arthur* ("The Death of Arthur"), first published in 1485, was reprinted in England to great acclaim. This work, and other medieval texts rediscovered around that time, encouraged a new scholarly study of medieval history and the appropriation of elements of medieval culture, which persists to this day. Many aspects of medievalism could be considered "wrong" by the standards of professional history, but it misses the point simply to describe what is "wrong" or "right" in popular medievalism. We need to understand why medieval fictions developed, when they first appeared (whether during the Middle Ages themselves, or in the early modern era, or only in the last century), and why they still persist. A combination of facts and fictions make up the most popular conceptions of the Middle Ages, not only in movies and video games, but also in textbooks and newspapers.

This metaphorical "medieval" world shapes not only our entertainment but also our politics, wars, and violence, especially since the terrorist attacks of September 11, 2001. In the immediate wake of those attacks, President George W. Bush described the new U.S. war on terrorism as a "crusade." Historians and informed journalists immediately condemned his use of the word, because it recalled medieval religious warfare, and the White House was careful after that not to use this medieval terminology for the wars in Afghanistan and Iraq. But the constant warfare in the Near East since 2001 has encouraged a wider separation between a mostly Christian "West" and a mostly Islamic "East," which has nonetheless perpetuated neomedieval crusading imagery, such as a military uniform patch reading "Pork Eating Crusader," which has been seen on soldiers in the Middle East.

More recently, the rise of white nationalism and extreme right-wing politicians in both Europe and America has encouraged extremist groups to appropriate violent medieval imagery. In 2017 violent alt-right protestors in Charlottesville, Virginia, carried shields bearing "medieval" Celtic crosses and the Black Eagle of the medieval Holy Roman Empire. Likewise, some American and Canadian white nationalists identify with "Vinland," the Norse name for lands on the eastern coast of North America visited by Leif Erikson and other Viking settlers around 1000 CE. They imagine that Vinland represents a mythical all-white medieval past, which they want to re-create in a racially diverse North America.

The scholarly study of medieval history has developed and changed at the same time and in the same cultures as popular medievalism. The field of medieval studies (which includes not just the history but the literature, art, philosophy, music, and science of the Middle Ages) has constantly been reinvented over the last two centuries to reflect the shifting interests of the leaders, media, and schools of Western civilization. The scholarly appreciation of the Middle Ages as a unique culture, and not merely as a despicable "Dark Age," began in the early nineteenth century as part of two movements in particular: the creation of history as a formal discipline and the rise of nationalism in the "Age of Revolutions" (1789–1848). The nations of Western Europe, especially Great Britain, France, and Germany, began to look proudly on their respective medieval pasts and to search for those historical elements that supposedly created their nations and made them unique.

Each of those nations produced in the first half of the nineteenth century great public historians who included the Middle Ages in their impressive surveys of national history. Each historian likewise sought the roots of his nation among the Germanic barbarians of northern Europe, rather than in ancient Greece or Rome, and they took some pride in how their nations had progressed during and since the Middle Ages. Among the most famous of these historians were Henry Hallam (1777–1859) and Thomas Macaulay (1800–1859) in Great Britain, Jules Michelet in France (1798–1874) who features prominently in the following chapters, and Leopold von Ranke in Germany (1795–1886). All these scholars, Ranke especially, established the modern study of history by relying on the empirical analysis of primary sources. But all of them also wrote powerful narratives in which their interests in great men (but rarely women), European politics, and the creation of their own nations took precedence.

The social and political movements of the nineteenth and twentieth centuries continued to shape the practice of history, medieval history included. The rise of Marxism and socialism partly inspired studies of the economics and social history of the Middle Ages. Regular people (now including women) and their labor—peasants, manors, and sheep—mattered as much as great men and wars. The rise of anthropology and other social sciences at the turn of the twentieth century helped shape new areas of medieval history, which looked at popular religion instead of just the Church and formal theology, the structures of typical families and communities instead of just royal dynasties, and broader mentalities rather than just the great philosophers.

The last half century has seen some of the most dramatic upheavals in medieval history, as scholars since the 1960s have seriously examined medieval gender roles, sexuality, disability and disease, race and racism, all of which reflect changing interests in modern politics and popular culture. Even more recently, some medieval historians have begun to work with scientists, like microbiologists and bioarchaeologists, who now have the ability to reconstruct the DNA from medieval skeletons, to better understand the bodies, lives, health, and illnesses of actual medieval people. This union of the humanities and sciences has totally transformed some areas of history, especially the study of medieval diseases like the Black Death (bubonic plague) and leprosy (Hansen's disease).

To fully understand the Middle Ages we have to address the influence of both popular culture and scholarly history in representing the period. The popular views of the Middle Ages outlined here are so widespread that it is often medievalism rather than the genuinely medieval that appears in history textbooks, political speeches, or documentaries. That is where this book comes in: to address some of the most persistent fictions about the Middle Ages. The book is organized from the broadest fictions about the nature of medieval history to more specific misconceptions about medieval religion, science, and culture. It begins with the biggest fiction of all, that the Middle Ages were simply the "Dark Ages," a backward millennium between classical Rome and the Italian Renaissance, in which there was little change except for the devastating loss of culture and civilization. According to that standard narrative of Western history, the last five hundred years have been dedicated to fixing the damage of the Middle Ages and moving beyond the supposed accomplishments of the Renaissance.

From there, we turn to fictions about the shape of the earth, the nature of medieval warfare, witches and peasants, the Church and science, medicine, and the Black Death. If you find that you previously believed one or more of the fictions described in this book, you must remember that it is probably not your fault. When teachers, historians, librarians, presidents, and captains of industry all repeat, for example, the claim that medieval people believed the earth was flat, why shouldn't you believe it too? But this example, like those in each chapter of this book, show just how deeply ingrained within our culture some of the fictions about the Middle Ages have become.

This book is addressed especially to students in the United States and Canada, with the understanding that many of these fictions began in Europe and still persist there too. Our North American cultures are far removed geographically from medieval Europe, but nonetheless we often claim a share of that medieval past because many of the founders of our countries came from England and France, the two nations that are most often used to represent a stereotypical "medieval" setting. But that medieval past becomes whatever we, in North America, want it to be: a dead zone in history, a romantic fairyland, centuries of unmitigated brutality, or a preindustrial and precapitalist utopia. "Medieval" thus becomes not a specific time period or location, but a feeling: the Middle Ages can represent an inversion (sometimes good, but usually bad) of however we see ourselves now.

1

The Middle Ages Were
the Dark Ages

What People Think Happened

You've probably heard this before, from a teacher, a website, or a history program: "Please don't call the Middle Ages the Dark Ages!" But why not? Everyone knows that life was horrible back then. It was a time of constant violence, filth, and ignorant superstition, an age without science, medicine, technology, sanitation, or naturalistic art. It took the Italian Renaissance to reintroduce these necessary aspects of civilization to Western European society (or so the popular fiction goes). Furthermore, medieval people had no rights, women were just property, and everyone was oppressed and even tortured by (take your pick) wicked lords, tyrannical kings, or the Catholic Church. In more eloquent language, the eighteenth-century historian Edward Gibbon summed up the fall of Rome and the start of the Middle Ages as "the triumph of barbarism and religion," by which he meant the Goths and the Church, both of whom Gibbon blamed for the "decline and fall of the Roman Empire."

The fictions outlined in every following chapter of this book reflect this stereotype of the Middle Ages as the Dark Ages. Medieval people were so intellectually backward that they thought Earth was flat (chapter 2), they shook in fear at the arrival of the year 1000 (chapter 4), and their medicine was nothing but ridiculous superstitions about elves and goblins (chapter 9). When faced with the devastation of the Black Death, their response was to chant rhymes about flowers and ashes and to seek help from clueless doctors in terrifying bird masks (chapter 11). They had so thoroughly abandoned the civilized culture of Greece and Rome that they never bathed, lived in filth, and ate rotten meat (chapter 3). Medieval Christians blindly followed a corrupt and repressive Church, which actively suppressed any scientific investigation (chapter 6) and cruelly sent thousands of children to die on a pointless Crusade (chapter 7). Yet this Church was also so clueless about its clergy that it accidentally elected a woman named Joan as pope (chapter 8). The hatred of women shown in medieval documents about this "Pope Joan" was taken to horrifying extremes in the medieval witch hunts, when (according to the popular narrative) millions of defenseless women were accused of witchcraft and burned at the stake (chapter 10).

Medieval historians have spent much of the last century and more pushing against these and other fictions about the Middle Ages, but often without success. It doesn't help when millions of people can watch a recent History Channel documentary on medieval history, which is still called *The Dark Ages* (dir. Christopher Cassel, 2007). Even though the film's producers sought to show that the Middle Ages were anything but "dark," their title only perpetuates the stereotype of the Middle Ages as nothing but the Dark Ages. This idea is reinforced by the cover of the DVD, which shows a worn and cracked human skull, embedded in a medieval stone wall, shrouded in darkness. An image like this aptly sums up what many people still believe about the medieval "Dark Ages." Violent and reductive stereotypes about the Middle Ages are further strengthened by fictional works, such as the *Game of Thrones* novels and shows. Although everyone understands that the series is fictional, with its dragons and ancient magic, much of the plot is made convincing and familiar, as it is based loosely on actual medieval events in the Wars of the Roses, the Hundred Years' War, and the Crusades (Marsden 2018). The Middle Ages, whether portrayed in a documentary or a fantasy epic, are usually equated with senseless brutality.

How true are such sweeping condemnations of the Middle Ages? And whether we use the term "Dark Ages" or "Middle Ages," what exactly do we mean about the chronology and culture of this historical period? In this chapter we will explore the "big myth" about the Middle Ages, namely that the era was nothing but a "dark age" that paled in comparison to the preceding Roman Empire or the Italian Renaissance that followed.

How the Story Became Popular

The first thing to understand about the Middle Ages—and this is a difficult starting point for a book about the subject—is that they do not actually exist. But how is that possible? Scholars and popular audiences have been talking about the Middle Ages for centuries as the millennium roughly between 500 and 1500 CE. Yes, the Middle Ages do exist as a term invented by scholars to refer to a period of time in history (usually Western European but the term is increasingly applied to all of Eurasia or even to the whole world), but the term "Middle Ages" does not refer to a specific place, event, form of government, or group of people, as is the case with other historical subjects like the Roman Republic, American Revolution, or Soviet Communism. "Medieval" is a problematic term because it refers not to what defines it, but to something it is not: it is not classical Greece and Rome and it is not the Italian Renaissance, but a "middle age" resting uneasily between them and lacking definition. Nobody living in the Middle Ages, therefore, would understand the concept of "medieval." The term itself appeared only in 1604, in the neo-Latin construction *medium aevum* ("middle age"), which then created the adjective *mediaevalis* ("medieval"). (It can be confusing that only English makes the term plural, Middle Ages, while other European languages follow the Latin in keeping it singular: *moyen âge*, *Mittelalter*, *medio evo*, and so on.)

The problems increase when we refer to the medieval period as the "Dark Ages." It is obviously a loaded term, one meant to trigger strong emotions. It is "dark" only in comparison to something "light," but that age or culture of light can change depending on your perspective. For some, the Middle Ages are dark because of the loss of the supposed splendors of classical Roman culture. The historian Edward Gibbon, in his monumental work *The Decline and Fall of the Roman Empire*, considered the second century CE in the Roman Empire (specifically the reigns of the "Five Good Emperors," 96–180 CE) to be the happiest and most prosperous age of humankind. Therefore he portrays all of the events that came after that period as increasingly unhappy and eventually "dark"— dark, that is, until the rise of enlightened modernity in his own time. For many other historians, the Middle Ages are dark because they have not yet become the Italian Renaissance of Petrarch, Michelangelo, and Leonardo, with their focus on individualism, humanism, naturalistic art, and three-dimensional sculpture.

It is usually a combination of these two approaches (the loss of Roman culture and the failure to be the Renaissance) that is found in recent works of popular history. For example, the author Barnet Litvinoff laments in his book *Fourteen Ninety Two: The Decline of Medievalism and the Rise of the Modern Age* (1991) the loss of Ancient Rome's "political sophistication, freedom of thought, splendid architecture and administrative genius" during the medieval period (Litvinoff 1991, 6). The Middle Ages are the very opposite of Ancient Rome for Litvinoff, who claims that "the Dark Ages, if one might dare a generalization, bequeathed to medieval man a kind of amnesiac void" (Litvinoff 1991, 7). In Litvinoff's book, "darkness" is defined by a failure to appreciate or emulate classical Greece and Rome, a definition by which the Middle Ages will always lose. Even if there is some utility in his approach to understanding Roman and medieval culture, Litvinoff also resorts to complete distortions of the past to paint the Middle Ages as "dark." For example, he claims that early medieval society justified slavery "as being ordained by god," even though slavery had almost entirely disappeared from medieval society at that time, while ancient Rome was thoroughly dependent on slavery, with 30–40 percent of the Roman population enslaved. He likewise claims, without any evidence, that an eighth-century pope destroyed multiple libraries out of fear that they might undermine Christianity. Litvinoff's book is one of the most egregious examples of distorting medieval history to support a proclassical or pro-Renaissance agenda, but it is hardly unique.

The darkness of the Dark Ages is promoted even more graphically by William Manchester, in his best-selling *A World Lit Only by Fire: The Medieval Mind and the Renaissance: Portrait of an Age* (1992). Most of his book examines the artists and explorers of the fifteenth and sixteenth centuries, but he begins his book with twenty-five pages in which he claims to define the "Medieval Mind." He vigorously defends the continued use of the term "Dark Ages," especially for the period 400–1000 CE. He claims (incorrectly) that "[v]ery little is clear about that dim era" and that throughout the medieval period "literacy was scorned" (Manchester 1992, 3). His first chapter is a catalogue of death, destruction, ignorance, and the constant failures of medieval society to be as great as Ancient Rome or Renaissance Italy. In the end, Manchester concludes that the medieval world was not even a civilization (a point that every modern history textbook would deny), for he defines a civilization as "a society which has reached a relatively high level of cultural and technological development" (Manchester 1991, 15). He demonstrates the failure of medieval culture to reach the status of a "civilization" by cherry-picking some of the bloodier and more anarchic stories from the fourth, fifth, and sixth centuries CE, and applying that violence to the next one thousand years. Litvinoff and Manchester provide us with just two of the more egregious examples of how the Middle Ages are unjustly depicted as nothing but the "Dark Ages," but where did this stereotype come from? In the following section we will explore the development of both the Middle Ages and the Dark Ages as historical constructs.

The construction of the Middle Ages as a specific period in history could only have come about once European thinkers began both to treasure the distant Greek or Roman past and to condemn the period they lived in or the one recently past. This happened first in the fourteenth and fifteenth centuries, primarily in northern Italy, in the period eventually known as the "Renaissance" (but first as *Rinascimento* in Italian), which supposedly saw the "rebirth" of classical culture. One of the first authors to promote this division of history was Francesco Petrarca (1304–1374), often known as Petrarch. Petrarch is credited with a lot: the founder of the Renaissance, founder of Italian humanism, model writer in the Italian language, and inventor of the sonnet. But he is best known for introducing to Western history a metaphorical division between "light" and "dark." These terms had been used throughout the Middle Ages for religious purposes, but Petrarch now applied them to the presence or absence of high-quality Latin literature. Thus Rome of the first centuries BCE and CE (the age of Julius Caesar and Augustus Caesar) was the true age of "light," while most of the millennium preceding his own life (roughly 300–1300 CE) was "dark." In one of his writings, Petrarch described the people of the medieval past: "amidst the errors [of the past] there shone forth men of genius, and no less keen were their eyes, although they were surrounded by darkness and dense gloom" (Mommsen 1942, 227). He recognizes that some medieval people were still intelligent, but their very age was so "dark" that they could not apply that intelligence.

Petrarch was hardly alone in embracing metaphors of a Roman age of light and a following age of darkness. His successors in the Italian Renaissance, such as Giovanni Boccaccio, Filippo Villani, and Lorenzo Ghiberti, stressed not only the classical age of light but also the rebirth in their own time of refined Latin literature, in the style of ancient Romans. Petrarch still imagined himself to be living in the "dark age," but these later scholars and artists credited him, along with Dante and Giotto, with reviving classical culture. Petrarch concluded his verse epic *Africa* with a message of hope for the future, written in a time of darkness: "My fate is to live among varied and confusing storms. But for you perhaps, if as I hope and wish you will live long after me, there will follow a better age. This sleep of forgetfulness will not last forever. When the darkness has been dispersed, our descendants can come again in the former pure radiance" (Mommsen 1942, 240). Where Petrarch imagined only two periods of history (light and darkness), his followers elevated their own period as a third age in a tripartite vision of history, defined by the promotion of Roman culture: classical, medieval, Renaissance (light, dark, light). The fifteenth-century scholars Leonardo Bruni and Flavio Biondo both employed this three-part division of history in their works.

But when exactly was this "middle age"? Historians and teachers to this day have trouble with this question, if they do not simply follow the shorthand of 500–1500 CE for the dates of the period. If you are looking for a specific date, medievalists often start the Middle Ages with the removal of the last Western Roman emperor, Romulus Augustulus, in 476 CE by the barbarian warlord Odoacer, but one can justifiably use the legalization of Christianity in 313 CE or the rise of Islam in 632 CE as other viable dates to divide the first and second ages. Flavio Biondo wrote numerous works of Italian, Roman, and European history, and in several of them he employed the Visigothic sack of Rome in 410 as the beginning of the second age, and his own youth in the 1440s as the start of the third, new age.

Renaissance scholars like Biondo could study documents from the later Roman Empire (third through sixth centuries CE) and see clear evidence for the collapse of Roman culture at the hands of uncultured barbarians, the very forces of darkness for a Romanophile humanist. Later Roman aristocrats like Ammianus Marcellinus (ca. 330–400) and Sidonius Apollinaris (ca. 430–489) left letters, poems, and histories about the external attacks of barbaric Franks, Goths, Vandals, and Alamanni, and the internal collapse of the Roman imperial government, army, and economy. They were witnesses, respectively, to the terrible Roman loss to Goths at the Battle of Adrianople in 378 and the disappearance of the last Western Roman emperor in 476. Likewise, the Byzantine Greek scholar Jordanes, a descendant of the Goths himself, described the many vicious attacks of Goths and other barbarian groups on the crumbling Roman Empire in his sixth-century work, *The History of the Goths*. Jordanes depicts the Goths as attacking and sacking cities in the eastern half of the empire, including Ephesus and Troy, and emphasizes the loss of their antiquity and culture to these barbarians (see the Primary Documents).

An author who was better known than Ammianus, Sidonius, or Jordanes throughout the Middle Ages and Renaissance was the Latin Church Father Saint Jerome (347–420). He is famous for translating the entire Bible into his contemporary Latin, the version known as the Vulgate Bible, but he was also a prolific letter writer, and dramatically recorded the sack of Rome by the Visigoths in 410 in two of his letters (see the Primary

Documents). That event would strike Jerome and his contemporaries, especially his fellow Church Father Augustine of Hippo, as unthinkable, a sign of the end of civilization. Jerome says of this event, "The City which had taken the whole world was itself taken," and "The renowned city, the capital of the Roman Empire, is swallowed up in one tremendous fire." Even though Jerome himself was not witness to these events, he paints them with vivid horror, recounting tales of cannibalism and the wanton destruction of Christian churches. It would be documents like these from Jerome and Jordanes that shaped visions of the Middle Ages for Renaissance and early modern historians. These later authors would apply to the entire Middle Ages the terrors described by these late Roman authors about the fifth century. For them, and still for many modern audiences, the whole millennium after 410 or 476 is unfairly colored by the barbaric sack of Rome, and they could not imagine a stable European culture without Roman dominance.

Renaissance scholars looked back on the period since the sack or fall of Rome as a clearly inferior time, but it would not be until the seventeenth century that the term "dark age" was actually used to refer to the Middle Ages. The Catholic scholar Caesar Baronius (1538–1607), cardinal-priest of Santi Nereo ed Achilleo, coined the term *saeculum obscurum* ("dark age") to refer to just the period ca. 900–1046 as a particularly bad time for the Church and the papacy, when very few documents were made or survived: "Behold, here begins the 900th year of the Redeemer . . . in which a new age begins, which it is customary to call an age of iron because of its harshness and the sterility of goodness, and an age of lead because of the deformity of exuberant evil, and a dark age because of the lack of writings" (Translation of Baronius, 1588–1607, 10:629). Even though Baronius did not intend to condemn the entire medieval, Catholic past, his use of the term "dark age" spread rapidly and came to apply to the entire period of European history when the Catholic Church was dominant.

What was meant by the "darkness" of the Dark Ages? These days the term "Dark Ages" usually brings up connotations of violence and anarchy, but for much of the last five centuries, the medieval darkness was an intellectual one, a period supposedly without books or learning. This is the attitude of a popular reference book from 1883, *The American Cyclopaedia*, which is still representative of popular ideas about the Middle Ages: "The DARK AGES is a term applied in its widest sense to that period of intellectual depression in the history of Europe from the establishment of barbarian supremacy in the fifth century to the revival of learning about the beginning of the fifteenth, thus nearly corresponding in extent with the Middle Ages" (Ripley and Dana 1883, 1:186). This book's conception of the Dark Ages as essentially the same period and culture as the Middle Ages persists to this day. Yet if we turn back to Petrarch's first quote about the medieval period, he did not see it as entirely ignorant. There were at that time "men of genius" with "keen eyes," but they were surrounded by a gloom caused by the lack of Roman leadership over the civilized world.

The shift in emphasis concerning the Middle Ages, from a gloomy period without Roman culture to a wholly ignorant age, does not come from the Italian Renaissance, but from the later periods of the Protestant Reformation and Enlightenment. Authors of both periods were more dedicated than the Renaissance figures to tarnishing the image of the Middle Ages: Protestant reformers wanted to make the entire Catholic past look corrupt and backward, and Enlightenment authors of the seventeenth and eighteenth centuries celebrated their own "Age of Reason" and denigrated the preceding "Age of Faith." For Enlightenment scholars like Immanuel Kant, Edward Gibbon, and Voltaire, even the Renaissance and the Reformation were still periods of darkness because they were dominated by religion (whether Catholic or Protestant). Voltaire (François-Marie Arouet, 1694–1778) in particular savaged the medieval past in his viciously polemical writings, such as his *Essay on the Customs and Spirit of Nations*, for its feudal institutions but especially for the ideas and activities of the Roman Catholic Church, most notoriously seen in his hatred of Scholastic philosophy, the Crusades, and the Inquisition (Bartlett 2001, 12). Voltaire's Middle Ages were barbaric, brutal, confused, tyrannical, and impoverished, all of which he blamed on the Church.

The most influential inheritor of these conceptions about the Middle Ages, both from the Renaissance and the Enlightenment, was the Swiss historian Jacob Burckhardt (1818–1897). His most important work was *The Civilization of the Renaissance in Italy* (*Die Kultur der Renaissance in Italien*, 1860), which is considered one of the foundational works in the historical study of the Renaissance and which shapes most popular conceptions of the Renaissance to this day. But in order to elevate the Italian Renaissance as the culture that, he argued, gave birth to modernity and invented individualism, Burckhardt necessarily had to push down the Middle Ages even farther. But Burckhardt's condemnation of the Middle Ages is highly appealing, especially when compared to the biting attacks of the Reformation and Enlightenment. For Burckhardt the Middle Ages are not "dark," but rather barely conscious or "childish" (see Primary Documents). Medieval people "lay dreaming or half awake beneath a common

veil." This veil, however, was not religion or the Church (the favorite enemies of earlier authors on the Middle Ages), but the bonds of medieval
society that kept people from becoming individuals and celebrating their
unique human natures. It was the special political and economic situation
of Italy in the later Middle Ages that allowed it to produce "individuals"
like Dante, Giotto, and Petrarch who established the Renaissance.

Almost every textbook of the history of Western civilization now
acknowledges that the views of the Middle Ages held by Gibbon, Voltaire,
Burckhardt, and others during the eighteenth and nineteenth centuries
are overly simplistic, if not pointlessly hostile. Most historians now recognize the medieval period as diverse and creative, containing numerous
cultures with their own place in history; they do not judge the medieval
period simply by its failure to perpetuate the Roman Empire. Nonetheless, there is still a reading market hungry for history books that keep the
hostile stereotypes of Gibbon alive, and that encourages popular writers
and even noted scholars to repeat the same uncritical fictions about the
Middle Ages as a long era of darkness that destroyed the light of the classical world and that itself was dispelled by the brilliance of the Renaissance.

The renowned Shakespearean scholar Stephen Greenblatt gave new
life to these antimedieval ideas in his best-selling and National Book
Award–winning volume *The Swerve: How the World Became Modern*,
which he also summarized in a 2011 *New Yorker* article. In that latter
piece, he reduces the entire Middle Ages to an empty age of fear and
ignorance: "It is possible for a whole culture to turn away from reading
and writing. As the Roman Empire crumbled and Christianity became
ascendant, as cities decayed, trade declined, and an anxious populace
scanned the horizon for barbarian armies, the ancient system of education fell apart. . . . Schools closed, libraries and academies shut their doors,
professional grammarians and teachers of rhetoric found themselves out
of work, scribes were no longer given manuscripts to copy" (Greenblatt
2011, 28). Greenblatt avoids the problematic phrase "Dark Ages," but
through his story of the Renaissance rediscovery of the ancient Roman
poem by Lucretius, *On the Nature of Things*, he paints the medieval period
as one of self-imposed darkness in which classical philosophy is forgotten
or intentionally destroyed.

Both popular authors and renowned scholars have found various reasons for describing the Middle Ages as a "dark age." This darkness could
be defined either by an absence (of Roman government and culture, of
modern scientific methods, of individualism) or by an oppressive presence (barbarian kingdoms, warrior lords, the Catholic Church). Recent

history texts, especially those for children, perpetuate all of these attitudes at once. Susan Wise Bauer, in her 2007 textbook *The Story of the World: History for the Classical Child,* compares the unity and stability of the Roman Empire with the disunity, ignorance, and desperation of the Middle Ages: "[Medieval people] lived in separate villages, speaking their different languages. And they no longer read the old books, written in Latin and Greek. They spent their days trying to grow enough food to stay alive and worrying about the next barbarian attack. . . . We call the centuries after Rome was destroyed the Middle Ages" (Bauer 2007, 318–19). In another passage Bauer pushes these stereotypes further by cloaking the entire Middle Ages with the darkness of ignorance about history, medicine, or even basic literacy. This darkness, she claims, was lifted only with the Renaissance invention of the printing press.

Bauer is not alone in teaching twenty-first-century children about a "Dark Ages" that is even more backward than Gibbon or Burckhardt ever would have claimed. In 2012, the online study site *ReadWorks* painted a brutal picture of the Middle Ages as nothing more than a period of post-Roman ignorance and laziness, religious mind control, and sheer physical exhaustion. The brief article concludes, "People were not as curious about the world around them. This is why the Middle Ages is sometimes called the Dark Age. During the Renaissance all of this changed. If the Middle Ages were dark, the Renaissance was the bright dawn of a new era" (*ReadWorks* 2012). Statements like this are problematic not simply because they oversimplify the millennium of medieval history, but also because they are based more on popular stereotypes than on actual historical evidence.

PRIMARY DOCUMENTS

JORDANES, *HISTORY OF THE GOTHS* (551 CE): THE DEVASTATION OF BARBARIAN ATTACKS

Jordanes was a bureaucrat and historian in the Eastern Roman (or "Byzantine") Empire in the sixth century. He was descended from Gothic settlers and proudly gave his people a formal, written history in his Getica, *or* History of the Goths, *in 551. He gives the Goths a lengthy, mostly fictional, past to show that they also have a long and worthy history like the Greeks and Romans. Jordanes focused especially on the military endeavors of the Goths and other "barbarian" groups like the Huns. This passage from the* Getica *shows how*

Jordanes imagined the violence and destruction of barbarism within the later Roman Empire.

[Chapter 20] While Gallienus [r. 260–268 CE] was given over to luxurious living of every sort, Respa, Veduc, and Thuruar, leaders of the Goths, took ship and sailed across the strait of the Hellespont to Asia. There they laid waste many populous cities and set fire to the renowned temple of Diana at Ephesus, which, as we said before, the Amazons built. Being driven from the neighborhood of Bithynia they destroyed Chalcedon, which Cornelius Avitus afterward restored to some extent. Yet even today, though it is happily situated near the royal city [Constantinople], it still shows some traces of its ruin as a witness to posterity. After their success the Goths recrossed the strait of the Hellespont, laden with booty and spoil, and returned along the same route by which they had entered the lands of Asia, sacking Troy and Ilium on the way. These cities, which had scarce recovered a little from the famous war of Agamemnon, were thus devastated anew by the hostile sword. After the Goths had thus devastated Asia, Thrace next felt their ferocity.

Source: Jordanes, *History of the Goths*. 1912–1913. In *Readings in Ancient History: Illustrative Extracts from the Sources*, edited by William Stearns Davis. 2 vols. Boston: Allyn and Bacon, 2:207.

SAINT JEROME, LETTERS ON THE SACK OF ROME (412–413 CE)

Saint Jerome (347–420), a Latin-speaking native of the Roman city of Stridon, possibly in modern Croatia, is one of the greatest "doctors of the Church," who shaped Christian belief through his writings. He is most famous for translating the entire Bible (Hebrew Old Testament and Greek New Testament) into Latin, and this translation, called the Vulgate Bible, was used for over the next one thousand years in Christian Europe. Jerome also wrote numerous commentaries on the books of the Bible, saints' lives, religious histories, and letters. In the two letters excerpted here, Jerome gives his heart-wrenching reaction to the Visigothic sack of Rome in 410. He sees it as a tragedy both for the loss of Christian lives but also because he imagines that the sack of Rome was equivalent to the destruction of all civilization. In fact, the Visigoths did not seriously damage Rome, and it quickly recovered after they moved on, but Jerome's dramatic accounts would be read throughout the Middle Ages and Renaissance, shaping the popular idea that the "fall of Rome" led to a "Dark Age."

From Letter 127 to Principia (412 CE)

12. Whilst these things were happening in Jebus a dreadful rumour came from the West. Rome had been besieged and its citizens had been forced to buy their lives with gold. Then thus despoiled they had been besieged again so as to lose not their substance only but their lives. My voice sticks in my throat; and, as I dictate, sobs choke my utterance. The City which had taken the whole world was itself taken; nay more famine was beforehand with the sword and but few citizens were left to be made captives. In their frenzy the starving people had recourse to hideous food; and tore each other limb from limb that they might have flesh to eat. Even the mother did not spare the babe at her breast. In the night was Moab taken, in the night did her wall fall down. [Isaiah 15:1] O God, the heathen have come into your inheritance; your holy temple have they defiled; they have made Jerusalem an orchard. The dead bodies of your servants have they given to be meat unto the fowls of the heaven, the flesh of your saints unto the beasts of the earth. Their blood have they shed like water round about Jerusalem; and there was none to bury them.

> *Who can set forth the carnage of that night?*
> *What tears are equal to its agony?*
> *Of ancient date a sovereign city falls;*
> *And lifeless in its streets and houses lie*
> *Unnumbered bodies of its citizens.*
> *In many a ghastly shape does death appear.*

13. Meantime, as was natural in a scene of such confusion, one of the bloodstained victors found his way into Marcella's house. Now be it mine to say what I have heard, to relate what holy men have seen; for there were some such present and they say that you too were with her in the hour of danger. When the soldiers entered she is said to have received them without any look of alarm; and when they asked her for gold she pointed to her coarse dress to show them that she had no buried treasure. However they would not believe in her self-chosen poverty, but scourged her and beat her with cudgels. She is said to have felt no pain but to have thrown herself at their feet and to have pleaded with tears for you, that you might not be taken from her, or owing to your youth have to endure what she as an old woman had no occasion to fear. Christ softened their hard hearts and even among bloodstained swords natural affection asserted its rights. The barbarians conveyed both you and her to the basilica of the apostle

Paul, that you might find there either a place of safety or, if not that, at least a tomb. Hereupon Marcella is said to have burst into great joy and to have thanked God for having kept you unharmed in answer to her prayer. She said she was thankful too that the taking of the city had found her poor, not made her so, that she was now in want of daily bread, that Christ satisfied her needs so that she no longer felt hunger, that she was able to say in word and in deed: naked came I out of my mother's womb, and naked shall I return there: the Lord gave and the Lord has taken away; blessed be the name of the Lord.

From Letter 128 to Gaudentius (413 CE)

4. The world sinks into ruin: yes! But shameful to say our sins still live and flourish. The renowned city, the capital of the Roman Empire, is swallowed up in one tremendous fire; and there is no part of the earth where Romans are not in exile. Churches once held sacred are now but heaps of dust and ashes; and yet we have our minds set on the desire of gain. We live as though we are going to die tomorrow; yet we build as though we are going to live always in this world. Our walls shine with gold, our ceilings also and the capitals of our pillars; yet Christ dies before our doors naked and hungry in the persons of His poor. The pontiff Aaron, we read, faced the raging flames, and by putting fire in his censer checked the wrath of God. The High Priest stood between the dead and the living, and the fire dared not pass his feet. On another occasion God said to Moses, Let me alone . . . that I may consume this people [Exodus 32:10], showing by the words let me alone that he can be withheld from doing what he threatens. The prayers of His servant hindered His power. Who, think you, is there now under heaven able to stay God's wrath, to face the flame of His judgment, and to say with the apostle, I could wish that I myself were accursed for my brethren? [Romans 9:3] Flocks and shepherds perish together, because as it is with the people, so is it with the priest [Isaiah 24:2]. Of old it was not so. Then Moses spoke in a passion of pity, yet now if you will forgive their sin; and if not, blot me, I pray you, out of your book [Exodus 32:32]. He is not satisfied to secure his own salvation, he desires to perish with those that perish. And he is right, for in the multitude of people is the king's honour [Proverbs 14:28].

Such are the times in which our little Pacatula is born. Such are the swaddling clothes in which she draws her first breath; she is destined to know of tears before laughter and to feel sorrow sooner than joy. And hardly does she come upon the stage when she is called on to make her exit. Let her then suppose that the world has always been what it is now. Let her know nothing of the past, let her shun the present, and let her long for the future.

These thoughts of mine are but hastily mustered. For my grief for lost friends has known no intermission and only recently have I recovered sufficient composure to write an old man's letter to a little child. My affection for you, brother Gaudentius, has induced me to make the attempt and I have thought it better to say a few words than to say nothing at all. The grief that paralyses my will will excuse my brevity; whereas, were I to say nothing, the sincerity of my friendship might well be doubted.

Source: *The Principal Works of St. Jerome.* 1893. Translated by W. H. Fremantle, G. Lewis, and W. G. Martley. In *Nicene and Post-Nicene Fathers,* 2d ser., vol. 6, edited by Philip Schaff and Henry Wace. New York: Christian Literature Publishing, 257, 260.

EDWARD GIBBON, *HISTORY OF THE DECLINE AND FALL OF THE ROMAN EMPIRE* (1776–1788)

Edward Gibbon's (1737–1794) History of the Decline and Fall of the Roman Empire *is widely considered one of the founding works of modern scholarly history. In six volumes, published over twelve years, Gibbon used primary sources to construct a rational and secular history of the Roman Empire, its fall, and the nature of the following Middle Ages. The book was hugely popular, going through numerous editions and hundreds of printings during Gibbon's life and throughout the following two centuries. He was one of the first historians to blame the rise of Christianity and the formation of the Church for the fall of Rome and ensuing "Dark Ages," an idea that was popular among Enlightenment philosophers and the Protestants of Great Britain and the United States of America. In the famous passage that follows, Gibbon sums up his longer arguments about the "triumph of barbarism and religion," which ended Roman dominance and led to the Middle Ages.*

[Chapter 71.2: The hostile attacks of the barbarians and Christians]

The crowd of writers of every nation, who impute the destruction of the Roman monuments to the Goths and the Christians, have neglected to inquire how far they were animated by a hostile principle, and how far they possessed the means and the leisure to satiate their enmity. In the preceding volumes of this *History*, I have described the triumph of barbarism and religion; and I can only resume, in a few words, their real or imaginary connection with the ruin of ancient Rome. Our fancy may create, or adopt, a pleasing romance, that the Goths and Vandals sallied from Scandinavia, ardent to avenge the flight of Odin; to break the chains, and to chastise the oppressors, of mankind; that they wished to burn the records of classic literature, and to found their national architecture on the broken members of the Tuscan and Corinthian orders. But in simple truth, the northern conquerors were neither sufficiently savage, nor sufficiently refined, to entertain such aspiring ideas of destruction and revenge. The shepherds of Scythia and Germany had been educated in the armies of the empire, whose discipline they acquired, and whose weakness they invaded: with the familiar use of the Latin tongue, they had learned to reverence the name and titles of Rome; and, though incapable of emulating, they were more inclined to admire, than to abolish, the arts and studies of a brighter period. In the transient possession of a rich and unresisting capital, the soldiers of Alaric and Genseric were stimulated by the passions of a victorious army; amidst the wanton indulgence of lust or cruelty, portable wealth was the object of their search; nor could they derive either pride or pleasure from the unprofitable reflection, that they had battered to the ground the works of the consuls and Caesars. Their moments were indeed precious; the Goths evacuated Rome on the sixth, the Vandals on the fifteenth, day: and, though it be far more difficult to build than to destroy, their hasty assault would have made a slight impression on the solid piles of antiquity. We may remember, that both Alaric and Genseric affected to spare the buildings of the city; that they subsisted in strength and beauty under the auspicious government of Theodoric; and that the momentary resentment of Totila was disarmed by his own temper and the advice of his friends and enemies. From these innocent Barbarians, the reproach may be transferred to the Catholics of Rome. The statues, altars, and houses, of the daemons, were an abomination in their eyes; and in the absolute command of the city, they might labor with zeal and perseverance to erase the idolatry of their ancestors. The demolition of the temples in the East affords to *them* an example of conduct, and to *us* an argument of belief; and it is probable that a portion of guilt or merit may be imputed with justice to the Roman proselytes. Yet their abhorrence was confined to the monuments of heathen superstition; and the civil structures that were dedicated to the business or pleasure of society might be preserved without injury or scandal. The change of religion was accomplished, not by a popular tumult, but by the decrees of the emperors, of the senate, and of time. Of the Christian hierarchy, the bishops of Rome were commonly the most prudent and least fanatic; nor can any positive charge be opposed to the meritorious act of saving or converting the majestic structure of the Pantheon.

Source: Gibbon, Edward. 1827. *The History of the Decline and Fall of the Roman Empire.* 12 vols. Oxford: D. A. Talboys, 8:379–81.

JACOB BURCKHARDT, *THE CIVILIZATION OF THE RENAISSANCE IN ITALY* (1860)

Just as the study of the fall of Rome was defined by Edward Gibbon (see the previous primary document), so the study of the Italian Renaissance as a historical period was defined by the Swiss historian Jacob Burckhardt (1818–1897). Before Burckhardt, most discussion of the Renaissance was confined to artistic production. Burckhardt defined the Renaissance in terms of politics, statecraft, customs, and religion, all of which he argued are reflected in the art and literature of the period. Burckhardt especially focused on the Renaissance promotion of the individual genius and his achievements, an emphasis that he claimed was entirely lacking in the Middle Ages.

In the Middle Ages both sides of human consciousness—that which was turned within as that which was turned without—lay dreaming or half awake beneath a common veil. The veil was woven of faith, illusion, and childish prepossession, through which the world and history were seen clad in strange hues. Man was conscious of himself only as member of a race, people, party, family, or corporation—only through some general category. In Italy this veil first melted into air; an *objective* treatment and consideration of the state and of all the things of this world became possible. The *subjective* side at the same time asserted itself with corresponding emphasis; man became a spiritual *individual*, and recognised himself as such. In the same way the Greek had once distinguished himself from the barbarian, and the Arabian had felt himself an individual at a time when other Asiatics knew themselves only as members of a race. It will not be difficult to show that this result was owing above all to the political circumstances of Italy. In far earlier times we can here and there detect a development of free personality which in Northern Europe either did not occur at all, or could not display itself in the same manner. The band of audacious wrongdoers in the sixteenth century described to us by Liudprand, some of the contemporaries of Gregory VII, and a few of the opponents of the first Hohenstaufen, show us characters of this kind. But at the close of the thirteenth century Italy began to swarm with individuality; the charm laid upon human personality was dissolved; and a thousand figures meet us each in its own special shape and dress. Dante's great poem would have been impossible in any other country of Europe, if only for the reason that they all still lay under the spell of race. For Italy the august poet, through the wealth of individuality which he set forth, was the most national herald of his time. But this unfolding of the treasures of human nature in literature and art—this many-sided representation and criticism—will be discussed in separate chapters; here we have to deal only with the psychological fact itself. This fact appears in the most decisive and unmistakeable form. The Italians of the fourteenth century knew little of false modesty or of hypocrisy in any shape; not one of them was afraid of singularity, of being and seeming unlike his neighbours.

Source: Burckhardt, Jacob. 1878. *The Civilization of the Renaissance in Italy.* Translated by S. G. C. Middlemore. London, 129–30.

What Really Happened

To describe what really happened in the Middle Ages, as part of an effort to correct misconceptions about the "Dark Ages," would take a lifetime and millions of words. In this small space, we can only begin to outline the problems with viewing the Middle Ages simply as the "Dark Ages," but every chapter in this book will also add to this effort in its own way. As we saw earlier, the Middle Ages are often viewed as "dark" either because of a supposed intellectual decline from the classical Romans or the presence of widespread and brutal violence. Renaissance and Enlightenment scholars focused on the intellectual decline, but modern audiences have preferred to focus on the supposedly endemic violence of the Middle Ages. Both stereotypes are true, to a certain extent, about parts of the Middle Ages, but primarily only in the in the first part of the Early Middle Ages, the fifth through eighth centuries, and not throughout the entire millennium of medieval history. Nonetheless, many fictions about the Middle Ages are due to a widespread belief in the uniformity of the Middle Ages, the idea that people and institutions changed little between the Fall of Rome and the Renaissance. So how can we counter the myth of the Dark Ages?

In the first place we must understand that the term itself of "Dark Ages" vanished from all works of serious scholarship over a century ago in recognition of the fact that it is unspecific, misleading, and incorrect when used to apply to a period of one thousand years. Even historians who still see the Middle Ages as hopelessly backward when compared to what came before or after now avoid the term (as seen with Stephen Greenblatt earlier). As history developed into a serious discipline during the nineteenth century, scholars recognized that the eleventh through fifteenth centuries were an age of population growth, urbanization, increased trade, revived artistic creativity, and expanding literacy, and thus should not be grouped together with the Early Middle Ages (ca. 500–1000 CE) under the same derogatory "Dark Ages." In 1904, when the British literary scholar W. P. Ker wrote a book called *The Dark Ages*, he was obliged to offer a sort of apology and explanation at the start: "The Dark Ages and the Middle Ages—or the Middle Age—used to be the same; two names for the same period. But they have come to be distinguished, and the Dark Ages are now no more than the first part of the Middle Ages, while the term mediaeval is often restricted to the later centuries, about 1100 to 1500, the age of chivalry, the time between the first Crusade and the Renaissance" (Ker 1904, 1). Even Ker's careful approach to the Middle Ages is generally rejected now, as scholars of that early medieval period that Ker would still call "dark" have shown how creative, original, and unique that era was as well, while scholars of the second half of the Middle Ages no longer reduce the entire period of 1100 to 1500 merely to an "age of chivalry." Nearly a century later, Roger Collins, the author of the most popular introduction to early medieval history (*Early Medieval Europe, 300–1000*), did not even acknowledge the term "Dark Ages." He instead demonstrates that "The centuries covered by this book constitute a period of the greatest significance for the future development, not only of Europe, but in the longer term, of much else of the world" (Collins 1999, xxiii).

But our concern here is to debunk the very idea of the "Dark Ages" and not simply to avoid the term. Yet how can we argue against an accusation of a medieval "darkness," which has been central to the definition of Western civilization for some six hundred years? For one, you can show that medieval people were not uncivilized or ignorant, but maintained many elements of Roman and Greek culture and also made other advances wrongly attributed to the later Renaissance. You can also show how the violence, dirt, and despair attributed to the Middle Ages actually belong to the classical and Renaissance worlds as well and are rather part of all premodern societies (granted, this is a depressing approach, but one that indirectly vindicates the medieval period). A third method breaks the Middle Ages free of the shadows of Rome and the Renaissance and argues that medieval society should be studied as its own culture, which produced many of the social and political structures of modern Western civilization.

We can address all three of these approaches if we return to the earlier quote from Stephen Greenblatt in which he claims the "whole culture" of medieval society "turn[ed] away from reading and writing" in a time when "cities decayed, trade declined, and an anxious populace scanned the horizon for barbarian armies" (Greenblatt 2011, 28). As Jim Hinch demonstrated in a scathing review of Greenblatt's book, nearly every statement Greenblatt makes about the Middle Ages is wholly incorrect or applies only to the period of invasions and migrations in the fifth through eighth centuries (Hinch 2012). Medieval society turned even more *toward* reading and writing than the classical Romans, as the Bible and other religious texts became the direct focus of their culture, learning, and art. But neither did medieval culture lose or abandon the classical past, because medieval clerics and scholars continued to read and copy the pagan Roman authors Virgil, Ovid, Horace, Pliny, and possibly even the supposedly lost Lucretius, to learn Latin grammar and rhetoric.

It is true that cities shrank and trade declined in Europe (the former western Roman Empire) in the difficult period of the fifth through eighth centuries. Recent archaeological investigations support the long-studied written documents which attest to the collapse of Roman civilization (Ward-Perkins 2005). But after that period, the opposite occurred in most areas of Europe, increasingly during the Carolingian era (751–888 CE) and especially by the turn of the first millennium: old cities grew again, new ones were founded, old trade routes revived, and new ones carved out, connecting Europe to cultures in Africa, the Near East, the Indian subcontinent, and even China. Even the Viking invasions of the ninth and tenth centuries, which inform so many popular fictions about the violent Middle Ages, did not halt the economic revival of Europe. In fact, they may have increased long-distance trade and cultural connections, despite the focus of contemporary European documents on their destructive cruelty.

Most of the Middle Ages was thus a period of growth and creativity in economics and politics. To claim that medieval people always "scanned the horizon for barbarian armies" is even more ludicrous, because most medieval Europeans were those very barbarians who invaded or settled in the later Roman era: Franks, Anglo-Saxons, Lombards, Visigoths (of Spain and Provence), and others all quickly became Christians, adopted some of the basic structures of Roman law and government, and created kingdoms that persist to this day as the nations or cultural regions of Europe. A significant group of historians, led by Peter Brown and Walter Goffart, have called for a reevaluation of the period of "barbarian invasions." Brown, in many of his publications, argues that the period ca. 300–700 CE should be known as "Late Antiquity," a period of vigorous cultural creativity that continued some aspects of Greco-Roman culture in a newly Christian society (Brown 1989; Brown 2013). Goffart argues that later Romans and Germanic tribes mixed cultures more peacefully than we have been led to believe in a process of "accommodation" that was more common and important than any violent invasions (Goffart 1980).

The Primary Documents that follow come from just the first half of the Middle Ages, that period which is still commonly called the "Dark Ages." Most of the sources in the following chapters 2–11 come from the eleventh through fifteenth centuries, the so-called "high" and "late" Middle Ages, periods of higher literacy rates and more extensive artistic and intellectual creativity. The sources here have been chosen to show the continuation of a creative and intellectual culture in early medieval Europe at a time when popular representations imagine little but barbarism and ignorance. It is true that in this period most writing and scholarship was practiced by members of the Church: monks and nuns, priests and bishops. Yet religion was not their sole focus, as is commonly believed. They inherited and developed the styles and intellectual tools of the Romans and applied them to not only the Bible but also to romance, literary criticism, and natural science.

The sources come from the sixth through ninth centuries CE in Western Europe, from women and men, laity and clergy, a monk and a worldly cleric. We know little about the Gaulish poet Eucheria, but she seems to have been of noble birth and was clearly well educated. Her one surviving poem, excerpted here, may be difficult for modern audiences to understand fully but it is a masterful composition, equivalent to much of the poetry in the Roman Empire. She, like many authors in the Middle Ages, is in full command of the Latin language and is still familiar with classical culture and mythology, even though she was certainly a Christian. The monk Bede is recognized as one of the finest historians and scientists of the early medieval period. In his work *Reckoning of Time*, excerpted here, Bede shows how detailed scientific and mathematical observations could be made in the service of the Christian faith. His calculation of the phases of the moon and its influence on the tides is more accurate than anything produced in Greek or Roman antiquity and influenced later medieval developments in astronomy and mathematics. The bishop Amalarius of

Metz lived and wrote in the early ninth century at the height of the Carolingian Empire. Like Bede, he wrote for the promotion and perfection of Christianity, but built on classical models to establish new forms of scholarship. In the prologue to his antiphonary (a type of liturgical book used in church services), he details his editorial methods, based on the close reading and comparison of numerous antiphonaries.

These three sources are only a tiny selection of the vast number of medieval works that could be quoted to show that the Middle Ages were not a "Dark Age" lacking intelligence, creativity, or a knowledge of the classical past. Yes, the unified administration and continental economy of the Roman Empire disappeared in the early middle ages, but this does not mean that Europe succumbed to mere barbarism and ignorance. Medieval people did not turn away from reading and writing, or from classical literature, as Stephen Greenblatt claims, nor did they lose the Latinity and manuscripts of their Roman predecessors, as claimed in many textbooks. Medieval authors, priests, scientists, builders, and farmers all combined elements of Mediterranean and Germanic cultures together with the themes and images of Christianity to create a wholly new medieval society that should not be judged simply by the interests of the Roman Empire or of the Italian Renaissance.

PRIMARY DOCUMENTS
EUCHERIA, SATIRICAL LOVE POEM (ca. 575 CE)

Eucheria was a woman poet in Frankish Gaul during the sixth century. It is not known if she was a member of the Church or a laywoman. Her poem excerpted here survives in an anthology of secular poems compiled around 575 CE. In this satirical Latin poem, she weaves together ancient mythology and dramatic images in a series of absurd and impossible unions in order to mock a poor slave named Rusticus, who was apparently seeking her affections. This and other poems from this period demonstrate the continuity of Roman Imperial culture within the early medieval "barbarian" kingdoms.

I wish to fuse golden threads, shining with harmonious metal, with masses
  of bristles.
Silken coverings, gem-studded Laconian fabrics,
I say, must be matched with goat skins.

Let noble purple be joined with a frightful red jacket;
let the gleaming gemstone be joined to ponderous lead.
Let the pearl now be held captive by its own brightness,
    and let it shine enclosed in dark steel. . . .
Let the rock-dwelling toad love the golden serpent,
    and likewise let the female trout seek for herself the male snail.
And let the lofty lioness be joined with the foul fox;
let the ape embrace the sharp-eyed lynx.
Now let the doe be joined to the donkey, and the tigress to the wild ass;
    now let the fleet deer be joined to the torpid bull.
Let now the foul silphium juice taint the nectared rose-wine,
    and let now honey be mixed with vile poisons.
Let us associate sparkling water with the muddy cesspool;
let the fountain flow saturated with a mixture of filth. . . .
Let the times manipulate these monstrosities with uncertain consequences,
    and in this way let the slave Rusticus seek Eucheria.

Source: Mathisen, Ralph W. 2003. *People, Personal Expression, and Social Relations in Late Antiquity.* Ann Arbor: University of Michigan Press, 38–40.

VENERABLE BEDE ON CALCULATING THE MOON AND THE TIDES, *RECKONING OF TIME* (ca. 725)

Bede (673–735) was an Anglo-Saxon monk at the double monastery of Wearmouth-Jarrow in the kingdom of Northumbria, now modern Yorkshire in England and southern Scotland. He is revered as a saint, hence his title "the Venerable." He is renowned as one of the greatest scholars of the early medieval period even though he never left his village and monastery. His most famous work is his Ecclesiastical History of the English People, *a masterpiece of history and literature that connects his "barbarian" race with the ancient histories of the Bible and the Romans. He also wrote several works on compu-tus, the medieval science of time, which was used primarily for the proper calculation of Easter and other Christian feasts. Bede and other "computists" sought to balance the Christian calendar with Roman secular calendars and also with careful observations of the sun, moon, and stars. Bede's longest work of computus is his* De temporum ratione, *or* Reckoning of Time, *in which he provides the following discussion of the relationship between the moon and the tides.*

But more marvellous than anything else is the great fellowship that exists between the ocean and the course of the Moon. For at [the Moon's] every rising and setting, [the ocean] sends forth the strength of his ardour, which the Greeks call "rheuma," to cover the coasts far and wide; and when it retreats, it lays them bare. The sweet streams of the rivers it abundantly mingles together and covers over with salty waves. When the Moon passes on, [the ocean] retreats and restores the rivers to their natural sweetness and level, without delay. It is as if [the ocean] were dragged forwards against its will by certain exhalations of the moon, and when her power ceases, it is poured back again into his proper measure.

For as we taught above, the Moon rises and sets each day 4 *puncti* later than it rose or set the previous day; likewise, both ocean tides, be they by day or by night, morning or evening, never cease to come and go each day at a time which is later by almost the same interval. Now a *punctus* is one-fifth of an hour, and five *puncti* make an hour. Furthermore, because the Moon in two lunar months (that is, in 59 days) goes around the globe of the earth 57 times, therefore the ocean tide during this same period of time surges up to its maximum twice this number of times, that is, 114, and sinks back again to its bed the same number of times. For in the course of 29 days, the Moon lights up the confines of Earth 28 times, and in the twelve hours which are added on to make up the fullness of the natural month, it circles half the globe of the Earth, so that, for example, the new Moon which emerged [from conjunction] last month above the Earth at noon, will this month meet up with the Sun to be kindled at midnight beneath the Earth. Through this length of time, the tides will come twice as often, and 57 times "the high seas swell, breaking their barriers and once again retreat unto themselves" [Vergil, *Georgics* 2.479–80]. Because the Moon in half a month (that is, in 15 days and nights) circles about the Earth 14 times, and once besides around half the Earth, it happens that it is in the east at evening when it is full, while earlier it was in the west at evening when it was new. In this period of time, the sea ebbs and flows 29 times. Just as the Moon in 15 days (as we said) is flung back by its natural retardation towards the east from its position in the west at evening, [so that while it] occupies the east today at morning, it will be in the west at morning 15 days from now, so also the ocean tide which now occurs at evening, will after 15 days be in the morning. On the other hand, the morning tide, impeded by this daily drag, will then rise at evening. And because the Moon in one year (that is, in 12 of its months, which makes 354 days) circles the globe of the Earth 12 fewer times (that is, 342 times), so the ocean tide within the same period washes up against the land and recoils 684 times.

The sea reflects the course of the Moon not only by sharing its comings and goings, but also by a certain augmenting and diminishing of its size, so that the tide recurs not only at a later time than it did yesterday, but also to a greater or lesser extent. When the tides are increasing, they are called *malinae*, and when they are decreasing *ledones*. In alternating periods of seven and eight days, they divide up every month among themselves in their fourfold diversity of change. Sometimes by equal shares both fill up their course in 7½ days; sometimes they will arrive earlier or later, or be more or less strong than usual when they are pushed onwards or forced back by the winds, or by the pressure of some other phenomenon or natural force, with the result that sometimes their order is upset, and the *malina* tide claims more in this month, and less in the next. Hence both directions will begin now in the evening, now in the morning. Indeed, when an evening tide occurs at the full or new Moon, it will be a *malina*, and for the next seven days this same *malina* tide will be greater and stronger than the morning tide. Similarly if a *malina* tide starts in the morning, the morning tide for days afterwards will cover the land with more sea. The evening tide, confined to the boundaries laid down by the morning tide, refrains from extending its course further, although in some months both tides grow at utterly different rates.

Source: Bede. 1999. *The Reckoning of Time.* Translated by Faith Wallis. Liverpool: Liverpool University Press, 82–84.

AMALARIUS OF METZ, PROLOGUE TO HIS ANTIPHONARY (ca. 840)

Amalarius of Metz (ca. 775–850) was a cleric and courtier for Charlemagne and his son Louis the Pious. He was also bishop of Trier and Lyon, but best known for his contributions to the Christian liturgy, or the performance of religious rituals. The following passage comes from the prologue Amalarius wrote to an antiphonary, or a collection of verses from the Psalms and other liturgical material to be sung in church services. He demonstrates that he closely read, compared, and collated multiple Frankish antiphonaries in order to critically edit a new and superior edition. This sort of scholarship would be practiced occasionally throughout the Middle Ages but was perfected only in the seventeenth and eighteenth centuries.

1. After I had long been vexed because of the antiphonaries in our province that disagreed with each other—for the modern ones ran in a manner different from the ancient ones—and I did not know which was the better one to retain, it pleased the One Who gives to all in abundance to free me

from this worry. For when a multitude of antiphonaries was discovered in the monastery of Corbie, that is, three volumes of the nighttime office and a fourth which only contained the daily office, I struggled to steer my ship from the high seas of curiosity to the port of tranquility. 2. Now then, when I was sent to Rome by our holy and most Christian emperor Louis to the holy and most reverend Pope Gregory IV, the pope said to me the following about the aforementioned volumes: "I do not have an antiphonary to send to my son the Lord Emperor, because those which we had, Wala took away with him to Francia when he was carrying out another legation here." 3. I compared these volumes with our antiphonaries and discovered that they diverged from ours not only in their order but also in the wording and in a multitude of the responsories and antiphons, which we do not sing. Indeed, in many matters I found our volumes to be more reasonably laid out than those were. 4. I wondered how it had happened that mother and daughter diverged so much from one another. I discovered in one volume of the above-mentioned antiphonaries on the basis of what was contained within it that it had been arranged long ago by Pope Hadrian. I recognized that our volumes are quite a bit more ancient than that volume of the city of Rome.

5. Nonetheless I also recognized that in some places our books could be corrected by them, and in some ours were set forth more reasonably and suitably, as I said before. I seized therefore upon a middle path between the two so as not to diverge from our [books] when they were better arranged, and I not neglect those places where they were able to be corrected by the volumes of the City, either in their order or language. 6. Where our modern cantors have set down their offices in authoritative words in a more reasonable manner, by dividing the antiphons and responses by days of the week and on feast days and by distributing their antiphons for the feasts of the saints on their individual vigils, I have first written down the Roman order, then that of our cantors. Where I found such an order to be lacking, we have added it from both volumes, just as the days and weeks before Christmas and Easter shall reveal themselves. 7. Where the order of responses and antiphons in the examined volumes seems to be at odds with the order of the books from which they have been taken and from the harmony which reason decrees, I have not hesitated to follow in our antiphonary those things which seemed to agree better with the history or rationale of this or that feast.

8. Where something in the Roman antiphonary seemed to me to be in a better order, there I have written "R" in the margin for the city of Rome; and where it seemed to be so in ours, I have written "M," for the

city of Metz; and where our own wit (*ingenium*) has thought that something could be put in a more reasonable order, [I have written] "I" and "C" for indulgence (*indulgentia*) and love (*caritas*). 9. I therefore entreat cantors that they not despise our [suggestions] before they discuss them in the light of the order of the books and the fullness of reason. And if they should find these things to suit the order of books less well, or [should find] any other reason, let them indulge my inexperience, but let them not despise taking the produce from our garden which a red head offers to them.

Source: Amalarius of Metz. 2018. https://apps.carleton.edu/curricular/mars/assets/Amalarius_of_Metz_Prologue_to_the_Liber_de_ordine_antiphonarii_for_MARS_website.pdf, translated by W. L. North from *Amalarii Episcopi Opera Liturgica Omnia*, edited by J. M. Hannssens. Vatican City: Biblioteca Apostolica Vaticana, 1958, 1:361–63.

Further Reading

Baronius. 1588–1607. *Annales Ecclesiastici.* 12 vols. Antwerp: Ex Officina Plantiniana.

Bartlett, Robert, ed. 2001. *Medieval Panorama.* Los Angeles: J. Paul Getty Museum.

Bauer, Susan Wise. 2007. *The Story of the World: History for the Classical Child.* Rev. ed. Volume 2, *The Middle Ages, from the Fall of Rome to the Rise of the Renaissance.* Charles City, VA: Peace Hill Press.

Bauer, Susan Wise. 2010. *The History of the Medieval World: From the Conversion of Constantine to the First Crusade.* New York: W. W. Norton.

Brown, Peter. 1989. *The World of Late Antiquity, AD 150–750.* New York: W. W. Norton.

Brown, Peter. 2013. *The Rise of Western Christendom: Triumph and Diversity, A.D. 200–1000.* Rev. ed. Chichester, UK: Wiley-Blackwell.

Burckhardt, Jacob. 1878. *The Civilization of the Renaissance in Italy.* Translated by S. G. C. Middlemore. London: George Allen & Unwin Ltd.

Collins, Roger. 1999. *Early Medieval Europe, 300–1000.* 2d ed. Basingstoke, UK: Palgrave Macmillan.

Davis, William Stearns, ed. 1912–1913. *Readings in Ancient History: Illustrative Extracts from the Sources.* 2 vols. Boston: Allyn and Bacon.

Gibbon, Edward. 1827. *The History of the Decline and Fall of the Roman Empire.* 12 vols. Oxford: D. A. Talboys.

Goffart, Walter. 1980. *Barbarians and Romans, A.D. 418–584. The Techniques of Accommodation.* Princeton, NJ: Princeton University Press.

Greenblatt, Stephen. 2011. "The Answer Man," *New Yorker,* August 8, 2011. https://www.newyorker.com/magazine/2011/08/08/the-answer -man-stephen-greenblatt.

Hinch, Jim. 2012. "Why Stephen Greenblatt Is Wrong—and Why It Matters." *Los Angeles Review of Books*, December 1, 2012. https://lareviewofbooks .org/article/why-stephen-greenblatt-is-wrong-and-why-it-matters/.

Ker, W. P. 1904. *The Dark Ages*. New York: Charles Scribner's Sons.

Litvinoff, Barnet. 1991. *Fourteen Ninety-Two: The Decline of Medievalism and the Rise of the Modern Age*. New York: Macmillan.

Manchester, William. 1992. *A World Lit Only by Fire. The Medieval Mind and the Renaissance: Portrait of an Age*. Boston: Little, Brown, and Co.

Marsden, Richard. 2018. "*Game of Thrones*: Imagined World Combines Romantic and Grotesque Visions of Middle Ages." *The Conversation,* October 17, 2018. https://theconversation.com/game-of-thrones-imagined -world-combines-romantic-and-grotesque-visions-of-middle-ages-105141.

Mommsen, Theodor E. 1942. "Petrarch's Conception of 'The Dark Ages.'" *Speculum* 17, no. 2: 226–42.

ReadWorks. 2012. "Non-fiction: The Renaissance—Introduction to the Renaissance." *ReadWorks.* https://www.readworks.org/article/The -Renaissance---Introduction-to-the-Renaissance/. No longer available December 1, 2018.

Ripley, George, and Charles Anderson Dana. 1883. *The American Cyclopaedia: A Popular Dictionary of General Knowledge*. New York: D. Appleton and Co.

Ward-Perkins, Bryan. 2005. *The Fall of Rome and the End of Civilization*. Oxford: Oxford University Press.

2

Medieval People Thought the Earth Was Flat

What People Think Happened

A common claim of those who see the Middle Ages as the "Dark Ages" is that medieval people were ignorant about even the most basic facts of modern science. One of the most pervasive examples of this ignorance is the idea that medieval people believed the earth was flat. The spherical shape of Earth is so central to our modern understanding of nature and the universe, that it seems logical (if you believe in the "Dark Ages") that foolish medieval people would not know Earth was round. The misconception that medieval people believed Earth was flat, which is widely held by people today who know Earth is round, should not be confused with the beliefs of modern "flat Earth societies," which have been active mostly in just the last century and promote the idea of a genuinely flat Earth.

According to this fiction, medieval people understood Earth and the solar system so little that when they looked at the world around them, they could only perceive the superficial impression that everything was flat. And if the world was flat, then it was dangerous, even impossible, to go sailing out on the oceans, for fear of ships going off the edge of the world. It was Christopher Columbus, so the story goes, who had the courage and intelligence to sail across the ocean and prove that the world was actually a sphere. But Columbus was not fighting against general ignorance; he was fighting against the oppression of the Catholic Church, which supposedly forced the people to believe only what they read in the

Bible and not to ask new and difficult questions about the world around them. Columbus is thus made even more important in this view of history: he did not just reach the Americas, but he also tore down a willfully blind medieval worldview and challenged the dominance of the Church.

How the Story Became Popular

This medieval fiction has risen up and been knocked down so many times that it can be called a "zombie fiction." While many misconceptions of the Middle Ages have some foundation in historical reality, this one is almost wholly false. It is the prime example of modern biases against the Middle Ages that found their start during the European Enlightenment (ca. 1675–1800). In that period of exciting intellectual and philosophical developments, European thinkers were rightly proud of their advances in science, mathematics, liberty, and government. Many of these thinkers were Protestants, deists (who believed in a creator god but were not necessarily Christian), or even atheists, who looked with hostility or pity on the Catholic culture of medieval Europe. They sought ways to separate themselves from that past by depicting the medieval era as the opposite of everything they valued: medieval people were unscientific, illiterate, intolerant, despotic where modern thinkers of the eighteenth century focused on science, reading, toleration, democracy, and the rights of men.

These Enlightenment ideals guided many of the founders of the United States of America and it was especially in that young nation that the myth of a medieval belief in a flat Earth took hold. Americans have always defined themselves as innovators and rule breakers, eager to embrace as their own the heroes of the Age of Exploration, like Christopher Columbus and Ferdinand Magellan, and to inflate or distort their achievements for the purposes of nationalistic mythmaking. The New York author Washington Irving (1783–1859), most famous today for his 1820 short stories "Rip Van Winkle" and "The Legend of Sleepy Hollow," also published a four-volume *History of the Life and Voyages of Christopher Columbus* in 1828. His *History* was one of the most popular English-language publications of the nineteenth century. It went through some 175 editions and remained the major English-language biography of Columbus until 1942.

Irving studied actual manuscripts from the time of Columbus as he prepared this work, but in the end his *History* is primarily a work of romantic historical fiction written to bolster Anglo-American beliefs about the backwardness of the Middle Ages and the Catholic Church and the importance of advances made between the Renaissance and the Enlightenment. Irving promoted, or perhaps even invented, the idea that most people in the time of Columbus believed Earth was flat and that representatives of the Catholic Church supported this belief and tried to stop Columbus from disproving it. Irving constructed entire scenes and events to support these myths about Columbus, such as a fictitious church council at the University of Salamanca, where Columbus tried to justify his plans to sail west across the Atlantic Ocean to reach Asia before a panel of angry and doubtful churchmen. In the first Primary Document, Washington Irving lays out the various arguments that those churchmen supposedly made against Columbus's claim for a round Earth.

Thanks to the popularity of Irving's *History*, the belief that premodern people thought Earth was flat became part of a basic U.S. education and could be used as a "fact" to support a wide variety of arguments. The English-born, U.S.-raised scientist and historian John William Draper treats the belief in a flat Earth almost as a conspiracy engineered by the Catholic Church, which is the explicit enemy in his book *History of the Conflict between Religion and Science*: "it is to be remembered that Catholicism had irrevocably committed itself to the dogma of a flat Earth, with the sky as the floor of heaven, and hell in the under-world" (Draper 1875, 294). Similarly, the U.S. lawyer Robert Green Ingersoll (1833–1899) gave lectures and wrote books promoting humanism and agnosticism. In one of his most famous lectures, "Individuality" (1873), excerpted in the Primary Documents, Ingersoll praised people who thought for themselves and stood up against the weight of authority, especially religious authority. He uses the example of Ferdinand Magellan, supposedly proving the world was round in the face of widespread belief in a flat Earth. This story about Magellan, while false, is actually more logical than Irving's stories about Columbus: Magellan and his crew could actually have proven the sphericity of Earth through their circumnavigation of the globe, while Columbus could not have done so simply by crossing the Atlantic Ocean. Nonetheless, his story is a complete fabrication.

Magellan makes a similar appearance in the hugely popular work of Andrew Dickson White (1832–1918), the first president of Cornell University in New York, *A History of the Warfare of Science with Theology in Christendom* (1896). As the title makes clear, White imagined an all-out battle between science and Christianity, in which the Christian (primarily Catholic) Church actively suppressed learning and creativity for much of the previous two thousand years before he was writing. White's work is still in print and shapes antimedieval and anti-Catholic opinions to this day. White depicts the Catholic Church and the pope in particular as setting up "theological barriers" to the "geographical truth" revealed by Columbus and Magellan. We will explore White's book in greater detail in chapter 6, concerning the fiction that the medieval Church was antiscience.

Some nineteenth-century authors who wanted to believe in medieval "flat-Earthers" recognized a problem: many ancient and medieval authors actually described a round Earth. They got around this problem by hunting for any possible exceptions that could support their own arguments. They found only two and both are essentially late Roman rather than medieval authors: Lactantius (ca. 265–345 CE), an early Latin Christian apologist, and Cosmas Indicopleustes, a Byzantine Greek author of *Christian Topography* (547 CE). Both of these authors wrote in the early centuries of Christianity, when there was still disagreement over whether Christians should read only the Bible (thereby rejecting the huge corpus of pagan Greek and Latin literature) for knowledge about the world. Most Christians, following St. Augustine of Hippo (354–430 CE), answered "no" to this question and argued that all writings and knowledge are open to Christians so long as they do not directly contradict the teachings of the faith. Augustine himself said that much of the Bible should be understood metaphorically and that it should not be used as the basis for scientific or geographic truths (Russell 1991, 21–23).

Lactantius and Cosmas each rejected a round Earth, but for different reasons. Lactantius could not accept or understand the possibility of people living upside-down in the antipodes, the opposite side of the world, so he therefore rejected outright the possibility of a round Earth. Most ancient and medieval authors accepted a round Earth, but still debated whether antipodeans (natives of the other side of the Earth) actually existed. Cosmas similarly argued against the existence of the antipodes and antipodeans, but he also took literally a passage in the Bible that described Earth in the shape of a tent (Psalm 104:2–3). Manuscripts of his *Christian Topography* include schematic maps showing a flat, rectangular Earth under a vaulted heaven. What is important to remember about Lactantius and Cosmas is that their views form a tiny minority of dissenters compared to the thousands of medieval authors who espoused a spherical Earth. Those two authors were forgotten for most of the Middle Ages and only resurrected in the modern period by those actively seeking medieval flat-Earthers.

This is a myth that simply will not go away, as it is repeated by some of the most prominent and educated people around. Daniel Boorstin, the former Librarian of Congress, claimed in *The Discoverers*, his 1983 popular study of historical innovation, that ancient Greeks knew Earth was round but that in the millennium 300–1300 CE, Europeans forgot that idea: "During those centuries Christian faith and dogma suppressed the useful image of the world that had been so slowly, so painfully, and so scrupulously drawn by ancient geographers" (Boorstin 1983, 100). Boorstin adds to his fanciful picture of medieval superstition and ignorance by making the wholly unfounded claim that "in Columbus' day, a pilot who used the magnetic compass might be accused of trafficking with Satan" (Boorstin 1983, 221). Medieval scholars were impressed with magnetism and navigational compasses, which they were using by the twelfth century, but they considered them wonders of nature, not tools of Satan.

President Barack Obama, in a 2012 speech, compared people who denied the reality of climate change to people in the time of Columbus who supposedly believed Earth was flat. Around the same time, television pundit Glenn Beck, in an attack on Bill Nye "the Science Guy," claimed that it was Galileo who set out to prove the world was round. Yet this double error about a flat Earth and Galileo is hardly new: President Thomas Jefferson also made it in his *Notes on the State of Virginia*: "Galileo was sent to the inquisition for affirming that the Earth was a sphere: the government had declared it to be flat as a trencher, and Galileo was obliged to abjured his error" (Jefferson 1801, 236). Everyone in Galileo's time knew Earth was a sphere; Galileo rather was forced to reject his belief that Earth moved around the sun. Jefferson can be admired for many reasons, but not for his knowledge of the Scientific Revolution!

This fiction has now been removed from all serious historical surveys, but persists in some books for children, such as Susan Wise Bauer's *The Story of the World*. She implies that belief in a flat Earth was widespread and that only the voyages of Columbus and other explorers could change ideas about the world: "But the Renaissance wasn't just a time when people relearned old ideas. It was a time of new discoveries. For the first time, ships were sailing all over the world. Explorers were realizing that their old ideas about the world (like boiling seas in the south and water that poured forever off the edge of the world) were wrong. So during the Renaissance, men and women began to make new theories about the world" (Bauer 2007, 321).When librarians, presidents, and textbook authors all repeat the myth of the medieval belief in a flat Earth, it's not surprising that it won't go away.

PRIMARY DOCUMENTS

WASHINGTON IRVING, *A HISTORY OF THE LIFE AND VOYAGES OF CHRISTOPHER COLUMBUS* (1828)

Washington Irving (1783–1859) published A History of the Life and Voyages of Christopher Columbus *in 1828. While some of his work is based on historical research, this meeting of Columbus with Church authorities at the "Council of Salamanca" is complete fiction. But this story confirmed popular notions that any sort of wrong thinking in the Middle Ages could lead to prosecution and execution for heresy, and helped establish the myth of Columbus as a humble, intelligent, open-minded explorer faced with the "errors and prejudices, the mingled ignorance and erudition, and the pedantic bigotry" of the late medieval Church.*

Columbus before the Council at Salamanca

The interesting conference relative to the proposition of Columbus took place in Salamanca, the great seat of learning in Spain. It was held in the Dominican Convent of St. Stephen, in which Columbus was lodged and entertained with great hospitality during the course of the examination.

Religion and science were at that time, and more especially in that country, closely associated. The treasures of learning were immured in monasteries, and the professors' chairs were exclusively filled from the cloister. The domination of the clergy extended over the state as well as the church, and posts of honour and influence at court, with the exception of hereditary nobles, were almost entirely confided to ecclesiastics. It was even common to find cardinals and bishops in helm and corslet at the head of armies, for the crosier had been occasionally thrown by for the lance, during the holy war against the Moors. The era was distinguished for the revival of learning, but still more for the prevalence of religious zeal, and Spain surpassed all other countries in Christendom in the fervor of her devotion. The Inquisition had just been established in that kingdom, and every opinion that savoured of heresy made its owner obnoxious to odium and persecution.

Such was the period when a council of clerical sages was convened in the collegiate convent of St. Stephen, to investigate the new theory of Columbus. It was composed of professors of astronomy, geography, mathematics, and the other branches of science, together with various dignitaries of the church, and learned friars. Before this erudite assembly, Columbus presented himself to propound and defend his conclusions.

He had been scoffed at as a visionary by the vulgar and the ignorant; but he was convinced that he only required a body of enlightened men to listen dispassionately to his reasonings, to ensure triumphant conviction. . . .

What a striking spectacle must the hall of the old convent have presented at this memorable conference! A simple mariner, standing forth in the midst of an imposing array of professors, friars and dignitaries of the church; maintaining his theory with natural eloquence, and as it were, pleading the cause of the new world. We are told that when he began to state the grounds of his belief the friars of St. Stephen alone paid attention to him; that convent being more learned in the sciences than the rest of the university. The others appear to have entrenched themselves behind one dogged position; that after so many profound philosophers and cosmographers had been studying the form of the world, and so many able navigators had been sailing about it for several thousand years, it was great presumption in an ordinary man to supposed that there remained such a vast discovery for him to make.

Several of the objections opposed by this learned body have been handed down to us, and have provoked many a sneer at the expense of the University of Salamanca, but they are proofs not so much of the peculiar deficiency of that institution, as of the imperfect state of science at the time, and the manner in which knowledge, though rapidly extending, was still impeded in its progress by monastic bigotry. All subjects were still contemplated through the obscure medium of those ages when the lights of antiquity were trampled out, and faith was left to fill the place of inquiry. Bewildered in a maze of religious controversy, mankind had retraced their steps, and receded from boundary line of ancient knowledge. Thus, at the very threshold of the discussion, instead of geographical objections, Columbus was assailed with citations from the Bible and the Testament: the book of Genesis, the Psalms of David, the orations of the Prophets, the epistles of the Apostles, and the gospels of the Evangelists. To these were added the expositions of various saints and revered commentators: St. Chrysostom and St. Augustine, St. Jerome and St. Gregory, St. Basil and St. Ambrose, and Lactantius Firmianus, a redoubted champion of the faith. Doctrinal points were mixed up with philosophical discussions, and a mathematical demonstration was allowed no weight, if it appeared to clash with a text of scripture, or a commentary of one of the fathers. . . .

More grave objections were advanced on the authority of St. Augustine. He pronounces the doctrine of antipodes incompatible with the historical foundations of our faith; since, to assert that there were inhabited lands on the opposite side of the globe, would be to maintain that there were nations not descended from Adam, it being impossible for them to have passed the intervening ocean. This would be, therefore, to discredit the Bible, which expressly declares, that all men are descended from one common parent.

Such were the unlooked-for prejudices which Columbus had to encounter at the very outset of his conference, and which certainly relish more of the convent than the university. To his simplest proposition, the spherical form of the earth, were opposed figurative texts of scripture. They observed, that in the Psalms, the heavens are said to be extended like a hide; that is, according to the commentators, the curtain, or covering of a tent, which, among the ancient pastoral nations, was formed of the hides of animals; and that St. Paul, in his epistle to the Hebrews, compares the heavens to a tabernacle, or tent, extended over the earth, which they thence inferred must be flat.

Columbus, who was a devoutly religious man, found that he was in danger of being convicted, not merely of error, but of heterodoxy. Others, more versed in science, admitted the globular form of the earth, and the possibility of an opposite and inhabitable hemisphere; but they brought up the chimera of the ancients, and maintained that it would be impossible to arrive there, in consequence of the insupportable heat of the torrid zone. Even granting this could be passed, they observed, that the circumference of the earth must be so great as to require at least three years to the voyage, and those who should undertake it must perish of hunger and thirst, from the impossibility of carrying provisions for so long a period. He was told, on the authority of Epicurus, that, admitting the earth to be spherical, it was only inhabitable in the northern hemisphere, and in that section only was canopied by the heavens; that the opposite half was a chaos, a gulph, or a mere waste of water.

Not the least absurd objection advanced, was, that should a ship even succeed in reaching, in this way, the extremity of India, she could never get back again; for the rotundity of the globe would present a kind of mountain, up which it would be impossible for her to sail with the most favourable wind.

Such are specimens of the errors and prejudices, the mingled ignorance and erudition, and the pedantic bigotry, with which Columbus had to contend throughout the examination of his theory. Can we wonder at the difficulties and delays which he experienced at courts, when such vague and crude notions were entertained by the learned men of university? We must not suppose, however, because the objections here cited are all which remain on record, that they are all which were advanced; these only have been perpetuated on account of their superior absurdity. They were probably advanced by but few, and those persons immersed in theological studies, in cloistered retirement; where the erroneous opinions derived from books, had little opportunity of being corrected by the experience of the day.

Source: Irving, Washington. 1828. *A History of the Life and Voyages of Christopher Columbus*. 3 vols. New York: G. & C. Carvill, 1:73–78.

ROBERT GREEN INGERSOLL, "INDIVIDUALITY" (1873)

Robert Green Ingersoll (1833–1899) was one of the most popular public thinkers of later nineteenth-century America, who wrote and lectured extensively on rationality and agnosticism. The following passage comes from his famous lecture "Individuality," given first in 1873, in which he praises pivotal individuals from the past who stood up to tradition (especially religious tradition) by using their reason and intelligence. Here, Ingersoll applies stories usually associated with Columbus to the Portuguese explorer Ferdinand Magellan. There is no evidence anywhere else for this quote he attributes to Magellan, but it is still widely cited as a genuine statement from the sixteenth century.

How fortunate it is for us all that it is somewhat unnatural for a human being to obey. Universal obedience is universal stagnation; disobedience is one of the conditions of progress. Select any age of the world and tell me what would have been the effect of implicit obedience. Suppose the church had had absolute control of the human mind at any time, would not the words liberty and progress have been plotted from human speech? In defiance of advice, the world has advanced.

Suppose the astronomers had controlled the science of astronomy; suppose the doctors had controlled the science of medicine; suppose kings had been left to fix the forms of government; suppose our fathers had taken the advice of Paul, who said, "be subject to the powers that be, because they are ordained of God"; suppose the church could control the world to-day, we would go back to chaos and old night. Philosophy would be branded as infamous; Science would again press its pale and thoughtful face against the prison bars, and round the limbs of liberty would climb the bigot's flame.

It is a blessed thing that in every age someone has had individuality enough and courage enough to stand by his own convictions—someone who had the grandeur to say his say. I believe it was Magellan who said,

"The church says the earth is flat; but I have seen its shadow on the moon, and I have more confidence even in a shadow than in the church." On the prow of his ship were disobedience, defiance, scorn, and success.

Source: Ingersoll, Robert Green. 1902. "Individuality." In *The Works of Robert G. Ingersoll.* 12 vols. New York: Dresden Publishing Co., 1:169–206, at 170–71.

ANDREW DICKSON WHITE, *A HISTORY OF THE WARFARE OF SCIENCE WITH THEOLOGY IN CHRISTENDOM* (1897)

Andrew Dickson White's A History of the Warfare of Science with Theology in Christendom *was the culminating work of decades of conflict and debates between religious and scientific figures in the later nineteenth century, kindled especially by Charles Darwin's publication of* On the Origin of Species *in 1859. White clearly takes the side of scientists who demanded that the study of the natural world be entirely separated from religious belief, and to make his point he endeavored to show that religious institutions, especially the Catholic Church, always had and still have the goal of suppressing and delegitimizing scientific progress (see chapter 6 for more on White's role in shaping this myth). In the passage excerpted here White claims that nobody knew before Columbus and Magellan that the world was round so he can thereby argue that the papacy tried to hide this "new" truth from the people.*

The warfare of Columbus the world knows well: how the Bishop of Ceuta worsted him in Portugal; how sundry wise men of Spain confronted him with the usual quotations from the Psalms, from St. Paul, and from St. Augustine; how, even after he was triumphant, and after his voyage had greatly strengthened the theory of the earth's sphericity, with which the theory of the antipodes was so closely connected, the Church by its highest authority solemnly stumbled and persisted in going astray. In 1493 Pope Alexander VI, having been appealed to as an umpire between the claims of Spain and Portugal to the newly discovered parts of the earth, issued a bull laying down upon the earth's surface a line of demarcation between the two powers. This line was drawn from north to south a hundred leagues west of the Azores; and the Pope in the plenitude of his knowledge declared that all lands discovered east of this line should belong to the Portuguese, and all west of it should belong to the Spaniards. This was hailed as an exercise of divinely illuminated power by the Church; but difficulties arose, and in 1506 another attempt was made by Pope Julius II to draw the line three hundred and seventy leagues west of the Cape

Verde Islands. This, again, was supposed to bring divine wisdom to settle the question; but, shortly, overwhelming difficulties arose; for the Portuguese claimed Brazil, and, of course, had no difficulty in showing that they could reach it by sailing to the east of the line, provided they sailed long enough. The lines laid down by Popes Alexander and Julius may still be found upon the maps of the period, but their bulls have quietly passed into the catalogue of ludicrous errors.

Yet the theological barriers to this geographical truth yielded but slowly. Plain as it had become to scholars, they hesitated to declare it to the world at large. Eleven hundred years had passed since St. Augustine had proved its antagonism to Scripture, when Gregory Reysch gave forth his famous encyclopaedia, the *Margarita Philosophica*. Edition after edition was issued, and everywhere appeared in it the orthodox statements; but they were evidently strained to the breaking point; for while, in treating of the antipodes, Reysch refers respectfully to St. Augustine as objecting to the scientific doctrine, he is careful not to cite Scripture against it, and not less careful to suggest geographical reasoning in favour of it.

But in 1519 science gains a crushing victory. Magellan makes his famous voyage. He proves the earth to be round, for his expedition circumnavigates it; he proves the doctrine of the antipodes, for his shipmates see the peoples of the antipodes. Yet even this does not end the war. Many conscientious men oppose the doctrine for two hundred years longer. Then the French astronomers make their measurements of degrees in equatorial and polar regions, and add to their proofs that of the lengthened pendulum. When this was done, when the deductions of science were seen to be established by the simple test of measurement, beautifully and perfectly, and when a long line of trustworthy explorers, including devoted missionaries, had sent home accounts of the antipodes, then, and then only, this war of twelve centuries ended.

Source: White, Andrew Dickson. 1897. *A History of the Warfare of Science with Theology in Christendom.* 2 vols. New York: D. Appleton & Co., 1:108–9.

What Really Happened

In simplest terms, almost no educated person in ancient or medieval Europe believed Earth was flat. While some of the earliest ancient peoples apparently believed in a flat Earth, from the time of the classical Greeks in the sixth and fifth century BCE, a round Earth has been common knowledge in Western culture. All of the greatest Greek philosophers and naturalists taught about a spherical earth: Pythagoras, Parmenides,

Plato, Aristotle, Euclid, Eratosthenes, and others. Their ideas were clarified and systematized by authors in the Roman Empire, such as Pliny the Elder (23–79 CE) and Claudius Ptolemy (90–168 CE), whose works on nature and geography were copied and read during the Middle Ages. The roundness of Earth is clear not only in scholarly writings but also appears frequently in the sculpture and paintings of the polytheistic Greeks and Romans as well as the monotheistic Jews, Christians, and Muslims of the Middle Ages. Kings, emperors, and God were all depicted holding a spherical Earth (an orb) in their hand as a sign of their earthly power.

Our main concern here, however, is with the later medieval centuries leading up to Columbus and Magellan (ca. 1100–1500). Rather than being a period of widespread belief in a flat Earth, these centuries are instead the great age of "spherical cosmology." According to medieval cosmology (the study of the structure of the universe), the planets and stars move along the surface of invisible spheres, the entire cosmos is spherical, and the movement of the stars and planets was said to produce the "music of the spheres." Every learned author, when writing on the nature of the world and the cosmos, describes both Earth and the universe as a sphere. Nor were these authors secular "freethinkers," working outside or against religious authority: almost every single medieval author who describes a spherical Earth was a member of the Catholic Church, from monks, nuns, and friars to priests, bishops, and popes. This is both because education and Latin literacy were primarily the concern of the clergy until the end of the Middle Ages and because the Church had no objection to the idea of a spherical Earth.

All of the following medieval primary sources describe a spherical Earth and all were written by members of the Catholic Church (one is even a saint): Adelard of Bath, John of Sacrobosco, and Saint Thomas Aquinas. Moreover, all of these sources treat the sphericity of Earth as an obvious fact that does not need to be proven. Instead they use a spherical Earth for deeper discussions about physics, optics, travel, logic, or theology. Adelard of Bath was a cleric and scientist in twelfth-century England. In his book *Natural Questions*, written around 1130, he presents in dialogue format his explanations for numerous questions about nature. These include "How the Globe Is Supported in the Middle of the Air" and "If a hole were made straight through the earth, in what direction would a stone thrown into it fall?" Both questions begin with the assumption that Earth is a "globe" and his real interest is instead with the nature of gravity on cosmic and local levels (even though his explanations are far removed from the gravitational physics of Newton or Einstein). What is especially important to note here is that his travels and scientific investigations were allowed and even encouraged by Church authorities.

In the thirteenth century, the clergyman and scholar John of Sacrobosco wrote a brief *Tractatus de Sphaera*, "Treatise on the Sphere," which describes and explains the spherical shape of Earth and the cosmos. His work was presenting little that was new, but is rather a university textbook summarizing widely held ideas, like those underlying the "questions" of Adelard of Bath. Sacrobosco's book was probably the most widely read treatment of the shape of Earth between the thirteenth and sixteenth centuries. It survives in many manuscripts copies and went on to be printed during the Renaissance era. Some manuscripts and printed copies contain illustrations (like the one in the Primary Documents) showing a round Earth for demonstrating its implications in areas such as navigation or the calculation of eclipses.

The last source printed here is especially revealing of medieval attitudes about the shape of Earth. Thomas Aquinas (1225–1274) was a Dominican friar, theologian, philosopher, and professor at the University of Paris. He was canonized as a saint soon after his death and he became known as the "Angelic Doctor" for the importance of his ideas in explaining and guiding Catholic Christianity. In his longest and most famous work, the *Summa Theologica*, he aimed to describe succinctly every topic that related to faith and reason in God's universe. This included scientific topics, because God created everything. Toward the very beginning of this massive (and unfinished) work, Aquinas discusses what types of knowledge are necessary for understanding God. For our purposes, what matters is an example Aquinas gives of a commonly known fact that can be proven with different sciences: "the astronomer and the physicist both may prove the same conclusion: that the earth, for instance, is round: the astronomer by means of mathematics . . . but the physicist by means of matter itself." Aquinas, one of the most influential voices of the medieval Church, took it for granted that Earth was round, that this knowledge could be gained in multiple ways, and that this fact in no way threatened the Church or Christian belief.

PRIMARY DOCUMENTS

ADELARD OF BATH, *NATURAL QUESTIONS* (ca. 1130)

Adelard was an English scholar of the twelfth century (ca. 1080–1150), who is best known for his work on mathematics and natural philosophy, influenced by Greek and Arabic learning from the Mediterranean. Little is known of his personal life, but he was almost certainly a cleric (an ordained member of the Church), probably in the service of Bishop John de Villula of the diocese of Bath and Wells (d. 1122). Adelard studied in France, like many English clerics of his day, but finding that education insufficient, he traveled throughout Greek lands and the Crusader states of the eastern Mediterranean. He was in Antioch (Syria) during an earthquake in 1114, a point he mentions in his work Quaestiones Naturales, *or* Natural Questions, *completed around 1130. This work, like many in the eleventh and twelfth centuries, takes the form of a dialogue, in imitation of Plato's Socratic dialogues. In it Adelard discusses numerous scientific questions with his "nephew" (who might be invented for this work). In the two questions excerpted here Adelard explains how Earth is suspended in space and explores the hypothetical question of what would happen to a stone dropped through the earth. In both cases, he takes for granted that Earth is a "globe", while he also demonstrates (as far as a twelfth-century scholar could) an understanding of gravity. Note that even though his explanations are not considered correct anymore according to modern physics, they are nonetheless based entirely on reason and the observation of nature.*

Chapter XLVIII. How the Globe Is Supported in the Middle of the Air

NEPHEW: . . . I will put the first question that comes into my head: How is it that this earth of ours which supports all weights (I am speaking not of simples, but of compounds), how is it that it remains in the same place, or by what is it supported? If all heavy bodies, such as stone, wood, etc., require support, and cannot through their weight be supported by the air, then much more does the earth, which is heavier than everything else put together, require to be supported, nor can it be held in position by so unstable a body as the air. Hence it is contrary to reason that it should maintain its position.

ADELARD: Certainly it is inexpedient that it should fall, and that we also shall not fall along with it. I will show that its remaining in its position is in accordance with reason. From the character of its primary qualities, we know that the earth has weight; that which has weight is more secure in the lowest position; and everything is naturally fond of that which preserves its life, and tends towards that for which it has a liking. It follows therefore that everything which is earthy tends towards the lowest possible position. But in the case of anything round, it is clear that the middle and the lowest are the same, and therefore all earthy things tend towards the middle position. Now the middle position is a simple and indivisible middle point, and it is therefore clear that all earthy things tend towards a local and simple point. But this local point is not several but one, and must necessarily be occupied by one thing, not by several; but to it, as has been said, all things tend: consequently each one thing presses on something else, since all and sundry are hastening to the same point. Now the point to which all weighty bodies are hastening is that to which they are falling, for the fall of weighty bodies is merely a hastening to a middle point. By the point to which they are falling I mean the fixed middle point. The place to which they are falling—the middle point—remains fixed; and therefore, while falling into a stable position, they yet remain fixed, unless some force be impressed on them as a result of which they are diverted from their natural course. The very opposite then is the case to what you thought; and you will now see clearly that it is what you thought to be a reason for falling which gives stability and coherence to heavy bodies. They are, therefore, in some way supported by the point to which they are hastening; and if it should move in any direction, all the things which are affected towards it would also of necessity move, though of course in that selfsame spot we have not the first but the second cause of stability: for, in accordance with the reason previously given, the first cause of this equilibrium is the property of the subject, the second the stability of the point which it makes for.

Chapter XLIX. If a hole were made straight through the earth, in what direction would a stone thrown into it fall?

NEPHEW: My next question is in no wise contrary to what has gone before; I see that this results from the mere coherence of things. My difficulty is this: Supposing the earth to be pierced, so that there were a passage straight through, and a stone be thrown in, what would be the direction of its fall?

ADELARD: That which causes the stationary position of the earth, would produce equilibrium in the stone.

NEPHEW: The answer satisfies me; for I understand that it would come to rest at the central point.

ADELARD: There is a further point I should like to make clear to you: as all nature loves its like, so it shuns the contrary. Fire is opposed to earth in the effective power of its qualities, and hence it follows that earth shuns fire. The whole of the upper space environing the world is the home of fire, and this upper space with its fire is therefore necessarily to be shunned by earth: but whatever flees from the central point will come into collision with that which it wants to avoid: therefore that it may not in unfortunate flight come into collision with that which it avoids, the earth seeks that point which is on all sides equally distant from the upper spaces. This position then it holds for two reasons, (1) through its own weight it seeks that for which it has a fondness, (2) because it shuns that which it does not like.

NEPHEW: If then, as explained by you, the centre and the lowest point are the same thing in the frame-work of the universe, how is it that Statius, the poet has contrasted them; for he says, "Either the lowest part of the earth or its centre, both adjoin the hidden universe"; by thus separating them, he has adjudged them to be opposites.

ADELARD: He has a two-fold object to gain: he is both hinting at the falsity of vulgar and self-contradictory belief, and openly setting forth a physical truth; for the common herd do not distinguish between circumference and containing plans. Consequently, with confused minds they wrongly trust the eye, and wrongly invent an hemispherical imperfection; and, therefore, from this stupid point of view the bottom of the earth will not be the centre. To right the mistake is, however, an easy task for the individual, and therefore outside the scope of the present treatise. It is now clear even to the unlearned that earth is both the bottom and the centre of this mundane mass.

Source: Adelard of Bath. 1920. *Natural Questions.* Printed with *Dodi Ve-Nechdi (Uncle & Nephew).* In *The work of Berachya Hanakdan*, edited and translated by H. Gollancz. Oxford: Oxford University Press, 137–39.

JOHN OF SACROBOSCO, *TREATISE ON THE SPHERE* (ca. 1230)

John of Sacrobosco (ca. 1195–ca. 1256) was most likely a monk or cleric and an astronomer who taught at the University of Paris in the thirteenth century. His name means "John of Hollywood," and he may have been English, but little is known about his life. He is best known for his textbook on astronomy and cosmology, Tractatus de sphaera, *"Treatise on the Sphere" (written ca. 1230). He also wrote books on mathematics and the religious calendar. The "sphere" of the* Tractatus *is the spherical universe, in which are nested the spheres on which the planets are thought to move and the spherical Earth, which was believed to be the center of the universe. There are few original ideas in this book (just like textbooks today), as it draws primarily on Ptolemy's* Almagest *and Islamic astronomical works.* Tractatus de sphaera *was one of the most widely read works on astronomy in Europe throughout the later Middle Ages and into the early modern period, appearing in both manuscript and print until the seventeenth century (after Galileo). Anyone with a basic education in science or mathematics would know from this book that the world was round.*

THE EARTH A SPHERE. That the earth, too, is round is shown thus. The signs and stars do not rise and set the same for all men everywhere but rise and set sooner for those in the east than for those in the west; and of this there is no other cause than the bulge of the earth. Moreover, celestial phenomena evidence that they rise sooner for Orientals than for westerners. For one and the same eclipse of the moon which appears to us in the first hour of the night appears to Orientals about the third hour of the night, which proves that they had night and sunset before we did, of which setting the bulge of the earth is the cause.

FURTHER PROOFS OF THIS. That the earth also has a bulge from north to south and vice versa is shown thus: To those living toward the north, certain stars are always visible, namely, those near the North Pole, while others which are near the South Pole are always concealed from them. If, then, anyone should proceed from the north southward, he might go so far that the stars which formerly were always visible to him now would tend toward their setting. And the farther south he went, the more they would be moved toward their setting. Again, that same man now could see stars which formerly had always been hidden from him. And the reverse would happen to anyone going from the south northward. The cause of this is simply the bulge of the earth. Again, if the earth were flat from east to west, the stars would rise as soon for westerners as for Orientals. which is false. Also, if the earth were flat from north to south and vice versa, the stars which were always visible to anyone would continue to be so wherever he went, which is false. But it seems flat to human sight because it is so extensive.

SURFACE OF THE SEA SPHERICAL. That the water has a bulge and is approximately round is shown thus: Let a signal be set up on the sea-coast and a ship leave port and sail away so far that the eye of a person standing at the foot of the mast can no longer discern the signal. Yet if the ship is stopped, the eye of the same person, if he has climbed to the top of the mast, will see the signal clearly. Yet the eye of a person at the bottom of the mast ought to see the signal better than he who is at the top, as is shown by drawing straight lines from both to the signal. And there is no other explanation of this thing than the bulge of the water. For all other impediments are excluded, such as clouds and rising vapors. Also, since water is a homogeneous body, the whole will act the same as its parts. But parts of water, as happens in the case of little drops and dew on herbs, naturally seek a round shape. Therefore, the whole, of which they are parts, will do so.

Source: John of Sacrobosco. 1949. *Tractatus de Sphaera*, translated by Lynn Thorndike. In *The Sphere of Sacrobosco and Its Commentators*. Chicago: University of Chicago Press, 121–22.

IMAGE FROM AN EARLY PRINTED COPY OF JOHN OF SACROBOSCO, *TREATISE ON THE SPHERE* (ca. 1550)

John of Sacrobosco's Treatise on the Sphere *was copied by hand throughout the rest of the Middle Ages and then printed during the early modern period. The image here comes from a sixteenth-century edition of his work, but represents the sort of illustrations found in many medieval copies of the* Treatise. *It illustrates the previous passage discussing how sailors know the surface of the sea is spherical by comparing what they can see from on deck and from on top of the mast.*

Source: Joannes de Sacrobosco (1550). *Libellus de Sphaerea* (Book on the Sphere). Wittenberg.

ST. THOMAS AQUINAS, *SUMMA THEOLOGICA* (1265–1274)

Thomas Aquinas (1225–1274) is considered a saint and a doctor of the Church because of the importance of his teaching and writings for clarifying and shaping Catholicism. His longest and most famous work is his Summa Theologica, *or "Summation of Theology," which has shaped Catholic thought to this very day and is also recognized as a central work of medieval philosophy outside of Catholicism. In the opening "articles" or questions from Book I of the* Summa, *Aquinas explores the nature and sources of knowledge, whether from the Bible or from philosophy. In this passage, he uses the sphericity of the earth as an example of basic knowledge gained through natural reason.*

Book I, Article 1: Whether, besides philosophy, any further doctrine is required?

Objection 1: It seems that, besides philosophical science, we have no need of further knowledge. For man should not seek to know what is above reason: "Seek not the things that are too high for thee" [Sirach 3:22]. But whatever is not above reason is fully treated of in philosophical science. Therefore any other knowledge besides philosophical science is superfluous.

Objection 2: Further, knowledge can be concerned only with being, for nothing can be known, save what is true; and all that is, is true. But everything that is, is treated of in philosophical science—even God himself; so that there is a part of philosophy called theology, or the divine science, as Aristotle has proved (*Metaphysics* VI). Therefore, besides philosophical science, there is no need of any further knowledge.

Reply to Objection 1: Although those things which are beyond man's knowledge may not be sought for by man through his reason, nevertheless, once they are revealed by God, they must be accepted by faith. Hence the sacred text continues, "For many things are shown to thee above the understanding of man" [Sirach 3:25]. And in this, the sacred science consists.

Reply to Objection 2: Sciences are differentiated according to the various means through which knowledge is obtained. For the astronomer and the physicist both may prove the same conclusion: that the earth, for instance, is round: the astronomer by means of mathematics (*i.e.* abstracting from matter), but the physicist by means of matter itself. Hence there is no reason why those things which may be learned from philosophical science, so far as they can be known by natural reason, may not also be taught us by another science so far as they fall within revelation. Hence theology included in sacred doctrine differs in kind from that theology which is part of philosophy.

Source: Thomas Aquinas. 1920. *The "Summa Theologica" of St. Thomas Aquinas. Part I. QQ I–XXVI.* Literally translated by the Fathers of the Dominican Province. 2d and rev. ed. London: Burns, Oates and Washbourne, 2–3.

Further Reading

Adelard of Bath. *Natural Questions.* 1920. Printed with *Dodi Ve-Nechdi (Uncle & Nephew).* In *The work of Berachya Hanakdan,* edited and translated by H. Gollancz, 85–161. Oxford: Oxford University Press.

Bauer, Susan Wise. 2007. *The Story of the World: History for the Classical Child.* Rev. ed. Vol. 2, *The Middle Ages, from the Fall of Rome to the Rise of the Renaissance.* Charles City, VA: Peace Hill Press.

Bishop, Louise. 2008. "The Myth of the Flat Earth." In *Misconceptions about the Middle Ages,* edited by Stephen J. Harris and Bryon Lee Grigsby. New York: Routledge.

Boorstin, Daniel. 1983. *The Discoverers.* New York: Random House, 1983.

Draper, John William. 1875. *History of the Conflict between Religion and Science.* New York: D. Appleton and Co.

Garwood, Christine. 2007. *Flat Earth: The History of an Infamous Idea.* New York: St. Martin's Press.

Jefferson, Thomas. 1801. *Notes on the State of Virginia.* 8th ed. Boston: David Carlisle.

Russell, Jeffrey Burton. 1991. *Inventing the Flat Earth: Columbus and Modern Historians.* Westport, CT: Praeger Publishers.

Thomas Aquinas. 1920–1922. *The "Summa Theologica" of St. Thomas Aquinas.* Literally translated by the Fathers of the Dominican Province. 2d and rev. edition. 10 vols. London: Burns, Oates and Washbourne.

Thorndike, Lynn. 1949. *The Sphere of Sacrobosco and Its Commentators.* Chicago: University of Chicago Press.

White, Andrew Dickson. 1897. *A History of the Warfare of Science with Theology in Christendom.* 2 vols. New York: D. Appleton and Co.

3

Peasants Never Bathed, and They Ate Rotten Meat

What People Think Happened

If there is one thing everyone knows about medieval people, it is that they were much dirtier than we are today. Most medieval people were peasants, agricultural laborers who worked and lived in dirt and manure, their bodies serving as permanent homes to lice and fleas. Soap and bathing, common among the Greeks and Romans, vanished during the Middle Ages for rich and poor alike. While peasants were covered in muck, the wealthy bathed maybe once a year but usually just covered their stench with expensive perfumes. Medieval towns and cities were even worse: without any toilets or sewers, urban streets and pathways were filled with human and animal waste and the garbage from cooking and industry. The dirtiness of these towns suggests there was at that time no concept of public hygiene and that medieval officials and governments cared nothing for the health of their people (these ideas are presented as a caricature by Thorndike 1928, 192). One writer of the nineteenth century, John William Draper, imagined that Europe did not change at all for one thousand years of filthiness, laziness, and emptiness (see Primary Documents).

These filthy towns, we are led to believe, were inevitable magnets for disease. Medieval people, because they never bathed, were more likely than modern people to contract horrible diseases—hence the supposed dominance of plague during the Middle Ages (see chapter 11 on this fiction). A recent children's book on the Crusades claims (without

evidence): "Because they did not bathe often, the crusaders were suscepti-
ble to disease and plagues" (Cartlidge 2002, 26), A recent popular website
on medieval diseases reinforces this stereotype, using the title "7 Outbreaks That Afflicted Europe during the Unsanitary Middle Ages." Those
"diseases" are St. Anthony's Fire, bubonic plague, the "dancing plague,"
the "Water Elf Disease," the "King's Evil" (scrofula), misbehaving nuns,
and the English sweating sickness (Bunn 2015). The Middle Ages are
here defined by a combination of outrageous diseases or behaviors and
the filthiness which supposedly caused them, even though most have no
connection to sanitation and several of them are postmedieval.

As if it were not enough that medieval peasants are imagined to be
filthy, lousy, and riddled with disease, some popular histories assert
that medieval people ate spoiled meat and masked its smell with spices.
Because medieval people (according to popular opinion) were desperately
poor and had no access to fresh food, they had to resort to eating potentially dangerous meat.

How the Story Became Popular: Bathing

The idea that people were invariably dirty through the entire Middle
Ages can be blamed almost entirely on one person, the French historian
Jules Michelet (1798–1874), whom you will meet in other chapters of
this book. He notoriously claimed that the Middle Ages were "a thousand
years without a bath" (Michelet 1862, 110). Michelet was a hugely popular author in nineteenth-century France, and his works were translated
into numerous other languages, carrying his extreme ideas about the Middle Ages around the world. Although Michelet seems to have knowingly
exaggerated the filthiness of the Middle Ages for the purpose of deriding
contemporary French conservatives, who admired the medieval era, many
people have taken his statement at face value.

Michelet's infamous quote about the Middle Ages was no throwaway
phrase, for it forms the heart of his argument about the physical and
spiritual backwardness of medieval society, represented best (he claims) by
the spread of leprosy in the thirteenth century. He attributes the spread
of leprosy to a variety of causes: European contact with Asia during the
Crusades, the growing desire among Europeans for exotic spices (not for
eating but for sexual stimulation), and especially the hatred of cleanliness
supposedly preached by body-hating Catholic saints and clergy (see Primary Documents). Michelet claims that all European peasants blindly
followed medieval monks, who taught such excessive hatred of bodies and

sexuality that they refused even to take off their clothes and thus wash themselves. Unsurprisingly, he offers no evidence for any of these claims, other than to say, "More than one saint boasted of having never washed even his hands" (Michelet 1863, 118).

John William Draper, Jules Michelet, and other nineteenth-century historians made the mistake of applying the acts of extreme asceticism and bodily punishment of a few saints to all medieval people. Draper, as seen in the Primary Documents, refers to a story about St. Thomas Becket, archbishop of Canterbury (1119–1170). When his body was searched after he was murdered by knights in the service of King Henry II of England, it was discovered that he wore rough and filthy animal skins, swarming with foul insects, under his luxurious clerical robes. Historians now recognize this as a singular act of religious devotion through bodily neglect, but Draper could only imagine that if one of the wealthiest and most powerful men in twelfth-century England was this filthy, the lower classes must be even worse. In a similar case of applying one medieval example to the entire Middle Ages, some modern historians misinterpret or exaggerate condemnations of bathing during the Black Death (Stapelberg 2016, 167). In 1348, representatives of the University of Paris medical faculty issued a public statement about the causes and treatment of the current plague (Horrox 1994, 163). This included a warning against bathing too much, which they feared might open the pores and allow in the poisoned air (*miasma*), which they thought caused or transferred the plague. While we might laugh at their misunderstanding of bacterial infection, the point here is that bathing was being restricted only in this particular instance and for people who bathed "too much." This is not a society against bathing in general.

Even though most twentieth- and twenty-first-century books on the Middle Ages avoid this sort of language or baseless conclusions about medieval bodies, the pervasive filthiness of medieval peasants, or even of all medieval people, remains a recurring theme in movies and television. In a stereotypical scene, the camera pans from the noble knights and ladies, clean of face and wearing rich garments, to a crowd of downtrodden peasants, their clothing barely held together and dirt smeared over their faces and hands. That dirt is supposed to add a touch of gritty realism, to show us the "real" Middle Ages, as opposed to the silly and saccharine costumes of older "medieval" movies. A clear demonstration of increasing dirt and grit in medieval movies can be seen in the progression from Errol Flynn's colorful and dashing *Adventures of Robin Hood* (1938, dir. M. Curtiz and W. Keighley), to the dusty camaraderie of Kevin Costner's

Robin Hood: Prince of Thieves (1991, dir. Kevin Reynolds), and at last to the deeply disturbing and "historically plausible gritty world" of Russell Crowe's *Robin Hood* (2010, dir. Ridley Scott) (Bildhauer 2016, 57–58). Dirt and violence go hand in hand in these medieval moves.

While we can realistically expect a bit of dirt on a band of forest outlaws like Robin and his Merry Men, an even clearer example of dirt being used to imply medieval realism is seen in the British television series *Last Kingdom* (BBC Two, 2015), based on the novels of Bernard Cornwell. The opening sequence of the first episode shows us the capital city of a fictional (but otherwise historically convincing) kingdom in Anglo-Saxon Northumbria, 866 CE, being attacked by Vikings. Nearly every Anglo-Saxon in this city, from the crowds of aimless peasants up to the king himself and his royal steward, has dirty clothes and a dirty face. The buildings and furniture are likewise poorly made and covered in dirt. We are led to believe that these people have no inclination or idea how to clean their own bodies, homes, or city. Yet this dirty realism is often convincing: surely these people without indoor plumbing or readily accessible mirrors were much dirtier than us, right?

How the Story Became Popular: Spices and Rotten Meat

A close corollary to the image of the filthy medieval peasant is the idea that medieval people, or at least poor ones, ate rotten meat and used spices to disguise the stench and taste. This myth builds upon several unfounded assumptions about medieval people: they were so uneducated in the basics of hygiene that they did not understand fresh from raw meat (see chapter 9 on medieval medicine); or they were often so poor (or perhaps careless) that they had to keep meat well past the point of spoilage; or that their stomachs were supposedly much tougher than ours and thus could handle eating rotten meat (van Winter 2007, 55–56).

The belief that medieval people regularly ate spoiled meat is still frequently invoked in the media, but it does not seem to be any older than a book from 1939. Sir Jack Cecil Drummond (1891–1952) was a British chemist and nutrition expert, who wrote *The Englishman's Food: Five Centuries of English Diet* in 1939 with his wife, Anne Wilbraham (1907–1952). (They were tragically murdered, along with their daughter Elizabeth, while on holiday in France in 1952, an event known since as the "Dominici affair," which is still studied by crime historians and police officials.) Most of *The Englishman's Food* is dedicated to the more recent history of English diet, nutrition, and cuisine. Only the very beginning provides a brief history of later medieval and early modern English food, and it is there that Drummond and Wilbraham repeated or invented myths about spoiled medieval meat.

Drummond and Wilbraham's description of medieval cooking is based mostly on later medieval London, which was home to many "cookshops," early restaurants where you could buy prepared meat pies or have your own meat cooked. There survives legislation from this period condemning the sale of spoiled meat in these cookshops, and Drummond and Wilbraham extrapolate from that the fiction that all medieval people regularly ate spoiled meat. So where the evidence shows us that the government of medieval London was actually quite modern in caring about health and food safety, Drummond and Wilbraham instead could only exaggerate to match popular stereotypes about filthy and sickly medieval people.

The authors further confused the issue by misunderstanding a 1594 recipe for improving "green" meat that called for wrapping it and burying it for a day. They took "green" to mean "spoiled" when it was actually a common English word at the time for meat of a freshly killed animal that needed aging or for uncured cheeses like cottage cheese and ricotta. Burying the meat hastens the aging process, which tenderizes and improves the flavor of some cuts of beef and wild game (Myers 2018). The authors make a leap of logic from "green" meat in 1594 to the medieval spice trade, claiming, "The popularity of strong seasoning for meat was undoubtedly due to the frequency with which it was necessary to mask taint." Exotic spices from the Orient were best for this purpose, the authors claim, but poorer folk could also use onions, garlic, and herbs for this purpose (Drummond and Wilbraham 1991, 37).

PRIMARY DOCUMENTS

JOHN WILLIAM DRAPER, *HISTORY OF THE CONFLICT BETWEEN RELIGION AND SCIENCE* (1875)

John William Draper (1811–1882) is remembered as a pioneer in the fields of chemistry and photography, famed for producing some of the first clear photographs around 1840. But he was also an amateur historian, writing books on the American Civil War and European intellectual history. He was an active promoter of the "conflict thesis," claiming that religion and science are always necessarily in conflict. This thesis is sometimes called the "Draper-White thesis" after him and his contemporary, Andrew Dickson White. In the following excerpt, Draper stresses how unbelievably filthy medieval Europe was as part of his broader effort to undermine the validity of medieval thought, religion, and culture. Draper returns in chapter 6 as a promoter of the fiction that the medieval Church actively suppressed scientific investigation and knowledge.

We may now examine somewhat more minutely the character of the resistances which thus, for a thousand years, kept the population of Europe stationary. The surface of the Continent was for the most part covered with pathless forests; here and there it was dotted with monasteries and towns. In the lowlands and along the river-courses were fens, sometimes hundreds of miles in extent, exhaling their pestiferous miasms [i.e., miasmas, poisoned air], and spreading agues far and wide. In Paris and London, the houses were of wood daubed with clay, and thatched with straw or reeds. They had no windows, and, until the invention of the saw-mill, very few had wooden floors. The luxury of a carpet was unknown; some straw, scattered in the room, supplied its place. There were no chimneys; the smoke of the ill-fed, cheerless fire escaped through a hole in the roof. In such habitations there was scarcely any protection from the weather. No attempt was made at drainage, but the putrefying garbage and rubbish were simply thrown out of the door. Men, women, and children, slept in the same apartment; not unfrequently, domestic animals were their companions; in such a confusion of the family, it was impossible that modesty or morality could be maintained. The best was usually a bag of straw, a wooden log served as a pillow. Personal cleanliness was utterly unknown; great officers of state, even dignitaries so high as the Archbishop of Canterbury, swarmed with vermin; such, it is related, was the condition of Thomas à Becket, the antagonist of the English king. To conceal personal impurity, perfumes were necessarily and profusely used. The citizens clothed himself in leather, a garment which, with its ever-accumulating impurity, might last for many years. He was considered to be in circumstances of ease, if he could procure fresh meat once a week for his dinner. The street had no sewers; they were without pavement or lamps. After nightfall, the chamber-shutters were thrown open, and slops unceremoniously emptied down, to the discomfiture of the wayfarer tracking his path through the narrow streets, with his dismal lantern in hand.

. . . Cabins of reeds plastered with mud, houses of wattled stakes, chimneyless peat-fires from which there was scarcely an escape for the smoke, dens of physical and moral pollution swarming with vermin, wisps of straw twisted round the limbs to keep off the cold, the ague-stricken peasant with no help except shrine-cure! How was it possible that the population could increase?

Source: Draper, John William. 1875. *History of the Conflict between Religion and Science*. New York: D. Appleton and Company, 264–65.

JULES MICHELET ON A "THOUSAND YEARS WITHOUT A BATH" (1862)

Jules Michelet (1798–1874) is considered one of the founders of modern history in France, and is known best for his lengthy Histoire de France *(1855). In this and other works he applied a secular, rationalist approach to the study of history, although his biases against the Catholic clergy and monarchy are frequently evident. As a staunch defender of modern republicanism, Michelet exhibits a deep loathing for the religious, monarchical Middle Ages, especially in his book* La Sorcière *("The Witch," 1862). This work produced Michelet's infamous claim that in the Middle Ages "There was no bathing for a thousand years!"*

Some Arab writers have asserted that the widespread eruption of skin-diseases [i.e., leprosy] which marks the thirteenth century, was caused by the taking of certain stimulants to re-awaken and renew the defaults of passion. Undoubtedly the burning spices brought over from the East, tended somewhat to such an issue. The invention of distilling and of divers fermented drinks may also have worked in the same direction.

But a greater and far more general fermentation was going on. During the sharp inward struggle between two worlds and two spirits, a third surviving silenced both. As the fading faith and the newborn reason were disputing together, somebody stepping between the caught hold of man. You ask who? A spirit unclean and raging, the spirit of sour desires, bubbling painfully within.

Debarred from all outlet, whether of bodily enjoyment, or the free flow of soul, the sap of life thus closely rammed together, was sure to corrupt itself. Bereft of light, of sound, of speech, it spoke through pains and ominous excrescences. Then happened a new and dreadful thing. The desire put off without being diminished, finds itself stopped short by a cruel enchantment, a shocking metamorphosis. [*Michelet adds here a lengthy footnote, copied after the document text, on the filthiness of medieval Europeans.*] Love was advancing blindly with open arms. It recoils groaning; but in vain would it flee: the fire of the blood keeps raging; the flesh eats itself away in sharp titillations, and sharper within rages the coal of fire, made fiercer by despair.

. . . Leprosy is the last stage, the apogee of this scourge; but a thousand other ills, less hideous but still cruel, raged everywhere. The purest and the most fair were stricken with sad eruptions, which men regarded as sin made visible, or the chastisement of God.

[*Michelet's footnote:*] Leprosy had been traced to Asia and the Crusades; but Europe had it in herself. The war declared by the Middle Ages against the flesh and all cleanliness bore its fruits. More than one saint boasted of having never washed even his hands. And how much did the rest wash? To have stripped for a moment would have been sinful. The worldlings carefully follow the teaching of the monks. This subtle and refined society, which sacrificed marriage and seemed inspired only with the poetry of adultery, preserved a strange scruple on a point so harmless. It dreaded all cleansing, as so much defilement. There was no bathing for a thousand years!

Source: Michelet, Jules. 1863. *La sorcière: The Witch of the Middle Ages*. Translated by L. J. Trotter. London: Simpkin, Marshall, and Co., 117–19.

CHARLES SHEPARD: A VICTORIAN DOCTOR'S MYTHOLOGY OF BATHING, 1892

Charles H. Shepard (1825–1910) was a New York physician and public health advocate. He is remembered for vigorously advocating public bathing, or "Turkish baths," for cleanliness and health. In the following excerpt from one of his several editorials on this issue, he offers a popular history of bathing in Europe over the last two millennia, in which he claims that bathing ended during the Middle Ages because of the influence of Christianity. He cites only the work of Jules Michelet (see previous document) as evidence. The backwardness and dirtiness of the Middle Ages is further stressed in comparison with the Greek and Roman obsession with bathing.

"Public Baths a Preventive of Disease"
By Charles H. Shepard, M.D.

There are baths of many kinds, the swimming bath, the plunge, shower, douche, warm water baths, medicated baths, mud baths, and the steam or Russian baths; lately the warm water shower bath has deservedly won much favor, but for completeness of adaptation to all classes and conditions of health and disease, no bath that ancient or modern science has yet devised, is equal to the hot air, or as it is more commonly called, the Turkish bath. It is a natural stimulus, and invigorates as nothing else can. It meets all the conditions, either local or general, where any bath is indicated, more fully that any other process.

. . . To more fully elucidate the subject [of the health benefits of bathing] let us refer to the ancient history of the Turkish bath, as well as the record it has made during the past thirty years or more.

As far back as 500 years before the Christian era, Hippocrates advised the use of baths in general, and the sudorific [sweat-inducing] bath in particular, for the alleviation of disease. In warm climates the practice of plunging into cold water for enjoyment and invigoration has been well-nigh universal, but the establishment of *thermae*, or hot air baths, was looked upon in the first instance as medicinal, though subsequently they were resorted to as a luxury.

Celsus prescribed these baths to his patients. Martial, in a celebrated epigram, recommended the dry heat of the *laconium*, and also baths in the cold water of Virgin and Martian, two streams in southern Italy famed for their purity. Galen left on record directions for treating *marasmus* by the use of these baths.

The early Christians, who led a severe and virtuous life, regarded public baths with horror. For many centuries baths and bathing were proscribed. Michelet speaks of the Middle Ages as "a thousand years without a bath." This long period was a time of terrible epidemics. Mysterious plagues, feeding, no doubt, upon the filth of the towns, swept away myriads of people.

. . . And where now is the bath? The Romans are gone. The Roman bath is apparently lost. Mr. Urquhart, the father of the modern bath, says: "A people which knows neither Greek nor Latin has preserved this great monument of antiquity on the soil of Europe, and presents to us, who teach our children only Latin and Greek, this institution in all its Roman grandeur and its Grecian taste. The ancient Roman bath lives in its modern offspring, the Turkish *hammam*."

In our schools are taught the language, literature and laws of the Romans, but one of their most important customs and sanitary measures, and one which very materially served to make them the all-powerful and great people that they were, that of the bath, has been entirely neglected.

Source: Shepard, Charles H. 1892. "Public Baths as Preventive of Disease." *Journal of the American Medical Association* 19, 429–30.

What Really Happened: Bathing

So how dirty were medieval people? It's a simple question without a simple answer, for some historians support the popular view that medieval people rarely bathed, while others claim that hygienic bathing was relatively common in the medieval period and practiced by members of all classes. Part of the difficulty for modern audiences to understand medieval cleanliness is that many of us now expect there to be clean and private toilets and baths in every household, and modern society encourages us to associate public toilets and public baths with physical and moral filthiness. But these attitudes are a product of just the last century and do not reflect attitudes toward cleanliness in the ancient, medieval, or even modern world up through the Victorian era. The nineteenth century in Europe was just as unsanitary as the Middle Ages, if not much more so, given the rise of tightly packed, industrial cities.

Despite the authority of Michelet and his claim that bathing did not exist in the Middle Ages, the evidence from archaeology and surviving medieval buildings, as well as from numerous medical, legal, and religious texts, overwhelmingly proves that bathing was relatively common during the Middle Ages, at least in urban areas, and that medieval people cared deeply about cleanliness and sanitation. This is not to say that bathing was as common during the Middle Ages as the ancient: the archaeological remains of massive public and private bathhouses dominate cities throughout the Roman Empire, from Bath, England, to Jerusalem, to Rome itself. Yet just because bathing seems to have become less common in the Middle Ages does not mean that it disappeared.

Typical medieval ideas about bathing were inherited from Greco-Roman antiquity, as seen in the writings of Hippocrates of Cos (ca. 460–370 BCE) and his many "Hippocratic" followers. A passage on bathing from his *On Regimen in Acute Diseases* can be found in the Primary Documents because that work and many other Hippocratic works were translated and read during the Middle Ages, especially after the eleventh century. Hippocrates viewed bathing in terms of its effects on the body, its humors, and elemental qualities, and medieval people were much the same. Medieval baths could be just as complicated as modern, as they were taken for cleaning, healing, or physical therapy. That said, however, we must grant that few medieval people outside of royalty and high nobility had indoor or private plumbing for bathing or toilets. This does not mean they therefore lived in utter filth and never cleaned themselves.

Public baths were common in the larger towns and cities of Europe by the twelfth century. The twelfth-century scholar Alexander Neckam describes bath attendants on the streets of Paris yelling that their water was hot. A thirteenth-century account from Paris records thirty-two public baths (Archibald 2005, 110–11). Fabiola I. W. M. Van Dam, a scholar of the history of bathing, has explored the different ways that bathing was understood during the Middle Ages. It was never as simple as saying "bathing is good" or "bathing is bad." Medieval people bathed for different reasons at different times, usually dictated by their understanding of bodily health. Nonetheless, Van Dam demonstrates that medieval authors of works as diverse as sermons, encyclopedias, or medical manuals usually approved of bathing (van Dam 2012). Later medieval preachers frequently condemned baths, not because they were against bathing or cleanliness itself, but because public bathhouses were unsurprisingly the location of immoral activities.

Some of the most popular baths in the Middle Ages were formed around natural mineral springs, such as the baths of Sulis Minerva in Bath, England, and the baths of Pozzuoli in Italy. Both existed during antiquity and may have fallen into disrepair during the early Middle Ages, but they were rebuilt and revived during the high Middle Ages. The benefits and variety of the baths at Pozzuoli were especially promoted by authors such as Peter of Eboli, as seen in the Primary Documents. As a final piece of evidence for medieval bathing, you can see Albrecht Dürer's (1471–1528) woodcut print from about 1496 of a public men's bathhouse, which was wisely kept segregated from the women's (which Dürer also published as a print). While this artwork is rightly considered a "Renaissance" masterpiece in its celebration of the naked human body, Dürer was depicting a normal activity in later medieval European communities.

It is true that almost no medieval people had their own bathroom, so they were undoubtedly a bit dirtier than most people in modern society. However, we cannot fall into the trap of imagining the "Dark Ages" as simply the opposite of today and assume that medieval people never bathed and even hated or feared bathing. Regular bathing, usually in public bathhouses, was an important element of medieval life.

What Really Happened: Spices and Rotten Meat

Exotic spices were an important part of both ancient Roman and medieval cuisine. While the availability of exotic spices decreased during the

Early Middle Ages, ca. 500–1000, with the reduction in long-distance trade, some remained available, such as pepper. Spices became more available in Europe, although expensive, starting in the eleventh century. The medieval category of "spices" was much broader than ours: they also included resins, perfumes, and medicines such as aloe, camphor, and scammony, besides the culinary spices used around the world today such as ginger, galangal, cinnamon, cloves, and saffron (Benito 2012, 53–54). What usually defined spices was their place of origin: they came from the "Orient," which could mean the Middle East, the Indian subcontinent, or China and the "spice islands" of modern Indonesia, as well as from islands in the Mediterranean and the Swahili Coast of East Africa. Spices were a valuable trade item for Italian and Arab merchants on the Mediterranean, who were the main intermediaries between the "Orient" and Western Europe. They sold these exotic goods directly to wealthy households, to spice vendors in large towns and cities, as well as to pharmacists and physicians.

In short, spices were expensive. They were not an item bought by the sort of people who felt they had to eat rotten meat. A historian of medieval food, Johanna Maria van Winter, makes this clear: the increase in highly spiced foods in the eleventh century was not due to increased consumption of spoiled meat and fish, but to a renewed awareness among European merchants of the high value and relatively low weight of spices. The trade in spices was highly profitable for those willing to take the risk of trade in the eastern Mediterranean (van Winter 2007, 23). Spices were not used for preservation, but because of their high cost were saved for elaborate culinary displays and for medicine.

Meat was far cheaper than spices, so if you were rich enough to afford spices, you could also afford fresh meat (Freedman 2008, 3–4). Van Winter reminds us that, "Although their food storage was perhaps less elaborate than in the modern Western world, it is nonsense to pretend that they always teetered on the edge of food-poisoning and tried to conceal this with heavy seasonings. . . . [T]hey knew what was healthy and what was not" (van Winter 2007, 56). This applied even to the lower classes during the later Middle Ages, when meat eating became more common thanks to dramatically lower populations after the Black Death (see chapter 11), increased wages for the survivors of the plague in many areas, and an increased meat supply from eastern Europe. Medieval peasants and nobility alike knew how to preserve and protect meat from spoilage using salt and vinegar, especially for making ham, bacon, and pork butt (Benito 2012, 47–48, 52).

PRIMARY DOCUMENTS

HIPPOCRATES, *ON REGIMEN IN ACUTE DISEASES* #18: BENEFITS OF BATHING (ca. 400 BCE)

The medical writings of Hippocrates (ca. 460–370 BCE) were widely read throughout the medieval world, equally in Islamic, Jewish, and Christian cultures, all of which embraced him as the "father of medicine." Some of the sixty works attributed to him are probably authentic, but many are by his "Hippocratic" followers in the fourth and third centuries BCE. The Hippocratic treatise On Regimen in Acute Diseases *is probably authentic or at least dates to Hippocrates's lifetime. Part of his "regimen," or system of treatments, for serious ("acute") diseases is therapeutic bathing, which assumes a large and professional bathhouse, with cleaning supplies and attendants. This and many other Hippocratic works were read and imitated in the Middle Ages, shaping medieval attitudes toward health and cleanliness.*

PART 18. The bath is useful in many diseases, in some of them when used steadily, and in others when not so. Sometimes it must be less used than it would be otherwise, from the want of accommodation; for in few families are all the conveniences prepared, and persons who can manage them as they ought to be. And if the patient be not bathed properly, he may be thereby hurt in no inconsiderable degree, for there is required a place to cover him that is free of smoke, abundance of water, materials for frequent baths, but not very large, unless this should be required. It is better that no friction should be applied, but if so, a hot soap must be used in greater abundance than is common, and an affusion of a considerable quantity of water is to be made at the same time and afterwards repeated. There must also be a short passage to the basin, and it should be of easy ingress and egress. But the person who takes the bath should be orderly and reserved in his manner, should do nothing for himself, but others should pour the water upon him and rub him, and plenty of waters, of various temperatures, should be in readiness for the douche, and the affusions quickly made; and sponges should be used instead of the comb (strigil), and the body should be anointed when not quite dry. But the head should be rubbed by the sponge until it is quite dry; the extremities should be protected from cold, as also the head and the rest of the body; and a man should not be washed immediately after he has taken a draught of ptisan or a drink; neither should he take ptisan as a drink immediately after the bath. Much will depend upon whether the patient, when in good health, was very fond of the bath, and in the custom of taking it: for such persons, especially, feel the want of it, and are benefited if they are bathed, and injured if they are not. In general it suits better with cases of pneumonia than in ardent fevers; for the bath soothes the pain in the side, chest, and back; concocts the sputa, promotes expectoration, improves the respiration, and allays lassitude; for it soothes the joints and outer skin, and is diuretic, removes heaviness of the head, and moistens the nose. Such are the benefits to be derived from the bath, if all the proper requisites be present; but if one or more of these be wanting, the bath, instead of doing good, may rather prove injurious; for every one of them may do harm if not prepared not prepared by the attendants in the proper manner. It is by no means a suitable thing in these diseases to persons whose bowels are too loose, or when they are unusually confined, and there has been no previous evacuation; neither must we bathe those who are debilitated, nor such as have nausea or vomiting, or bilious eructations; nor such as have hemorrhage from the nose, unless it be less than required at that stage of the disease (with those stages you are acquainted), but if the discharge be less than proper, one should use the bath, whether in order to benefit the whole body or the head alone. If then the proper requisites be at hand, and the patient be well disposed to the bath, it may be administered once every day, or if the patient be fond of the bath there will be no harm, though he should take it twice in the day. The use of the bath is much more appropriate to those who take unstrained ptisan, than to those who take only the juice of it, although even in their case it may be proper; but least of all does it suit with those who use only plain drink, although, in their case too it may be suitable; but one must form a judgment from the rules laid down before, in which of these modes of regimen the bath will be beneficial, and in which not. Such as want some of the requisites for a proper bath, but have those symptoms which would be benefited by it, should be bathed; whereas those who want none of the proper requisites, but have certain symptoms which contraindicate the bath, are not to be bathed.

Source: Hippocrates. 1868. "On Regimen in Acute Diseases." In *The Genuine Works of Hippocrates,* edited by Charles Darwin Adams, #17. New York: Dover.

PETER OF EBOLI, *DE BALNEIS PUTEOLANIS* (*ON THE BATHS OF POZZUOLI*), ca. 1200

Peter was a monk and Latin author from Eboli in southern Italy. He was a favorite court poet in the years 1196–1220 for Henry VI and his son

Frederick II, both of whom were king of Sicily and Holy Roman emperor. One of his several books focuses on the thermal baths around Pozzuoli, outside of Naples (which belonged to the Kingdom of Sicily). These baths were a popular tourist attraction, and Peter emphasizes the healing and regenerative properties of each different natural "bath." Emperor Frederick II spent much time at the baths in 1227 when he fell ill during his preparations for a crusade.

The bath that brings relief to man. From reality it takes its name the bath that brings relief to the sick, and gratified it is that its efficacy corresponds to its name. It restores the lungs to health, relieves the spleen from pressure, with an effective therapy it purifies the swollen liver, and eliminates the cause of melancholy from the chilled heart. The wave gently washes away abdominal humours, and removes inappetence from the stomach, strengthening it, in order that it can once again appreciate normal, appetizing foods. It clears the voice, and makes any kind of pain disappear. The bathers who indulge regularly in this wave will be restored to health. It also eases chronic podagra and offers the limbs a period of repose.

Saint Anastasia's bath. After your name, O Anastasia, men call this bath that produces countless remedies for humanity. It regenerates sick limbs and its wave gives the body new strength. It is wonderful: if you dig out the sand, hot water will gush out from the middle of the ditch. As it flows out of its spring, it will remove the sick person's symptoms. If instead the water is taken away from its source, it will be of no use. And it is of no benefit if it gets a little cold. So those who wish to be relieved from their pains, will have beneficial results if they renew the water.

The bath named Cantarello. Midst the waves of the sea there gushes a very hot water, enclosed by a dam of bricks to prevent it from being dispersed. When the sea is foaming, the barrier is lashed by the waves. Only with great difficulty can a sick person reach this pace. The Cantaro [another name for *Cantarello*] has the power to medicate human beings. In fact, it hardens sores old and new. The suppurating ulcers that impair the skin are healed by the Cantaro. It brightens the eyes, and coagulates any blood that flows. It is beneficial to arthritics, a medicine for the feet, useful in curing fevers and shivers. But continual use of this water is harmful to the lungs.

The so-called bath of the Meadow. There is a water that people call baths of the Meadow. Many believe it to be the work of Cicero. A rough path leads down to the lower part where the sick person can find the water he seeks. It is said to be good for sick intestines; it soothes the tired body made sluggish by inertia. It is said to be marvellous for loosening up the muscles and for making head and shoulders function again. It clears bleary eyes and cleanses ulcers. Likewise it helps the whole body. He who is bathed in sweat should avoid the cold for the moment. And, while his limbs are overheated, he should not drink.

The bath named Tripergola. There is a wide lake where Christ broke the doors of hell and withdrew his dead. Here there is a double house rightly named Tripergola: one houses the clothes, the other contains the water. For those who sweat excessively, this very useful water removes tiredness from the mind and heaviness from the feet. It keeps away various stomach troubles and eliminates aching weariness from the whole body. We advise those who are weak and lazy and lacking in energy to make frequent use of this water. He who loves this water will not fear symptoms of sickness and will always be pleased with his healthy body.

Source: Pietro da Eboli. 1987. *De Balneis Puteolanis (sec. XV).* Edited by Pietro Migliorini and Massimo Rodella, Italian translation by Carlo Marcora, English translation by Jane Dolman. 2 vols. Milan: Edizioni Il Mondo Positivo, 1:22–31.

ALBRECHT DÜRER, *THE MEN'S BATH* (1497)

Albrecht Dürer (1471–1521) is one of the greatest painters and printmakers of the Northern or German Renaissance. Around 1496 he published a pair of prints showing men and women at their separate public bathhouses. The secular theme and the focus on the naked human form define these works as "Renaissance" creations, but Dürer was showing a common element of later medieval urban life. Baths were not just for cleaning, but also for relaxing, exercising, and socializing.

Source: Albrecht Dürer, *Das Männerbad* (The Men's Bath). Metropolitan Museum of Art, Accession Number 19.73.155. https://www.metmuseum.org/art/collection/search/387563.

Further Reading

Archibald, Elizabeth. 2005. "Did Knights Have Baths? The Absence of Bathing in Middle English Romance." In *Cultural Encounters in the Romance of Medieval England*, edited by Corinne Saunders, 101–15. Woodbridge, Suffolk, UK: Boydell.

Benito, Pere. 2012. "Food Systems." Translated by Leah Ashe. In *A Cultural History of Food in the Medieval Age*, edited by Massimo Montanari, 37–55. London: Bloomsbury.

Bildhauer, Bettina. 2016. "Medievalism and Cinema." In *The Cambridge Companion to Medievalism*, edited by Louise D'Arcens. Cambridge: Cambridge University Press.

Bunn, Curtis. 2015. "7 Outbreaks That Afflicted Europe during the Unsanitary Medieval Ages." *Atlanta Black Star*, February 13, 2015. https://atlantablackstar.com/2015/02/13/7-outbreaks-that-afflicted-europe-during-the-unsanitary-medieval-ages/.

Cartlidge, Cherese. 2002. *The Crusades: Failed Holy Wars.* San Diego, CA: Lucent Books.

Draper, John William. 1875. *History of the Conflict between Religion and Science.* New York: D. Appleton and Co.

Drummond, J. C., and Anne Wilbraham. 1991. *The Englishman's Food: Five Centuries of English Diet.* London: Pimlico. [Reprint of 1957 edition, originally published 1939]

Freedman, Paul. 2008. *Out of the East: Spices and the Medieval Imagination.* New Haven, CT: Yale University Press.

Horrox, Rosemary, ed. 1994. *The Black Death.* Manchester: Manchester University Press.

Michelet, Jules. 1862. *La sorcière.* Paris: E. Dentu.

Michelet, Jules. 1863. *La sorcière: The Witch of the Middle Ages.* Translated by L. J. Trotter. London: Simpkin, Marshall, and Co.

Myers, Daniel. 2018. "Drummond's Rotten Meat: When Good Sources Go Bad." *Medieval Cookery.* http://medievalcookery.com/notes/drummond.pdf.

Shepard, Charles H. 1892. "Public Baths a Preventive of Disease." *Journal of the American Medical Association* 19:429–32.

Stapelberg, Monica-Maria. 2016. *Through the Darkness: Glimpses into the History of Western Medicine.* Crux Publishing.

Thorndike, Lynn. 1928. "Sanitation, Baths, and Street-Cleaning in the Middle Ages and Renaissance." *Speculum* 3, no 2: 192–203.

van Dam, Fabiola I. 2002. "Permeable Boundaries: Bodies, Bathing and Fluxes, 1135–1333." In *Medicine and Space: Body, Surroundings and Borders in Antiquity and the Middle Ages*, edited by Patricia Baker, 117–43. Leiden: Brill.

van Winter, Johanna Maria. 2007. *Spices and Comfits: Collected Papers on Medieval Food*. Totnes, UK: Prospect Books.

4

People Were Terrified
of the Year 1000

What People Think Happened

On the eve of the third millennium, in the year 1999, people around the world were gripped with a fear over what would happen during "Y2K," or the turn of the millennium at 12:00 a.m. on January 1, 2000. Many people were convinced that a "millennium bug" (not an actual computer virus, but a coding problem in computer systems) would lead to the widespread failure of important computer systems, such as those governing power plants, financial data, and hospitals. While no serious problems actually occurred during Y2K, this fear encouraged many people to ask what happened on the eve of "Y1K," or the year 1000: What were people afraid of then? Did society fall apart, but for different reasons?

Many media reports from around 2000 gave people what they already thought they knew about the year 1000, or rather, about the year 999. On the eve of the first millennium, the superstitious peasants of Europe lived in mortal terror of the impending Day of Judgment. At the turn of the year 1000, many feared the dead would rise from their graves and Christ would come back to judge the living and the dead. The terrified medieval people either huddled together in fear or rushed to the monasteries and churches to do penance and pour out what little wealth they had, so that the clergy could pray for their souls and help them get to heaven. Their fears were reinforced by the sermons and writings of the Catholic clergy, who are depicted in modern accounts either as just as superstitious as the peasants or as greedy and cynical manipulators of the uneducated (Landes 2000, 97–98).

How the Story Became Popular

This stereotype of a universal belief in the impending end of the world, whether in 999, 1000, 1001, or another nearby year, is a product of the modern era, and mostly of authors since the mid-nineteenth century. One of the earliest authors, however, to claim that medieval people thought the Antichrist would come at the end of the first millennium was Italian Catholic cardinal Caesar Baronius (1538–1607). He wrote a massive history of the Church in twelve volumes called *Annales Ecclesiastici* (1588–1607). He begins the eleventh volume of his work with the year 1001, which he says some people "foretold as the world's last, or nigh thereto, when Antichrist should be revealed" (Burr 1901, 430). To support this statement, Baronius refers to the medieval authors Abbo of Fleury and Rodulphus Glaber, who will be discussed later.

Cardinal Baronius, however, did not claim that people panicked in the year 1000. It would take the vigorous writers of the nineteenth century to elaborate this idea and turn medieval apocalyptic beliefs into a full-fledged millennial panic. Charles Mackay (1814–1889), the Scottish author of the influential *Extraordinary Popular Delusions and the Madness of Crowds*, depicted the millennial panic of 1000 as a significant precursor to the First Crusade of 1095–1099: "A strange idea had taken possession of the popular mind at the close of the tenth and the commencement of the eleventh century. It was universally believed that the end of the world was at hand: that the thousand years of the Apocalypse were near completion, and that Jesus Christ would descend upon Jerusalem to judge mankind. All Christendom was in commotion. A panic terror seized upon the weak, the credulous and the guilty, who in those days formed more than nineteen-twentieths of the population. Forsaking their homes, kindred, and occupation, they crowded to Jerusalem to await the coming of the Lord, lightened, as they imagined, of a load of sin by their weary pilgrimage" (Mackay 1852, 2:3).

Mackay's French contemporary, the historian Jules Michelet (1798–1874), elaborated even more on the credulity of the medieval Christians in the year 1000, the terrors they felt, and the ridiculous lengths they went to in preparation for the Second Coming. An extended passage is given in the Primary Sources from his 1855 *Histoire de France* (translated as *History of France* in 1887). Without referring to any actual sources,

Michelet tells a tragic and pathetic story of a repressed peasantry looking forward with both fear and hope to the return of Christ. Without the Roman Empire or the empire of Charlemagne, Michelet implies, what could these serfs possibly have to live for?

Since the time of Mackay and Michelet, the practice of a scientific history, based on the analysis of primary sources, has advanced considerably and numerous historians have written essays and books debunking the supposed panic of the first millennium. As early as 1873, the French historian François Plaine wrote an essay titled "Les prétendues terreurs de l'an mille" ("The false terrors of the Year 1000"), and in 1901 George Lincoln Burr dismissed any "Terror of the Year 1000" in his influential essay "The Year 1000 and the Antecedents of the Crusades" (Palmer 2014, 4–6). Similarly, the celebrated French art historian Henri Focillon (1881–1943) wrote a book addressing the myth of a benighted Year 1000, published as *L'An mil* in 1952 and translated as *The Year 1000* in 1969.

But the arguments of these serious historians against the "terror of the Year 1000," appearing now for nearly a century a half, have not stopped popular historians even at the end of the twentieth century from promoting the fiction that Europe and Europeans essentially shut down on the eve of the year 1000. A notable example is the dramatically titled 1988 book, *A.D. 1000: A World on the Brink of Apocalypse*, by Richard Erdoes (1912–2008). Erdoes was a prolific author, artist, and photographer, but not a trained medievalist; most of his books were on Native American cultures. In the excerpt that follows from Erdoes's book, he presents an evocative scene of Europe in 999, which is clearly inspired by the older works of Mackay and Michelet. He describes a scene in which Pope Sylvester II (r. 999–1002) preaches to cowering peasants at the stroke of midnight, December 31, 999. Erdoes admits that this scene is made up, but he nonetheless presents his book as a work of history, not fiction. A nearly identical story is told by the journalist James Reston, Jr., in one of his many popular histories, *The Last Apocalypse: Europe at the Year 1000 A.D.* (Reston 1998, 204–6).

Yet Erdoes, Reston, and other authors like them did have a genuine medieval source that they could rely upon for apocalyptic imagery: an eleventh-century monk and historian named Rodulphus Glaber ("Ralph the Bald," 985–1047). Glaber wrote a work known as *History in Five Books* about events in France and around Christian Europe between the years 900 and 1044. He is especially famous for his vigorous apocalyptic theology, as he explains many events, good and bad, in relation to his belief in the impending Second Coming of Christ. He dates events, such as royal coronations or the appearance of a giant whale, according to how many years they occurred before "the thousandth year after the birth of our Lord and Savior," namely 1000 CE (Rodulphus Glaber, in Coulton 1910, 5). Richard Erdoes especially highlighted the natural disasters described by Glaber: medieval people before the year 1000 thought an early thunderstorm in March was God's voice announcing the Second Coming. Likewise the eruption of Mount Vesuvius in Italy during the year 993 is compared to the mouth of hell and linked both with a contemporary fire at St. Peter's church in Rome and the "fire" of the disease (possibly ergotism) then known as St. Anthony's Fire: all of these fiery events, Glaber implies, are signs of the impending Last Judgment.

Apart from Glaber, there is only one other medieval author who is frequently quoted for evidence of panic at the first millennium. Abbo of Fleury (945–1004) was a French monk and author of numerous works, and is now considered a saint. Toward the end of his life, he mentions in a letter that he had heard as a youth (so perhaps around 960, when he was a teenager) a preacher saying the Antichrist would come in the year 1000 (or perhaps 1001). Some modern authors have used Abbo's statement as representative of medieval Christian belief, but they fail to mention that Abbo also says this preacher was immediately refuted by the religious authorities and he implies that this millennial belief is wrong and ridiculous. Even if Abbo did embrace this belief, he says nothing of a panic either in 960 or 1000 about the Antichrist or the Last Judgment.

Popular opinions about the supposed "Terrors of the Year 1000" are shaped both by uncritical histories of the period, which rely almost entirely on Glaber's account, and by developments in modern Christianity. For example, modern descriptions of terrified medieval Christians are probably influenced by eighteenth- and nineteenth-century Protestant theology about the "Rapture" (known by theologians under the technical term "premillennial dispensationalism"). This belief, which is now found primarily among U.S. evangelical Christians, states that specially chosen Christians (living and dead) will disappear or rise up into the sky ("raptured") with Christ before the actual Second Coming. Most human beings will remain on Earth and suffer through a time of "Tribulation," often said to be an actual or metaphorical period of 1,000 years. While medieval theologians debated extensively about the nature of the Last Judgment, there is little evidence of medieval belief in the Rapture. Nonetheless, modern descriptions of the supposed utter terror of medieval peasants before the year 1000 appear to be shaped by equally modern ideas about those "left behind" after the Rapture.

PRIMARY DOCUMENTS

RODULPHUS GLABER, *HISTORY IN FIVE BOOKS* (ca. 1045)

Rodulphus Glaber, or "Ralph the Bald" (985–1047), was a French monk and the author of several works, including his History in Five Books, *written at the request of William of Volpiano, abbot of the French monastery of Saint-Bénigne. In this work Glaber discussed many political and religious events, primarily in France during his own lifetime, but he is most famous for the passage that follows. He describes terrifying events around Europe soon before and after the year 1000, and he associates them with the coming Apocalypse and "Last Days."*

Warned by the prophecy of Holy Writ, we see clearer than daylight that in process of the Last Days, as love waxed cold and iniquity abounded among mankind, perilous times were at hand for men's souls. For by many assertions of the ancient fathers we are warned that, as covetousness stalks abroad, the religious Rules or Orders of the past have caught decay and corruption from that which should have raised them to growth and progress. . . . From this also proceed the constant tumult of quarrels at law, and frequent scandals arise, and the even tenor of the different Orders is rent by their transgressions. Thus also it cometh to pass that, while irreligiousness stalks abroad among the clergy, froward and incontinent appetites grow among the people, until lies and deceit and fraud and manslaughters, creeping abroad among them, draw almost all to perdition! And, since the mist of utter blindness hath darkened the eye of the Catholic Faith (that is, the prelates of the Church), therefore their flocks, ignorant of the way to salvation, fall into the ruin of their own perdition. . . . For whensoever religion hath failed among the pontiffs, and strictness of the Rule hath decayed among the abbots, and therewith the vigor of monastic discipline hath grown cold, and by their example the rest of the people are become prevaricators of God's commandments, what then can we think but that the whole human race, root and branch, is sliding willingly down again into the gulf of primeval chaos. . . . And because, in fulfilment (as we see) of the Apostle's prophecy, love waxeth cold and iniquity aboundeth among men that are lovers of their own selves, therefore these things aforesaid befell more frequently than usual in all parts of the world about the thousandth year after the birth of our Lord and Savior.

For, in the seventh year before that date, Mount Vesuvius (which is also called Vulcan's Cauldron) gaped far more often than his wont and belched forth a multitude of vast stones mingled with sulphurous flames which fell even to a distance of three miles around; and thus by the stench of his breath he began to make all the surrounding province uninhabitable. . . . It befell meanwhile that almost all the cities of Italy and Gaul were ravaged by flames of fire, and that the greater part even of the city of Rome was devoured by a conflagration. During which fire, the flames caught the beams of St Peter's church, beginning to-creep under the bronze tiles and lick the carpenters' work. When this became known to the whole multitude that stood by, then, finding no possible device for averting this disaster, they turned with one accord and, crying with a terrible voice, hastened to the Confession [an area of the Church] even of the Chief of the Apostles, crying upon him with curses that, if he watched not over his own, nor showed himself a very present defender of his church, many throughout the world would fall away from their profession of faith. Whereupon the devouring flames straightway left those beams of pine and, died away. . . .

At this same time a horrible plague raged among men, namely a hidden fire which, upon whatsoever limb it toned, consumed it and severed it from the body. Many were consumed even in the space of a single night by these devouring flames. . . . Moreover, about the same time, a most mighty famine raged for five years throughout the Roman world, so that no region could be heard of which was not hunger stricken for lack of bread, and many of the people were starved to death. In those days also, in many regions, the terrible famine compelled men to make their food not only of unclean beasts and creeping things, but even of men's, women's, and children's flesh, without regard even of kindred; for so fierce waxed this hunger that grown-up sons devoured their mothers, and mothers, forgetting their maternal love ate their babes.

Source: Rodulphus Glaber. 1910. *History in Five Books*. Translated by G. G. Coulton. In *A Medieval Garner: Human Documents from the Four Centuries preceding the Reformation*. London: Constable & Company, 4–6. Spelling and punctuation modified slightly.

ABBO OF FLEURY REMEMBERS A PREACHER ON THE APOCALYPSE, (ca. 994–996)

Abbo of Fleury (945–1004) was a French monk and abbot who served in both French and English monasteries. He was a prolific author and an active figure in religion and politics at the turn of the millennium, including the introduction of reformed monastic rules and customs from France into England. Toward the end of the first millennium, Abbo wrote a long letter, known as the Apologeticus ad Hugonem et Rodbertum reges Francorum, *to King Hugh Capet of France and his son and co-king Robert II, who ruled together 987–996 CE. The letter touches on many religious matters, calling on the kings to lead the way in the reform of the French church and the protection of the Christian faith. Abbo ends the letter with a description of several unorthodox and potentially heretical beliefs abroad in France, and includes his own reminiscence of hearing, as a young man in Paris, a preacher claiming that the Antichrist would come in the year 1000. Abbo is clear that he does not believe this idea and sought to fight it at the time with his knowledge of scripture.*

Firstly, I believe something must be said about faith, which I have heard varies with alternating choirs both in France and within the church of the English. Some speak, as I understand it, according to the words of Athanasius: "holy spirit from the Father and from the Son, neither made, nor created, nor begotten but proceeding." But others only say: "Holy Spirit from the Father and Son, neither made, nor created, but proceeding," and these people, when they subtract that phrase "nor begotten," believe that they are following the synodal statute of Lord [Pope] Gregory, where it is thus written: "Holy Spirit is neither begotten, not unbegotten, but only proceeding."

And also concerning the end of the world, when I was a teenager I heard a sermon before the people at the church of Paris, saying that the Antichrist would come immediately at the number of a thousand years, and that the Universal Judgment would follow not long after. I stood up to this preaching with all the power I could muster, using the Gospels and the Apocalypse and the Book of Daniel.

Finally also my abbot of happy memory, Richard, drove out with his wise spirit the error which was growing about the end of the world, after he received letters from the people of Lorraine, to which he ordered me to respond. For a rumor had filled almost the entire world that, when the divine Annunciation happened on the day of Parasceve, it occurred without any notion of the end of the world. Also concerning the start of Advent which is celebrated every single year before the Nativity of the Lord, a most serious error sometimes has occurred, with some people beginning after the fifth Kalends of December, others before, although Advent never has more than four weeks and at least one day. And since differences of this sort are apt to increase disagreements within the Church, it must be determined by a council, in such a way that all those who live within that Church may savor of one thing. May this be granted by your [Hugh and Robert II, co-kings of France, 987–996 CE] industriousness, you wish to see us living with a single spirit in your house.

Source: New translation of Abbo of Fleury, *Apologeticus ad Hugonem et Rodbertum reges Francorum.* In *Patrologia Latina* 139, edited by J.-P. Migne. Paris, 1853, cols. 471–72.

JULES MICHELET, *HISTORY OF FRANCE* (1855)

Jules Michelet (1798–1874) created one of the greatest works of modern historiography with his nineteen-volume Histoire de France, *completed in 1855. He displays his deep nationalist pride in France as well as his disdain for much of medieval history in this and other books. (See chapters 3 and 10 for discussions of his book* La Sorcière, *on medieval witchcraft.) In the following passage, Michelet dramatically re-creates without any reference to evidence the terror that uneducated, overly religious Europeans supposedly felt on the eve of the year 1000.*

It was the universal belief of the middle age, that the thousandth year from the Nativity would be the end of the world. In like manner, before Christianity, the Etrusci had fixed ten centuries as the term of their empire; and the prediction had been fulfilled. Christianity, a wayfarer on this earth, a guest, exiled from heaven, readily adopted a similar belief. The world of the middle ages was without the external regularity of the ancient city, and the firm and compact order within was not easily discernible. It only saw chaos in itself; but longed for order, and hoped to find it in death. Besides, in those days of miracles and legions, in which every thing assumed a strange hue, as if seen through the somber medium of a stained casement, it might well be doubted whether all that met the eye in this apparently tangible world were other than a dream. . . .

The idea of the end of the world, sad as that world was, was at once the hope and terror of the middle age. Look at those antique statues of the tenth and eleventh centuries—mute, meager, and their pinched and stiffened lineaments grinning with a look of living suffering, allied to the repulsiveness of death. See how they implore, with clasped hands, that desired yet dreaded moment, that second death of the resurrection, which is to redeem them from their unspeakable sorrows, and raise them from nothingness into existence, and from the grave to God. Here is imaged the poor world itself and its hopelessness, after having witnessed so many ruins. The Roman empire had crumbled away; so had that of Charlemagne. Christianity had then believed itself intended to do away with sorrow here below; but suffering still went on. Misfortune succeeded misfortune, ruin, ruin. Some other advent was needed; and men expected that it would arrive. The captive expected it in the gloomy dungeon, and in the bonds of the sepulchral *in pace* [in peace]. The serf expected it while tracing the furrow under the shadow of his lord's hated tower. The monk expected it amidst the privations of the cloister, amidst the solitary tumults of his heart, amidst temptations and backslidings, repentances and strange visions, the wretched puppet of Satan who malignantly gamboled around him, and who at night would draw aside his coverlet, and laughingly chuckle in his ear—"thou art mine."

All longed to be relieved from their suffering, no matter at what cost! Better were it for them to fall once for all into God's hands, and rest forever, though on a bed of fire, than remain as they are. Nor could that moment be without its charm, when the shrill and withering trump of the archangel should peal in the ear of their tyrants; for then—from dungeon, cloister, and from furrow—one tremendous shriek of laughter would burst forth from the stricken and oppressed.

This fearful hope of the arrival of the judgment-day grew with the calamities that ushered in the year 1000, or that followed hard upon. It seemed as if the order of the seasons had been inverted, and the elements had been subjected to new laws. A dreadful pestilence made Aquitaine a desert. The flesh of those who were seized by it was as if struck by fire, for it fell rotting from their bones. The high roads to the places of pilgrimage were thronged with these wretched beings. They besieged the churches, particularly that of St. Martin's at Limoges, and crowded its portals to suffocation, undeterred by the stench around it. Most of the bishops of the south repaired thither, bringing with them the relics of their respective churches. The crowd increased, and so did the pestilence; and the sufferers breathed their last on the relics of the saints.

Source: Michelet, Jules. 1887. *History of France.* Translated by G. H. Smith. New York: D. Appleton and Co., 1:184–85.

RICHARD ERDOES, *A.D. 1000: A WORLD ON THE BRINK OF APOCALYPSE* (1988)

Richard Erdoes (1912–2008) was a German-American author and artist, illustrating many magazines as well as books by Dr. Seuss. Much like Barnet

Litvinoff, discussed in chapter 1, Erdoes was a popular historian who did not specialize in medieval history and wrote on the topic in just one book. His work A.D. 1000: A World on the Brink of Apocalypse, *therefore, must be understood as a semifictional representation of the Middle Ages and not a work of scholarship. Erdoes used scenes from real medieval sources, especially the history of Rodulphus Glaber, but expanded them liberally to create this dramatic scene of utter terror in Rome itself on the eve of the year 1000. There is no historical evidence for this midnight mass of Pope Sylvester II.*

On the last day of the year 999, according to an ancient chronicle, the old basilica of St. Peter's at Rome was thronged with a mass of weeping and trembling worshipers awaiting the end of the world. This was the dreaded eve of the millennium, the Day of Wrath when the earth would dissolve into ashes. Many of those present had given away all their possessions to the poor—lands, homes, and household goods—in order to assure for themselves forgiveness for their trespasses at the Last Judgment and a good place in heaven near the footstool of the Almighty. Many poor sinners—and who among them was without sin?—had entered the church in sackcloth and ashes, having already spent weeks and months doing penance and mortifying the flesh.

At the altar the Holy Father, Pope Sylvester II, in full papal regalia, was celebrating the midnight mass, elevating the host for all to see. Many did not dare to look, lying face down upon the multicolored marble floor, their arms spread out in the shape of a cross. A few were seized by holy ecstasy, waiting to be united with Christ. As the minutes passed and the fateful hour was about to strike, a deathly silence filled the venerable basilica. Only the voice of the pope was heard intoning the hallowed phrases, and, at the words *ite missa est* [concluding Latin words of the Roman Catholic Mass], the great bell began to ring.

The crowd remained rooted, motionless, transfixed, barely daring to breathe, "not a few dying from fright, giving up their ghosts then and there." This description was written from hearsay, and things might not have happened just that way, but it gives a good idea of the all-pervading dread of the apocalypse that held humankind in its grip. Legends set the period against an apocalyptic background and associate the end of the first millennium with some vague terror of judgment day. The historical truth is that not only the year 999, but the whole century that preceded it was a period of obscurity during which people, "blinded with blood, groped their way fearfully through a quagmire of filth."

This is not to say that everybody believed in the impending doom. Many did not. Prelates and abbots inveighed against the belief that the earth was about the burn up. But the common people, the lower nobles, village priests, and peasants, took it as an absolute truth that the "nightfall of the universe was at hand."

Some were certain that the Second Coming of Christ would fall of the last day of the year 999, at the very stroke of midnight. Others were equally convinced that Armageddon would happen a little earlier, on the eve of the nativity when "the Children of Light would join in battle with Gog's army of hellish fiends." Some fixed the date on the day of the summer or winter solstice in the thousandth year after our Lord's passion.

In France and Lorraine wise men scoffed at the idea. They had it on good authority that the end would come when the Feast of the Annunciation fell on a Good Friday "when darkness will cover the earth and the stars fall upon it." Though people quarreled about the exact day and hour, they all agreed, in the words of Raoul Glaber, that "Satan will soon be unleashed because the thousand years have been completed."

. . . Many expected the Last Judgment to be held at Jerusalem, and, throughout the year 999, the number of pilgrims converging upon the Holy City were compared to an immense, desolating army. Often these pious wayfarers had also sold their worldly possessions to finance their pilgrimage.

. . . Signs and prodigies prompted faith in the apocalypse. If one is to believe contemporary chronicles, many such signs appeared. One early scribe told of the sky splitting open, letting fall down to earth a gigantic torch, which left behind it a long trail of light like a lightning bolt. Its thunderclap frightened not only people surprised in the open fields but also those who at the moment were safely indoors. The gap in the sky closed again, but then the shape of [a] dragon with blue feet appeared, its head continuing to grow until it filled the horizon from end to end.

Source: Erdoes, Richard. 1988. *A.D. 1000: A World on the Brink of Apocalypse.* Berkeley, CA: Seastone, 1–4.

What Really Happened

All medieval Christians were supposed to believe in the Second Coming of Christ and the Last Judgment. This is the subject of the final book of the Bible, the Apocalypse or Revelation of St. John of Patmos.

These beliefs are also central to the Nicene-Constantinopolitan Creed (statement of faith) of 381, used throughout the Middle Ages and by many Christian churches to this day, which states that Christ "shall come again, with glory, to judge the quick and the dead." Medieval beliefs in the Last Judgment were usually accompanied by less-well-defined ideas about the Apocalypse, based on interpretations of the biblical Revelation of John, and about a figure called the Antichrist who would also come to sow discord and work against both Christ and good Christians in their attempt to unite and save Christianity and at the end of time. Numerous medieval theologians wrote learned treatises about the Second Coming, Apocalypse, and the Antichrist. Among the best known were the English monk Bede (672–735) and the French monk Adso of Montier-en-Der (ca. 920–992). The latter wrote a short work specifically on the Antichrist for Queen Gerbera of France, around the year 950. Historians have long debated just how concerned medieval people actually were with the end of the world, but there is no doubt that some people, especially members of the learned clergy, thought the end could be coming in their own time.

If this description of medieval beliefs in the Apocalypse is true, why is this chapter included among "fictions" of the Middle Ages? There are two major problems with the apocalyptic panic described by modern authors like Mackay, Michelet, Erdoes, and Reston: first, the very notion of a "panic," and second, the "year 1000" itself. In the first place, there is no evidence of a widespread panic at any time in medieval Europe about the Apocalypse. Where there is panic, or at least fear, about the Second Coming, it is found not among the peasantry (for whom we have little evidence) but among a minority of learned clerics, who had time to muse on theology and the possibility of Christ's imminent return. What is more, there is little evidence of medieval Christians fearing or even acknowledging the year 1000 as the time specifically when Christ would return and end the world. Some modern scholars, especially Richard Landes, still vigorously assert that the year 1000 was important to medieval Christians, but not as a time to be feared, but rather a sign of hope; the Apocalypse was not the violent end of the world but the return of Christ ushering in an age of rewards for the faithful. To Landes and other like-minded historians, the year 1000 was a focus for medieval people, not as the actual year of the end of the world but as the keystone in a century of vigorous change in Christian society that extended some fifty years on either side of the millennium (Landes, Gow, and Van Meter 2003, v–ix).

Rodulphus Glaber, as we have seen, was fixated on the year 1000, but he never describes a panic at the coming of that year. Rather, he speaks of people being disturbed by extraordinary signs from nature, and wondering if those signal the eventual return of Christ. The very fact that Glaber was writing some thirty years after the year 1000 (and using the same dating system as us) shows that he was not trying to justify the year 1000 as the time of the Apocalypse, but as a year of significant heavenly signs. Glaber's message is not one of terror, but of great optimism about the state of Christendom after the year 1000: his was a time of religious revival of the cult of saints and of church building, of peace councils and monastic splendor (Head and Landes 1992, 12). Glaber, moreover, is just one voice and not necessarily representative of his era. His close contemporary, Thietmar, prince-bishop of Merseburg (975–1018), described the year 1000 in his chronicle with obvious joy and optimism: "When the thousandth year since the salvific birth of the Immaculate Virgin had come, a radiant dawn rose over the world" (Focillon 1969, 60).

But what about the date itself of 1000 CE? Surely that year would have registered with medieval Europeans as important, if not actually apocalyptic. The fact is that few people would have recognized the year 1000 in the way we do now. There was no widespread agreement at this time in the Middle Ages on what the year actually was, or what numbering system they should use to indicate the year. The system of dating from the birth of Christ (AD, *Anno Domini*, "in the Year of the Lord") was developed in the sixth century by the monk Dionysius Exiguus, and first applied systematically by the Anglo-Saxon monk Bede in a treatise he wrote around the year 725. But this system of dating was still not used widely in Europe by our year 1000 (Riddle and Black 2016, 245). For example, Christians in medieval Spain used a calendar that differed from ours by thirty-eight years! The so-called Spanish Era begins in 38 BCE, and this method was used in parts of Europe until the end of the Middle Ages. So even if medieval people did greatly fear the year 1000, it would occur at different times in different regions.

To complicate the issue of dating further, many people now assume that a "millennial" belief in the return of Christ would be based on the date of his birth. But this choice of date reflects modern obsessions with Christmas rather than medieval concerns about the life of Christ. For medieval Christians, his death and resurrection at 33 years old (33 CE according to medieval dating) were considered far more important than his birth. We therefore find more medieval authors concerned about the year 1033 CE than about the year 1000, while others pinpoint the Apocalypse at 968, 979, 992, or a variety of years well after 1000. Scholars at the Center for Millennial Studies at Boston University, led by Dr. Richard Landes, have gathered a dossier of all known evidence for Apocalyptic beliefs in the tenth and eleventh centuries ("The Apocalyptic Dossier," 967–1033), which demonstrates significant concerns about the Second Coming, but very few examples from the actual year 1000 CE. Conversely, many of the passages recorded in the "Dossier" indicate strange events around the year 1000, but do not explicitly connect them to the end of the world.

A final complication comes from a misunderstanding of the word "millennial" in relation to apocalyptic fears. So-called millennial or millenarian beliefs are often thought to concern the coming of Christ at one of the major millennial milestones (1000 CE, 2000 CE, etc.). But, in fact, the term refers rather to beliefs in a thousand-year period of peace and prosperity between the Second Coming of Christ and the actual end of the world. Millenarian beliefs do not specify the date of the Second Coming or Apocalypse but are instead concerned with the calendar of events at the end of time. For example, the aforementioned Center for Millennial Studies is named after their study of the Christian end times, and not after beliefs about the year 1000 or 2000 (Landes 2000, 101).

How do we make sense of medieval beliefs in the Second Coming and the year 1000? To be sure, medieval apocalyptic beliefs are no fiction: they are a significant aspect of medieval culture and have been studied extensively by some of the finest medieval scholars (Richard Landes, Richard Emmerson, Bernard McGinn, Carol Walker Bynum, James Palmer, just to name some of the prominent English-language authors). And these scholars sometimes disagree deeply about the extent and definition of medieval apocalypticism, millenarianism, and the meaning of the year 1000 to actual medieval people (Steinfels 1999). Were some medieval people worried about the religious significance of the year 1000? Almost certainly. Did they panic about (or hope for) the Apocalypse at that time? Probably not. There is little evidence of that, and we find more panic about the religious implications of worldly events during the mid-tenth century, the mid-eleventh century, or on the eve of the First Crusade in 1095 (Focillon 1969, 60–61). The so-called Terrors of the Year 1000, while rooted in some genuine medieval beliefs, are mostly a fantasy of modern authors who want to imagine the Middle Ages as so thoroughly wrapped up in supernatural beliefs that their entire society temporarily collapsed in the face of a number.

PRIMARY DOCUMENT

RODULPHUS GLABER, *HISTORY IN FIVE BOOKS* (ca. 1030)

This selection from Glaber's History in Five Books *immediately follows the selection in the "Fiction" Primary Documents, which provided the details that support most popular accounts of the "Terrors of the Year 1000." But if we read the entire passage, we can see that Glaber imagined a wide range of positive and negative events occurring all around the millennium after Christ's birth. These events occur throughout the period ca. 990 to ca.1030 and are not fixed on just the year 1000. Nor does Glaber express any sense of panic concerning these events, but rather highlights the connections he sees between the marvelous events and this important anniversary of the "Incarnation of our Saviour."*

So on the threshold of the aforesaid thousandth year, some two or three years after it, it befell almost throughout the world, but especially in Italy and Gaul, that the fabrics of churches were rebuilt, although many of these were still seemly and needed no such care; but every nation of Christendom rivaled with the other, which should worship in the seemliest buildings. So it was as though the very world had shaken herself and cast off her old age, and were clothing herself everywhere in a white garment of churches. Then indeed the faithful rebuilt and bettered almost all the cathedral churches, and other monasteries dedicated to divers saints, and smaller parish churches. . . . When therefore, as we have said, the whole world had been clad in new church buildings, then in the days following that is, in the eighth year following the aforesaid thousandth year after the Incarnation of our Saviour—the relics of very many saints, which had long lain hid, were revealed by divers proofs and testimonies; for these, as if to decorate this revival, revealed themselves by God's will to the eyes of faithful, to whose minds also they brought much consolation. This revelation is known to have begun first in the city of Sens in Gaul, at the church of the blessed Stephen, ruled in those days by the archbishop Leoteric, who there discovered certain marvellous relics of ancient holy things; for, among very many other things which lay hidden, he is said to have found a part of Moses' rod, at the report whereof all the faithful flocked together not only from the provinces of Gaul but even from well-nigh all Italy and from countries beyond the sea; and at the same time not a few sick folk returned thence whole and sound, by the intervention of the saints. But, as most frequently befalls, from that source whence profit springs to men, there they are wont to rush to their ruin by the vicious impulse of covetousness; for the aforesaid city having, as we have related, waxed most wealthy by reason of the people who resorted thither through the grace of piety, its inhabitants conceived an excessive insolence in return for so great benefits. . . . At that time, moreover, that is in the ninth year after the aforesaid thousandth anniversary, the church at Jerusalem which contained the sepulchre of our Lord and Saviour was utterly overthrown at the command of the prince of Babylon. . . . After that it had been over-thrown, as we have said, then within a brief space it became full evident that this great iniquity had been done by the wickedness of the Jews. When therefore this was spread abroad through the whole world, it was decreed by the common consent of Christian folk that all Jews should be utterly driven forth from their lands or cities. Thus they were held up to universal hatred and driven forth from the cities; some were Slain with the sword or cut off by manifold kinds of death, and some even slew themselves in divers fashions; so that, after this well-deserved vengeance had been wreaked, scarce any were found in the Roman world. Then also the bishops published decrees forbidding all Christians to associate them-selves with Jews in any matter whatsoever; and ordaining that, whosoever would be converted to baptismal grace and utterly eschew the customs or manners of the Jews, he alone should be received. Which indeed was done by very many of them for love of this present life, and impelled rather by fear of death than by the joys of the life everlasting; for all such of them as simulated this conversion returned impudently within a brief while to their former way of life. . . .

After the manifold signs and prodigies which came to pass in the world, some earlier and some later, about the thousandth year from our Lord's birth, it is certain that there were many careful and sagacious men who foretold other prodigies as great when the thousandth year from His Pas-sion should draw nigh. Then were innumerable sick folk healed in those conclaves of Holy men; and, lest men should think lightly of mere bursten skin or rent flesh in the straightening of arms and legs, much blood flowed forth also when the crooked limbs were restored; which gave faith to the rest who might have doubted. At this all were inflamed with such ardour that through the hands of their bishops they raised the pastoral staff to heaven, while themselves with outspread palms and with one voice cried to God: Peace, peace, peace! that this might be a sign of perpetual cov-enant for that which they had promised between themselves and God; on condition that, after the lapse of five years, the same covenant should marvellously be repeated by all men in the world in confirmation of that peace. That same year, moreover, so great was the plenty and abundance of corn and wine and other fruits of the earth, that men dared not hope to have so much during all the five years next to come; for no human food was aught accounted of save flesh or choice Victuals, and this year was like unto the great Jubilee of ancient Mosaic times. Next year again, and again in the third and fourth years, the fruits were no less abundant. But, alas for shame! The human race, forgetful of God's loving kindness and prone from its very beginning to evil, like the dog returning to his own vomit again or the sow that was washed to her wallowing in the mire, made the covenant of their own promise of none effect in many ways; and, as it is written, they waxed fat, and grew thick, and kicked. For even the princes of both orders, spiritual and secular, turned to covetousness and began to sin in theft and greed as grievously as before, or even worse. Then those of middle rank and the poorer people, following the example of the greater, declined into horrible Crime. For who ere now had heard of such incests, adulteries, and illicit alliances between close kindred, such mockery of concubines and such emulation of evil men? Moreover, to fill up the measure of so great wickedness, since there were few or none among the people to correct the rest, and to rebuke such crimes, therefore the prophecy was fulfilled which says, "And it shall be as with the people, so with the priest"; seeing especially that all the rulers in those days, both secular and spiritual were mere boys. For in those days through the sins of the people, that saying of Solomon's was fulfilled: "Woe to you, O land, when your king is a child." For even the universal Pope of Rome himself, the nephew of the two popes Benedict and John who had preceded him was a boy scarce ten years old, whose money and treasures had procured his election by the Romans; by whom in process of time he was dishonourably treated and oftentimes cast forth, so that he had no power. Moreover, as we have already said, the rest of the prelates in those days owed their promotion rather to their gold and silver than to their merit. Alas for shame! It is of such that the Scripture says—nay rather God's own mouth—"They have been princes, and I knew not." At this same time so innumerable a multitude began to flock from all parts of the world to the sepulchre of our Saviour at Jerusalem, as no man could before have expected; for the lower orders of people led the way, after whom came those of middle rank, and then all the greatest kings and counts and bishops; lastly (a thing which had never come, to pass before), many noble ladies and poorer women journeyed thither. For many purposed and desired to die before they should see their homes again. . . . Moreover, some of those were then most concerned in these matters, being consulted by many concerning the signification of this concourse to Jerusalem, greater than the past age had ever heard of, answered with some caution that it portended no other than advent of that reprobate Antichrist, whose coming at the of this World is prophesied in Holy Scripture.

Source: Rodulphus Glaber. 1910. In *History in Five Books,* translated by G. G. Coulton. In *A Medieval Garner: Human Documents from the Four Centuries preceding the Reformation.* London: Constable & Co, 6–11. Spelling and punctuation modified slightly.

Further Reading

"The Apocalyptic Dossier: 967–1033." 1998–2005. *Center for Millennial Studies at Boston University.* www.bu.edu/mille/scholarship/1000/1000 -dos.html

Burr, George Lincoln. 1901. "The Year 1000 and the Antecedents of the Crusades." *American Historical Review* 6, no 3: 429–39.

Coulton, G. G. 1910. *A Medieval Garner: Human Documents from the Four Centuries preceding the Reformation.* London: Constable and Co.

Erdoes, Richard. 1988. *A.D. 1000: A World on the Brink of Apocalypse.* Berkeley, CA: Seastone.

Focillon, Henri. 1969. *The Year 1000.* Translated by Fred D. Wieck. New York: Frederick Ungar Publishing.

Glaber, Rodulfus. 1989. *The Five Books of Histories.* Edited and translated by John France. Oxford: Clarendon Press.

Head, Thomas, and Richard Landes. 1992. Introduction to *The Peace of God: Social Violence and Religious Response in France around the Year 1000,* 1–20. Ithaca, NY: Cornell University Press.

Landes, Richard. 2000. "The Fear of an Apocalyptic Year 1000: Augustinian Hagiography, Medieval and Modern." *Speculum* 75, no. 1: 97–145.

Landes, Richard, Andrew Gow, and David C. Van Meter, eds. 2003. *The Apocalyptic Year 1000: Religious Expectation and Social Change, 950–1050.* Oxford: Oxford University Press.

Mackay, Charles. 1852. *Extraordinary Popular Delusions and the Madness of Crowds.* 2d ed. 3 vols. London: Office of the National Illustrated Library.

McGinn, Bernard, trans. 1995–2014. "Letter on the Origin and Time of the Antichrist by Adso of Montier-en-Der." *PBS: Frontline.* www.pbs .org/wgbh/pages/frontline/shows/apocalypse/primary/adsoletter.html

Michelet, Jules. 1887. *History of France*. Translated by G. H. Smith. New York: D. Appleton and Co.

Palmer, James T. 2014. *The Apocalypse in the Early Middle Ages*. Cambridge: Cambridge University Press.

Reston, James, Jr. 1998. *The Last Apocalypse: Europe at the Year 1000 A.D.* New York: Doubleday.

Riddle, John M., and Winston Black. 2016. *A History of the Middle Ages, 300–1500*. 2d ed. Lanham, MD: Rowman and Littlefield.

Steinfels, Peter. 1999. "Beliefs; Millennial Fears in the Year 1000: Apocalypse Then, Apocalypse Now, and Apocalypse Forever." *New York Times*. July 17, 1999. www.nytimes.com/1999/07/17/nyregion /beliefs-millennial-fears-year-1000-apocalypse-then-apocalypse-now -apocalypse.html

5

Medieval Wars Were Fought
by Knights on Horseback

What People Think Happened

The knight in shining armor, astride his mighty warhorse, is the ultimate symbol of the Middle Ages. He represents both the violence and the honor that many people assume to have defined medieval warfare and chivalry. According to popular tradition, the entire Middle Ages is treated as a "feudal" society in which knights fight honorably (or not) for their lords against other knights and lords. The economy of this society is structured entirely to support mounted warfare and pay for expensive arms and armor. A typical medieval battle therefore featured heavily armored, elite warriors, each on horseback and equipped with a lance and a sword, fighting alone or supported by just a few foot soldiers or archers. These battles were defined by duels between opposing pairs of knights, each seeking glory for himself and his lord.

In numerous modern accounts (especially on the internet), the mounted knight is compared to a "medieval tank": a heavily armored, unstoppable force when faced with soldiers on the ground (for example, see *It's History*, 2018). Yet in other accounts, the medieval knight is seen as a hindrance to the professionalization of warfare: poorly disciplined, too independent, and extremely vulnerable if he fell off his horse in his bulky armor (McGlynn 1994). A foot soldier could easily kill him with a knife through an opening in his armor. But whether historians and popular authors have imagined knights as an asset or a liability to medieval warfare, almost all of them depict knights on horseback as the central feature of medieval warfare.

These knights have not only been used to define medieval warfare, but medieval behavior as well. *Chivalry* and *cavalry* come from the same medieval Latin word (by way of French), *caballarius*, for a warrior on horseback (Bouchard 1998, 103–5). Chivalry is the behavior expected of the best cavalry knights. A chivalrous knight must honor his lord and lady, protect the weak, women, and children, and in all respects serve as a model of good behavior for the people of Christian Europe. Stories about heroic medieval knights, especially those about Arthur, Lancelot, and Galahad, are frequently interpreted as fictional representations of realistic medieval warfare.

How the Story Became Popular

The fiction of this chapter is subtler than in others, for it is a fiction of scale, concerning the extent to which knights were actually involved in medieval warfare. Knights on horseback did exist, of course, but they have been taken out of context and used to represent the entire medieval period and are assumed to take the central role in medieval warfare. This is a common approach to the medieval era in literature throughout the last two centuries, movies and television shows, as well as in children's history books. For example, the 2001 book . . . *If You Lived in the Days of the Knights* treats the entire Middle Ages as "the days of the knights": "The days of the knights were a long time ago. This time in history is known as the Middle Ages" (McGovern 2001, 5). The author does go on to specify that she is describing England around 1250, and the interior text examines many aspects of medieval culture, but the message most children would take away from the book is that "medieval = knights."

The knight is likewise one of the most powerful units and the defining figure of the medieval period in the video game series *Sid Meier's Civilization*. According to the online "Wiki" for *Civilization 6*, "A veritable mountain of iron armor, the Knight is a specialist in charging and breaking the enemy line. With its superior Combat Strength, a force of Knights can lay waste not only to armies, but also to poorly defended cities" ("Knight [Civ6]," 2018). This description is a mix of fantasy and genuine medieval battle tactics, but because the game purports to be founded on established historical facts, players are led to assume this description of medieval knights is accurate. Since the many iterations of the game have sold millions of copies since its initial release in 1991, it is likely one of the most influential creations in shaping contemporary views of the medieval knight.

This is a fiction, however, that took root in the Middle Ages themselves, as the warrior noblemen, who were often trained to fight on horseback, privileged representations of that form of fighting in their favorite art and literature. An early example of this tendency is seen in the famous Bayeux Tapestry, embroidered around 1085 to celebrate William of Normandy's (afterward William "the Conqueror") conquest of England in 1066 at the Battle of Hastings. Nearly every battle scene in the tapestry shows Norman knights dominating Anglo-Saxon foot soldiers and archers. Even though historians agree that mounted warriors provided the Normans with an edge over the native English, the tapestry exaggerates their centrality in the battle. Rather, other sources indicate that the Normans masterfully combined archers, infantry, and cavalry shock troops to break through the well-trained English soldiers and their shield wall (Patterson 2008, 91). The tapestry was designed by and for the Norman elites who wanted to emphasize their favorite form of fighting as mounted knights, especially William the Conqueror and his half-brother, Bishop Odo of Bayeux, both of whom are portrayed fighting from horseback in the tapestry (see an image in the Primary Documents).

The epics and romances of the High Middle Ages likewise frequently feature warrior nobles as the protagonists, who fight from horseback in battles, duels, and tournaments. One of the best-known stories of chivalry is *The Song of Roland*, first written down around 1100 CE. The story is based on real events from the later eighth century, but it essentially reflects the culture of the Crusades and mature feudalism of the High Middle Ages. Roland and his companions are usually described as knights fighting other knights with lances. Battles are deadly imitations of jousting, with warriors of both sides—the good Christian knights and the wicked "Saracens"—usually remaining in the saddle until death or victory.

This mostly fictional style of fighting remained central to stories of chivalry throughout the rest of the Middle Ages. This included later stories starring Roland, but especially romances about King Arthur and the Knights of the Round Table. The most famous Arthurian stories were crafted in the twelfth century by romantic authors like Chrétien de Troyes and Marie de France. These stories were meant to entertain and were hardly a realistic depiction of High Medieval knights and society. As the historian Constance Bouchard points out, "what chivalric literature reveals most clearly are a host of contradictions and opposing goals. It was truly impossible to be fully chivalrous" (Bouchard 1998, 113). She is referring here mostly to the social and courtly behaviors expected of a chivalrous knight, but the origin of chivalry was the behavior of a warrior on the battlefield. The warriors of literature are almost all great, mounted warriors, famous for fighting other mounted warriors in single combat. The supposed rules of chivalry are based on this form of fighting that rarely occurred on a real battlefield. These romances also condemn the use of longbows and crossbows as unchivalrous, even though they were used in every major medieval battle. They likewise insist that a good knight on horseback would never strike an enemy on the ground, although this certainly happened as well (Bouchard 1998, 117).

One of the last great Arthurian works of the Middle Ages was *Le Morte d'Arthur* ("The Death of Arthur"), a compilation of numerous stories written by Thomas Malory perhaps in the 1460s but first published in 1485 by the printer William Caxton. Many modern works about Arthur use Malory's story as their main source, including T. H. White's *The Once and Future King* (1938–1958), the basis for Walt Disney's *Sword in the Stone* (1963), and the 1981 film *Excalibur*. This work in particular is important for understanding our fiction because *Le Morte d'Arthur* was reprinted in 1816 to great acclaim, and this event can be used to date the start of the modern fascination with the Middle Ages and the creation of a partially factual "medievalism" (see the Introduction for more on medievalism). The warfare of the Arthurian stories is usually limited to heroic adventures and duels between knights, which often begin with jousting on horseback and proceed to a sword battle on foot.

The nineteenth-century revival of *Le Morte d'Arthur* and other medieval works of "chivalry" was encouraged by, and further encouraged, Romantic novelists who wrote books set in the Middle Ages and featuring medieval knights. The most famous by far was Sir Walter Scott, whose novels like *Ivanhoe: A Romance* (1820) promoted an image of the Middle Ages dominated by chivalrous knights. British and French antiquaries had shown a scholarly interest in the Middle Ages throughout the eighteenth century, but Scott is credited for dramatically increasing popular medievalism. Scott's books spurred a vogue for "medieval" art throughout the nineteenth century, especially among the "Pre-Raphaelite Brotherhood" of artists, founded in 1848, who sought a return to the methods and subjects of later medieval artists. In the United States, Mark Twain joined this medievalizing movement (although in his own humorous fashion), publishing *A Connecticut Yankee in King Arthur's Court* in 1889. Twain satirized both the chivalry of the Middle Ages and the contemporary obsession with medieval chivalric knights, by weaving direct quotes from *Le Morte d'Arthur* into his new tale of U.S. time travel.

All of these literary and visual works of the nineteenth century emphasize the centrality of the knight in medieval culture and warfare, so it is hardly surprising that a work of historical scholarship from this era had the same focus. Even though many historians have seriously examined medieval soldiers and warfare over the last century and more, much of our basic understanding of the subject is still shaped by a book from 1885. Charles Oman (1860–1945) was a significant military historian in the later nineteenth and early twentieth centuries. He wrote many books, and especially on the medieval period, but his very first, *The Art of War in the Middle Ages*, written when he was only twenty-five years old, continues to be reprinted and is widely available online in the public domain. Sean McGlynn notes that much of Oman's work is still considered valuable, but his first book was flawed for focusing almost entirely on knights as the essential force of medieval battles. This generalization has been repeated in books of military history for one and a quarter centuries, many of which are written by retired soldiers and enthusiasts who neglect the actual primary sources of medieval battles (McGlynn 1994). These sources, as will be discussed, show the equal or greater importance of infantry, archers, and siege warfare when compared to mounted knights.

PRIMARY DOCUMENTS

BAYEUX TAPESTRY (ca. 1085), SCENE OF NORMAN KNIGHTS CHARGING

The Bayeux Tapestry (technically an embroidered cloth rather than a woven tapestry) was produced around 1085 in southern England or northern France to celebrate William the Conqueror's victory over Anglo-Saxons forces at the Battle of Hastings in 1066. It is not certain who commissioned the tapestry, but most historians lean toward Bishop Odo of Bayeux, a participant in the Norman Conquest, and the half-brother of William, who made Odo the earl of Kent. The actual battle takes up about half of the surviving tapestry and clearly focuses on the successes of the Norman knights, who are shown in most cases overwhelming the Anglo-Saxon infantry. A few archers are shown accompanying the knights, but the Norman army is presented as almost entirely composed of cavalry.

Source: Bayeux Tapestry, Scene 51. Bayeux Museum, La Tapisserie de Bayeux. Photo by Myrabella.

THE SONG OF ROLAND (ca. 1100): EPIC BATTLE BETWEEN CHRISTIAN AND SARACEN KNIGHTS

The Song of Roland *is one of the most famous epic poems of the Middle Ages. It presents a mythologized and fantastical version of a real event in the year 778: a surprise attack on the rearguard of Charlemagne's troops as they marched through the Ronceveaux (or Roncesvalles) Pass in the Pyrenees from Islamic Spain into Frankish territory. In the actual battle, a force of Christian Basques ambushed the Franks, but over the following centuries, poets turned the story into an epic battle between the Christian Franks and a massive host of monstrous pagans and "Saracens" (Muslims). The* Song *follows the exploits of the Frankish commander Roland, who was killed in the real battle, along with his chivalrous companions. The oldest version of the* Song *is written in Old French and survives in a manuscript from about 1100. It reflects more the knightly culture of that time than any realities of eighth-century Frankish warfare. The following passage describes the meeting of Roland and his companions with the "heathen" and "Saracen" enemies. All of the fighting is described in terms of armored knights on horseback clashing with spears and swords.*

XCVI. King Marsil's nephew, Aelroth his name,
Vaunting in front of the battle came,
Words of scorn on our Franks he cast:
"Felon Franks, ye are met at last,
By your chosen guardian betrayed and sold,
By your king left madly the pass to hold.
This day shall France of her fame be shorn,
And from Karl [Charlemagne] the mighty his right arm torn."
Roland heard him in wrath and pain!
He spurred his steed, he slacked the rein,
Drove at the heathen with might and main,
Shattered his shield and his hauberk broke,
Right to the breast—bone went the stroke;
Pierced him, spine and marrow through,
And the felon's soul from his body flew.
A moment reeled he upon his horse,
Then all heavily dropped the corpse;

Wrenched was his neck as on earth he fell,
Yet would Roland scorn with scorn repel.
"Thou dastard! never hath Karl been mad,
Nor love for treason or traitors had.
To guard the passes he left us here,
Like a noble king and chevalier.
Nor shall France this day her fame forego.
Strike in, my barons; the foremost blow
Dealt in the fight doth to us belong:
We have the right and these dogs the wrong."

XCVII. A duke was there, named Falsaron,
Of the land of Dathan and Abiron;
Brother to Marsil, the king, was he;
More miscreant felon ye might not see.
Huge of forehead, his eyes between,
A span of a full half-foot, I ween.
Bitter sorrow was his, to mark
His nephew before him lie slain and stark.
Hastily came he from forth the press,
Raising the war-cry of heathenesse [paganism].
Braggart words from his lips were tossed:
"This day the honour of France is lost."
Hotly Sir Olivier's anger stirs;
He pricked his steed with golden spurs,
Fairly dealt him a baron's blow,
And hurled him dead from the saddle-bow.
Buckler and mail were reft and rent,
And the pennon's flaps to his heart's blood went.
He saw the miscreant stretched on earth:
"Caitiff, thy threats are of little worth.
On, Franks! the felons before us fall;
Montjoie!" 'Tis the Emperor's battle-call.

XCVIII. A king was there of a strange country,
King Corsablis of Barbary;
Before the Saracen van he cried,
"Right well may we in this battle bide;
Puny the host of the Franks I deem,
And those that front us, of vile esteem.
Not one by succor of Karl shall fly;

The day hath dawned that shall see them die."
Archbishop Turpin hath heard him well;
No mortal hates he with hate so fell:
He pricked with spurs of the fine gold wrought,
And in deadly passage the heathen sought;
Shield and corselet were pierced and riven,
And the lance's point through his body driven;
To and fro, at the mighty thrust,
He reeled, and then fell stark in dust.
Turpin looked on him, stretched on ground.
"Loud thou liest, thou heathen hound!
King Karl is ever our pride and stay;
Nor one of the Franks shall blench this day,
But your comrades here on the field shall lie;
I bring you tidings: ye all shall die.
Strike, Franks! remember your chivalry;
First blows are ours, high God be praised!"
Once more the cry, "*Montjoie!*" he raised.

XCIX. Gerein to Malprimis of Brigal sped,
Whose good shield stood him no whit in stead;
Its knob of crystal was cleft in twain,
And one half fell on the battle plain.
Right through the hauberk, and through the skin,
He drove the lance to the flesh within;
Prone and sudden the heathen fell,
And Satan carried his soul to hell.

C. Anon, his comrade in arms, Gerier,
Spurred at the Emir with levelled spear,
Severed his shield and his mail apart,
The lance went through them, to pierce his heart.
Dead on the field at the blow he lay.
Olivier said, "'Tis a stirring fray."

CI. At the Almasour's shield Duke Samson rode
With blazon of flowers and gold it glowed;
But nor shield nor cuirass availed to save,
When through heart and lungs the lance he drove.
Dead lies he, weep him who list or no.
The Archbishop said. "'Tis a baron's blow."

CII. Anseis cast his bridle free;
At Turgis, Tortosa's lord, rode he:
Above the centre his shield he smote,
Broke his mail with its double coat,
Speeding the lance with a stroke so true,
That the iron traversed his body through.
So lay he lifeless, at point of spear.
Said Roland, "Struck like a cavalier."

CIII. Engelier, Gascon of Bordeaux,
On his courser's mane let the bridle flow;
Smote Escremis, from Valtierra sprung,
Shattered the shield from his neck that swung;
On through his hauberk's vental pressed,
And betwixt his shoulders pierced his breast.
Forth from the saddle he cast him dead.
"So shall ye perish all," he said.

CIV. The heathen Estorgan was Otho's aim:
Right in front of his shield he came;
Rent its colors of red and white,
Pierced the joints of his harness bright,
Flung him dead from his bridle rein.
Said Otho, "Thus shall ye all be slain."

CV. Berengier smote Estramarin,
Planting his lance his heart within,
Through shivered shield and hauberk torn.
The Saracen to earth was borne
Amid a thousand of his train.
Thus ten of the heathen twelve are slain;
But two are left alive I wis
Chernubles and Count Margaris

CVI. Count Margaris was a valiant knight,
Stalwart of body, and lithe and light:
He spurred his steed unto Olivier,
Broke his shield at the golden sphere,
Pushed the lance till it touched his side;
God of his grace made it harmless glide.

Margaris rideth unhurt withal,
Sounding his trumpet, his men to call.

CVII. Mingled and marvellous grows the fray,
And in Roland's heart is no dismay.
He fought with lance while his good lance stood;
Fifteen encounters have strained its wood.
At the last it brake; then he grasped in hand
His Durindana [usually "Durendal"], his naked brand.
He smote Chernubles' helm upon,
Where, in the centre, carbuncles shone:
Down through his coif and his fell of hair,
Betwixt his eyes came the falchion bare,
Down through his plated harness fine,
Down through the Saracen's chest and chine,
Down through the saddle with gold inlaid,
Till sank in the living horse the blade,
Severed the spine where no joint was found,
And horse and rider lay dead on ground.
"Caitiff, thou camest in evil hour;
To save thee passeth Mohammed's power.
Never to miscreants like to thee
Shall come the guerdon of victory."

CVIII. Count Roland rideth the battle through,
With Durindana, to cleave and hew;
Havoc fell of the foe he made,
Saracen corpse upon corpse was laid,
The field all flowed with the bright blood shed;
Roland, to corselet and arm, was red
Red his steed to the neck and flank.
Nor is Olivier niggard of blows as frank;
Nor to one of the peers be blame this day,
For the Franks are fiery to smite and slay.
"Well fought," said Turpin, "our barons true!"
And he raised the war-cry, "*Montjoie*" anew.

CIX. Through the storm of battle rides Olivier,
His weapon, the butt of his broken spear,
Down upon Malseron's shield he beat,

Where flowers and gold emblazoned meet,
Dashing his eyes from forth his head:
Low at his feet were the brains bespread,
And the heathen lies with seven hundred dead!
Estorgus and Turgin next he slew,
Till the shaft he wielded in splinters flew.
"Comrade!" said Roland, "what makest thou?
Is it time to fight with a truncheon now?
Steel and iron such strife may claim;
Where is thy sword, Hauteclere by name,
With its crystal pommel and golden guard?"
, "Of time to draw it I stood debarred,
Such stress was on me of smiting hard."

CX. Then drew Sir Olivier forth his blade,
As had his comrade Roland prayed.
He proved it in knightly wise straightway,
On the heathen Justin of Val Ferrée.
At a stroke he severed his head in two,
Cleft him body and harness through;
Down through the gold-encrusted saddle,
To the horse's chine, the falchion fell:
Dead on the sward lay man and steed.
Said Roland, "My brother, henceforth, indeed
The Emperor loves us for such brave blows!"
Around them the cry of "*Montjoie!*" arose.

CXI. Gerein his Sorel rides; Gerier
Is mounted on his own Pass-deer:
The reins they slacken, and prick full well
Against the Saracen Timozel.
One smites his cuirass, and one his shield,
Break in his body the spears they wield;
They cast him dead on the fallow mould.
I know not, nor yet to mine ear was told,
Which of the twain was more swift and bold.
Then Espreveris, Borel's son,
By Engelier unto death was done.
Archbishop Turpin slew Siglorel,

The wizard, who formerly had been in hell,
By Jupiter thither in magic led.
"Well have we escaped," the archbishop said:
"Crushed is the caitiff," Count Roland replies,
"Olivier, brother, such strokes I prize!"

CXII. Furious waxeth the fight, and strange;
Frank and heathen their blows exchange;
While these defend, and those assail,
And their lances broken and bloody fail.
Ensign and pennon are rent and cleft,
And the Franks of their fairest youth bereft,
Who will look on mother or spouse no more,
Or the host that waiteth the gorge before.
Karl the Mighty may weep and wail;
What skilleth sorrow, if succour fail?
An evil service was Gan's that day,
When to Saragossa he bent his way,
His faith and kindred to betray.
But a doom thereafter awaited him
Amerced in Aix, of life and limb,
With thirty of his kin beside,
To whom was hope of grace denied.

Source: *The Song of Roland.* 1880. Translated by John O'Hagan. London: C. Kegan Paul, 115–24. Text and punctuation slightly modified.

CHARLES OMAN, *THE ART OF WAR IN THE MIDDLE AGES A.D. 378–1515* (1885)

Charles Oman (1860–1945) was one of the founders of modern military history. He carefully described the methods and patterns of warfare in dozens of publications. Many of his works focus on medieval warfare, including his first book, The Art of War in the Middle Ages. *The following excerpt is from that book, in which Oman imagines "feudal" warfare to be concerned solely with armored knights, claiming that "Infantry was in the twelfth and thirteenth centuries absolutely insignificant." Yet he does not praise the "feudal horseman" for his chivalry or military prowess, but rather constantly and anachronistically condemns knights of that period for lacking the discipline and military science of the nineteenth century.*

Chapter IV. The Supremacy of Feudal Cavalry. A.D. 1066–1346.

Between the last struggles of the infantry of the Anglo-Dane, and the rise of the pikemen and bowmen of the fourteenth century lies the period of the supremacy of the mail-clad feudal horseman. The epoch is, as far as strategy and tactics are concerned, one of almost complete stagnation. . . .

The feudal organization of society made every person of gentle blood a fighting man, but it cannot be said that it made him a soldier. If he could sit his charger steadily, and handle lance and sword with skill, the horseman of the twelfth or thirteenth century imagined himself to be a model of military efficiency. That discipline or tactical skill may be as important to an army as mere courage, he had no conception. Assembled with difficulty, insubordinate, unable to manoeuvre, ready to melt away from its standard the moment that its short period of service was over—a feudal force presented an assemblage of unsoldierlike qualities such as has seldom been known to coexist. Primarily intended to defend its own borders from the Magyar, the Northman, or the Saracen, the foes who in the tenth century had been a real danger to Christendom, the institution was utterly unadapted to take the offensive. When a number of tenants-in-chief had come together, each blindly jealous of his fellows and recognizing no superior but the king, it would require a leader of uncommon skill to persuade them to institute that hierarchy of command, which must be established in every army that is to be something more than an undisciplined mob. Monarchs might try to obviate the danger by the creation of offices such as those of the constable and Marshal, but these expedients were mere palliatives. The radical vice of insubordination continued to exist. It was always possible that at some critical moment a battle might be precipitated, a formation broken, a plan disconcerted, by the rashness of some petty baron or banneret, who could listen to nothing but the promptings of his own heady valour. When the hierarchy of command was based on social status rather than on professional experience, the noble who led the largest contingent or held the highest rank, felt himself entitled to assume the direction of the battle. The veteran who brought only a few lances to the array could seldom aspire to influencing the movements of his superiors. . . .

The army of a feudal force was stereotyped to a single pattern. As it was impossible to combine the movements of many small bodies, when the troops were neither disciplined nor accustomed to act together, it was usual to form the whole of the cavalry into three great masses, or 'battles,' as they were called, and launch them at the enemy. The refinement of keeping a reserve in hand was practised by a few commanders, but these were men distinctly in advance of their age. Indeed it would often have been hard to persuade the feudal chief to take a position out of the front line, and to incur the risk of losing his share in the hard fighting. When two 'battles' men, a fearful *mêlée* ensued, and would often continue for hours. Sometimes, as if by agreement, the two parties wheeled to the rear, to give their horses breath, and then rushed at each other again, to renew the conflict till one side grew overmatched and left the field. An engagement like Brenville or Bouvines or Benevento was nothing more than a huge scuffle and scramble of horses and men over a convenient heath or hillside. The most ordinary precautions, such as directing a reserve on a critical point, or detaching a corps to take the enemy in flank, or selecting a good position in which to receive battle, were considered instances of surpassing military skill. Charles of Anjou, for instance, has received the name of a great commander, because at Tagliacozzo he retained a body of knights under cover, and launched it against Conradin's rear, when the Ghibellines had dispersed in pursuit of the routed Angevin main-battle. Simon de Montfort earned high repute; but if at Lewes he kept and utilized a reserve, we must not forget that at Evesham he allowed himself to be surprised and forced to fight with his back to a river, in a position from which no retreat was possible. The commendation of the age was, in short, the meed [gift] of striking feats of arms rather than of real generalship. If much attention were to be paid to chroniclers, we should believe that commanders of merit were numerous; but, if we examine the actions of these much-belauded individuals rather than the opinion of their contemporaries, our belief in their ability almost invariably receives a rude shock. . . .

Infantry was in the twelfth and thirteenth centuries absolutely insignificant: foot-soldiers accompanied the army for no better purpose than to perform the menial duties of the camp, or to assist in the numerous sieges of the period. Occasionally they were employed as light troops, to open the battle by their ineffective demonstrations. There was, however, no really important part for them to play. Indeed their lords were sometimes affronted if they presumed to delay too long the opening of the cavalry charges, and ended the skirmishing by riding into and over their wretched followers. At Bouvines the Count of Boulogne could find no better use for his infantry than to form them into a great circle, inside which he and his horsemen took shelter when their chargers were fatigued and needed a short rest. If great bodies of foot occasionally appeared upon the field, they came because it was the duty of every able-bodied man to join the *arrière-ban* [a king's call to arms to his vassals] when summoned, not because the addition of 20,000 or 100,000 half-armed peasants and burghers was calculated to increase the real strength of the levy. The chief cause of their military worthlessness may be said to have been the miscellaneous nature of their armament. Troops like the Scotch Lowlanders, with their long spears, or the Saracen auxiliaries of Frederick II, with their cross-bows, deserved and obtained some respect on account of the uniformity of their equipment. But with ordinary infantry the case was different; exposed, without discipline and with a miscellaneous assortment of dissimilar weapons, to a cavalry charge, they could not combine to withstand it, but were ridden down and crushed. A few infantry successes which appear towards the end of the period were altogether exceptional in character. The infantry of the 'Great Company,' in the East beat the Duke of Athens, by inducing him to charge with all his men-at-arms into a swamp. In a similar way the victory of Courtrai was secured, not by the mallets and iron-shod staves of the Flemings, but by the canal, into which the headlong onset of the French cavalry thrust rank after rank of their companions. . . .

The military efficiency of the mercenary of the thirteenth century was, however, only a development of that of the ordinary feudal cavalier. Like the latter, he was a heavily-armed horseman; his rise did not bring with it any radical change in the methods of war. Though he was a more practised warrior, he still worked on the old system—or want of system—which characterised the cavalry tactics of the time.

Source: Oman, C. W. C. 1885. *The Art of War in the Middle Ages, A.D. 378–1515.* Oxford: B. H. Blackwell, 49–52, 54–56.

What Really Happened

The problem with medieval knights is not that they are fictional, but that they are a relatively rare example of warfare in the Middle Ages and should not be used to represent the entire period. Most medieval armies were composed of infantry, and even those soldiers honored with the title "knight" frequently fought on foot. The medieval mounted knight is imagined to be an unstoppable force, but there was never a time when cavalry dominated medieval warfare. Rather, mounted knights formed one small element of shock troops, which were helpless without the support of a large army of foot soldiers and archers. Even then, cavalry can overcome only poorly trained or disorganized infantry; a disciplined group of foot soldiers with spears or pikes could always withstand a cavalry charge (Patterson 2008, 91).

Mounted knights were not used much in warfare until about 1000 CE, at which time the stirrup became common through Europe (although probably invented at a much earlier date), allowing a knight to hold his position firmly while holding a lance. It is still frequently claimed that the age of knights began in 732, when mounted Frankish warriors under Charles Martel defeated Muslim Arab and Berber invaders at the Battle of Poitiers because they were able to launch devastating cavalry charges using couched lances thanks to the use of stirrups (Contamine 1984, 179–84). However, many historians now reject this theory, insisting that the opposite occurred at Poitiers, with the Franks winning the battle on foot against mounted Muslim warriors. Contemporary evidence of the Battle of Poitiers describes a powerful cohort of Frankish foot soldiers "standing shoulder-to-shoulder using their spears and swords to repel repeated charges of [Muslim] horseman" (Hanson 2001, 138).

The most important military manual of the Middle Ages scarcely mentions mounted warriors at all. Medieval military commanders and clerics concerned with warfare closely read and commented on the late Roman treatise *De Re Militari* ("Concerning Military Matters") of Vegetius, written ca. 380 CE (McGlynn 1994), Vegetius briefly treats cavalry as a small portion of a legion, which is composed primarily of foot soldiers and archers. All of his descriptions of training and battle formation assume large groups of infantry. Medieval battles may have depended more on horse than did the Romans, but nonetheless it was works like Vegetius's that shaped the military theory of the medieval period (Contamine 1984, 210–11). What is more, many of the horses brought to medieval battles were used for transportation and not combat. Large and well-trained cavalry horses were rare in medieval Europe (Hanson 2001, 163): all the more reason to celebrate their use in poetry and art! These rare knights on horseback were thus impressive and dangerous, but "the idea of entire armies of heavy horsemen sweeping all before them is once again largely a myth" (Hanson 2001, 164).

As we saw earlier, medieval and modern audiences preferred to focus on the heroic clash of heavily armored knights, but in reality medieval warfare was usually not about battles between soldiers (whether on horse or on foot) as about fortifications, artillery, and siege machines. Warfare, especially in the era of the Crusades and afterward (ca. 1100–1400), primarily meant defending or capturing strategically important strongholds, be they cities or castles. This can clearly be seen in chronicles of the Crusades, in which most "battles" take the form of lengthy sieges of Muslim-held cities like Antioch, Jerusalem, and Acre (Claster 2009, 61–63). This would remain the case until the invention of effective cannons in the fifteenth century, which could finally break through stone walls. For most of the history of medieval warfare, open battle was the exception, but this does not make for an exciting story of chivalry! Complicating the matter further is that the much of the so-called age of chivalry in the twelfth and thirteenth centuries saw the most extended periods of peace in the entire Middle Ages (Contamine 1984, 65). The very period that created our most cherished images of knighthood saw those knights mostly involved in mock tournaments.

If we return to the Battle of Hastings in 1066, we can look to other sources than the Bayeux Tapestry for an indication of the type of soldiers actually active in a large medieval battle. I have chosen this battle in particular because it is often cited as an example of the superiority of Norman cavalry over the Anglo-Saxon foot soldiers. While it is no doubt true that the Norman warhorses gave them an advantage at times during the battle, the actual number and importance of mounted knights is frequently exaggerated, probably influenced by images like that from the tapestry. The tapestry focuses on William and his bodyguard of mounted knights and barely shows any Norman soldiers on the ground, whereas the native English forces are shown entirely on foot, often in huddled masses. But if we accept that the tapestry is propaganda, designed by and for the ruling, knightly class, then we have to find a more dependable source for the actual makeup of the battle. That can be found in William of Poitier's *Gesta Guillelmi* ("Deeds of William"), which describes significant numbers of French infantry and archers on foot playing the main role in the battle (Lawson 2000, 73). In the passage excerpted in the Primary Documents, the bulk of the fighting is done by foot soldiers. Knights on horseback support them in times of trouble and for an occasional charge, but the main purpose of horses is to keep the commanders above the fray so they can see and make commands.

Effectively riding a horse in battle is a difficult and dangerous task, which took young knights-in-training years to perfect. Members of the knightly class were undeniably proud of this skill and sought to promote it in art and literature, even if it was rarely employed in actual battles. Most medieval sources that depict knights in battle are fictional, like the Arthurian tales and *The Song of Roland*, or are propagandistic retellings of real events, like the Bayeux Tapestry. In order to understand the real nature of medieval warfare, historians need to reject the stories of heroism and pay closer attention to the records and chronicles of actual battles, which are more apt to show us the real numbers and impact of the foot soldiers and archers.

PRIMARY DOCUMENT

WILLIAM OF POITIERS, *THE DEEDS OF WILLIAM, DUKE OF THE NORMANS AND KING OF THE ENGLISH* (ca. 1090)

William of Poitiers (ca. 1020–1090) was a warrior and priest from Normandy who accompanied Duke William on the Norman Conquest in 1066. In his later years he wrote a short history of William's reign as duke and then king, Gesta Guillelmi ducis Normannorum et regis Anglorum *("The Deeds of William, Duke of Normandy and King of England"). It is considered one of the most accurate, eyewitness accounts of the Battle of Hastings, as William of Poitiers closely observed the composition and organization of the armies of Duke William and King Harold II of England. He distinguished between the bulk of the* pedites, *or foot soldiers, and the supporting minority of* equites, *or knights.*

Now this is the well-planned order in which he [William of Normandy] advanced behind the banner which the pope had sent him. He placed footsoldiers in front, armed with arrows and cross-bows; likewise footsoldiers in the second rank, but more powerful and wearing hauberks; finally the squadron of mounted knights, in the middle of which he himself rode with the strongest force, so that he could direct operations on all sides with hand and voice. If any author of antiquity had been writing of Harold's line of march he would have recorded that in his passage rivers were dried up and forests laid flat. For huge forces of English had assembled from all the shires. Some showed zeal for Harold, and all showed love of their country, which they wished to defend against invaders even though their cause was unjust. The land of the Danes (who were allied by blood) also sent copious forces. However, not daring to fight with William on equal terms, for they thought more formidable than the king of the Norwegians, they took their stand on higher ground, on a hill near to the wood through which they had come. At once dismounting from their horses, they lined up all on foot in a dense formation. Undeterred by the roughness of the ground, the duke with his men climbed slowly up the steep slope.

The harsh bray of trumpets gave the signal for battle on both sides. The Normans swiftly and boldly took the initiative in the fray. Similarly, when orators are engaged in a lawsuit about theft, he who prosecutes the crime makes the first speech. So the Norman footsoldiers closed to attack the English, killing and maiming many with their missiles. The English for their part resisted bravely each one by any means he could devise. They threw javelins and missiles of various kinds, murderous axes and stones tied to sticks. You might imagine that our men would have been crushed at once by them, as by a death-dealing mass. The knights [*equites*] came to their rescue, and those who had been in the read advanced to the fore. Disdaining to fight from a distance, they attacked boldly with their swords. The loud shouting, here Norman, their foreign, was drowned by the clash of weapons and the groans of the dying. So for a time both sides fought with all their might. The English were greatly helped by the advantage of the higher ground, which they held in serried ranks without sallying forward, and also by their great numbers and densely-packed mass, and moreover by their weapons of war, which easily penetrated shield and other protections. So they strongly held or drove back those who dared to attack them with drawn swords. They even wounded those who flung javelins at them from a distance. So, terrified by this ferocity, both the footsoldiers and the Breton knights and other auxiliaries on the left wing turned tail; almost the whole of the duke's battle line gave way, if such a thing may be said of the unconquered people of the Normans. The army of the Roman empire, containing royal contingents and accustomed to victory on land and sea, fled occasionally, when it knew or believed its leader to have been killed. The Normans believed that their duke and lord had fallen, so it was not too shameful to give way to flight; least of all was it to be deplored, since it helped them greatly. [*William lifts his helmet to show his men that he is still alive. The Normans and allies rally.*]

. . . When the Normans and the troops allied to them saw that they could not conquer such a solidly massed enemy force without heavy loss, they wheeled round and deliberately feigned flight. They remembered how, a little while before, their flight had brought about the result they desired. There was jubilation among the foreigners, who hoped for a great victory. Encouraging each other with joyful shouts, they heaped curses on our men and threatened to destroy them forthwith. As before, some thousands of them dared to rush, almost as if they were winged, in pursuit of those they believed to be fleeing. The Normans, suddenly wheeling round their horses, checked and encircled them, and slaughtered them to the last man.

Having used this trick twice with the same result, they attacked the remainder with greater determination: up to now the enemy line had been bristling with weapons and most difficult to encircle. So a combat of an unusual kind began, with one side attacking in different ways and the other standing firmly as if fixed to the ground. The English grew weaker, and endured punishment as though confessing their guilt by their defeat. The Normans shot arrows, smote and pierced; the dead by falling seemed to move more than the living. It was not possible for the lightly wounded to escape, for they were crushed to death by the serried ranks of their companions. So fortune turned for William, hastening his triumph.

Source: William of Poitiers. 1998. *Gesta Guillelmi.* Edited by R. H. C. Davis and Marjorie Chibnall. Oxford: Oxford University Press, 127, 129, 133.

Further Reading

Adkins, Jan. 2006. *What If You Met a Knight?* New Milford, CT: Roaring Brook Press.

Bouchard, Constance Brittain. 1998. *Strong of Body, Brave and Noble: Chivalry and Society in Medieval France.* Ithaca, NY: Cornell University Press.

Claster, Jill N. 2009. *Sacred Violence: The European Crusades to the Middle East, 1095–1396.* Toronto: University of Toronto Press.

Contamine, Philippe. 1984. *War in the Middle Ages.* Translated by Michael Jones. Oxford: Basil Blackwell.

Elgin, Kathy. 2005. *Knights and Chivalry.* Mankato, MN: Smart Apple Media.

Hanson, Victor. 2001. *Carnage and Culture: Landmark Battles in the Rise of Western Power.* New York: Doubleday.

It's History. 2018. "Medieval Tank—The 13th Century Knight." *YouTube.* https://www.youtube.com/watch?v=81p_sqrVvwU.

"Knight (Civ6)." 2018. *Civilization Wiki.* http://civilization.wikia.com /wiki/Knight_(Civ6).

Lawson, M. K. 2000. "Observations upon a Scene in the Bayeux Tapestry, the Battle of Hastings and the Military System of the Late Anglo-Saxon State." In *The Medieval State: Essays Presented to James Campbell*, edited by J. R. Maddicott and D. M. Palliser, 73–92. London: Hambledon Press.

McGlynn, Sean. 1994. "The Myths of Medieval Warfare." *History Today* 44. https://deremilitari.org/2013/06/the-myths-of-medieval-warfare/.

McGovern, Ann. 2001. . . . *If You Lived in the Days of the Knights*. Illustrated by Dan Andreasen. New York: Scholastic.

Murrell, Deborah. 2005. *The Best Book of Knights and Castles*. Kingfisher.

Oman, C. W. C. 1885. *The Art of War in the Middle Ages, A.D. 378–1515*. Oxford.

Patterson, James G. 2008. "The Myth of the Mounted Knight." In *Misconceptions about the Middle Ages*, edited by Stephen J. Harris and Bryon L. Grigsby, 90–94. Routledge.

Scott, Walter. 1820. *Ivanhoe: A Romance*. Edinburgh: Archibald Constable.

The Song of Roland. 1880. Translated by John O'Hagan. London: C. Kegan Paul.

6

The Medieval Church Suppressed Science

What People Think Happened

Popular ideas about the Middle Ages frequently emphasize either the backwardness or the corruption of the Church. Medieval clergy were either blinded by their religion from recognizing the facts of the natural world or, in more nefarious versions of the story, they actively hid scientific truths to keep the medieval peasants in thrall to their power. Such ideas were especially popular among early modern Protestants, who explicitly wanted to undermine Catholicism, but during the Enlightenment they became a standard part of knowledge about the Western past. In popular belief, whether among modern Catholics or Protestants or people of any or no religion, the medieval Church stands opposed to progress and modernity: it actively hindered intellectual and technological progress to support its authoritarian rule over people's souls and to protect the vast wealth of the clergy and monasteries. The Church, led by grasping and power-hungry popes, sought to keep medieval Europeans ignorant and superstitious, to better control their minds and purses. In support of this story, modern accounts often refer to just the trial of Galileo in 1633 for the "heresy" of teaching that Earth was not stationary at the center of the universe, but orbited around the sun. In doing so, they imply that the entire Middle Ages before this could not possibly have been any better, that the Church had always suppressed science and persecuted scientists.

How the Story Became Popular

One of the most pervasive beliefs about the medieval Church is that it was actively opposed to scientific investigation. Systematic knowledge of the natural world, it is commonly believed, would undermine religious belief for medieval people and thus the Church's worldly authority. Some Christians believed this from the foundation of the faith and to the modern day. One of the clearest warnings against "science," which in the Roman Empire and the Middle Ages usually meant the pagan Greek natural philosophy of Aristotle, came from the early Christian author Tertullian of Carthage (ca. 160–220 CE). In his religious treatise, *Prescription against Heretics*, he associated the study of Greek science and philosophy with the worship of demons, and in this context uttered his most famous phrase: "What indeed has Athens to do with Jerusalem?" By this rhetorical question, he meant the teachings of ancient Greek philosophers (Athens) have nothing to do with Christ and his teachings (Jerusalem). (See the Primary Documents for more of this work.)

Beyond this statement from Tertullian, there are two historical episodes that are frequently invoked as evidence that the medieval Church was against scientific progress, even though neither is actually medieval: the murder of Hypatia of Alexandria (415) and the condemnation of Galileo before the Catholic Inquisition (1633). In the first case, Hypatia was a famous teacher of philosophy and mathematics in late Roman Alexandria, and a rare example of a woman in this role. She was a pagan at a time when most of the Roman Empire was converting to Christianity, but nonetheless worked closely with and taught Christians. According to the popular version of her story, she angered the Christians of Alexandria by defending science and mathematics against faith, and an angry mob of willfully uneducated Christians attacked her with sharp oyster shells, shredding the flesh from her bones.

Anti-Catholic writers of the early modern period made much of her murder, connecting it with their broader criticism of the medieval Church. This is especially evident in John Toland's elaborately titled 1720 polemic, *Hypatia: Or the History of a most beautiful, most vertuous, most learned, and every way accomplish'd Lady; who was torn to pieces by the Clergy of Alexandria, to gratify the pride, emulation, and cruelty of their Archbishop, commonly, but undeservedly, stil'd St. Cyril.* Toland introduced many elements of this myth that persist to this day, such as that she was supposedly young and beautiful (she may have been about sixty years old at the time) or that she was killed by monks or members of the clergy (the earliest sources say she was killed by local laymen). In reality, Hypatia's death had little to do with religion or science, but rather she was killed as part of a political struggle between Orestes, the imperial prefect of Alexandria, and Cyril, the city's archbishop, who were in conflict over control of the city. Cyril wanted to defame Orestes by claiming that his friend, Hypatia, practiced illegal magic. Whether Cyril intentionally stirred up a mob of his supporters to kill her is unclear, but what is clear is that she was not defending her science nor were they punishing her paganism (Lindberg 2009, 8–9).

In the hands of influential Enlightenment authors like Voltaire and Edward Gibbon (see Primary Documents), Hypatia's murder became the death blow for ancient science at the hands of close-minded and vicious Catholic clergy. Even though this view of Hypatia has been debunked numerous times in the last century, any author who wants to portray the medieval Church and Catholicism in a negative light can return to Talbot's or Gibbon's version of the story. Their version obviously appeals to Charles Freeman who, in his 2003 monograph *The Closing of the Western Mind: The Rise of Faith and the Fall of Reason*, obviously sees medieval Catholic faith as the enemy of rational science. Freeman uncritically follows Gibbon's account because it suits his argument on the "fall of reason" at the start of the Middle Ages (Freeman 2003, 249). Even more recently, this version of Hypatia's story came to the big screen in the film *Agora* (dir. Alejandro Amenábar, 2009), starring Rachel Weisz as Hypatia. The Alexandrian Christians are portrayed as violent fanatics in the face of Hypatia's mathematical reasoning and often as darker-skinned Africans and Arabs, in comparison to Weisz's white and "European" Hypatia. The Christians are made out to be destroyers of art, books, and lives, the very instigators of the "Fall of Civilization" in the words of the film's official trailer.

At the other end of the Middle Ages is the famous story of Galileo Galilei (1564–1642) and his condemnation before the Catholic Inquisition for his scientific ideas. This story is used even more than Hypatia's as proof that there was no scientific progress in the Middle Ages, and that when it began again in the early modern "Scientific Revolution," it was necessarily seen as an attack on the Catholic Church. Galileo is popularly believed to have been imprisoned and tortured by the Inquisition for publicly supporting Copernicus's heliocentric theory and publishing further observational and mathematical proofs that Earth moves around the sun. These are not new ideas; already during the eighteenth century philosophers and historians widely believed that "the celebrated Galileo . . . was put in the inquisition for six years, and put to the torture, for saying, that the earth moved" (Giuseppe Baretti, 1757, quoted in Finocchiaro 2009, 68).

But what does Galileo, living well after the usual dates for the Middle Ages, have to do with our fiction about the medieval Church? Simply put, Galileo's condemnation is used as proof of a millennium-long repression of science by the Church. His imprisonment is seen as an inevitable consequence of medieval theology and Church teachings. This attitude is seen in numerous recent books, from children's histories to lengthy, complex monographs. Marty Gitlin, in the 2016 children's book *The Totally Gross History of Medieval Europe*, claims that medieval people resorted only to prayer to heal sickness, because they supposedly had no natural knowledge of disease or any conception of medical science (Gitlin 2016, 24). Gitlin, and many other popular authors, assume a binary system of science or religion: if you have one, you cannot have the other. Charles Freeman, although writing for adults in his book *The Closing of the Western Mind*, builds on the same basic idea: "the subversion of the natural order of things by miracles becomes one of the distinguishing features of Christianity and, necessarily, goes hand in hand with the waning of scientific thought" (Freeman 2003, 321). Freeman also claims that the later medieval theologian St. Thomas Aquinas (1225–1274) argued that faith (which includes the Bible) must be the foundation of rational thought, which included explorations of the nature of the universe. Because the Bible says that "the earth was fixed on its foundation, not to be moved forever" (Psalm 103), medieval and early modern Catholics could not believe otherwise. Therefore, Freeman says, "The famous clash between Galileo and the Catholic Church was the result" (Freeman 2003, 332). This statement comes at the end of a book, not about Galileo or early modern science, but about the rise of the Christian Church in Late Antiquity (the third through the sixth centuries CE). By skipping over the entire Middle Ages between the fall of Rome and the trial of Galileo, he subsumes the medieval period into that single episode of Galileo and the Inquisition.

Thus far we have danced around the actual medieval period. What ideas are commonly held about the medieval Church itself (and not that of the later Roman Empire or early modern period) and its reaction to science? As we have seen, many of the false assumptions about medieval science took form during the eighteenth-century Enlightenment. But it was especially in the later nineteenth century that we find some of the most powerful condemnations of medieval religion, in regard to science, in the persons of John William Draper (1811–1882) and Andrew Dickson White (1832–1918), both U.S. scientists and historians. White was also the first president of Cornell University, 1866–1885. They wrote similarly titled books on our topic: Draper wrote *History of the Conflict between*

Religion and Science (1875) and White spoke publicly for decades after his 1869 lecture titled "The Battle-Fields of Science," which culminated in his book *A History of the Warfare of Science with Theology in Christendom* (1896). Together these authors are credited with the so-called Draper-White Thesis or Conflict Thesis, which argues that there is inevitable conflict and hostility between religion and science by their very natures. The conflict thesis is still widely and popularly accepted despite the efforts of historians of science and religion for decades to prove it false. Draper and White both began writing in the midst of heated public debates in the United Kingdom and the United States over Darwin's theory of biological evolution in relation to Christian beliefs. Both of their works are shaped by Anglo-American Protestantism and an overt hostility to Catholics and Continental Europeans.

Draper's book catalogued all the areas of science over which faith came into conflict with reason: nature of the soul, nature of the world, age of Earth, criteria of truth, government of the universe (Draper 1875). "Faith" for Draper typically means medieval Catholic Christianity, for he praises medieval Muslims and Hindus for their superior grasp of mathematics and astronomy. In one of his final chapters, after showing how ignorant medieval Europe was of science and mathematics, Draper clearly places the blame on the Church: "Latin Christianity is responsible for the condition and progress of Europe from the fourth to the sixteenth century" (Draper 1875, 255). In fact, Draper's work is not so much a work of history or sociology but a vicious diatribe against Catholics in the Middle Ages and, by implication, in his own day. Draper's younger contemporary, Andrew Dickson White, produced a more carefully historical work, but one that was nonetheless destined from the start to shame and condemn medieval and modern Catholicism. Unlike Draper, White recognized that there were significant changes during the Middle Ages in population, culture, education, and theological doctrine. Nonetheless, he shared with Draper the overriding theme that the medieval Church was most to blame for delaying scientific advances until the age of Newton and Galileo.

In the last century, fewer historians are so openly hostile to religion, and Catholicism in particular, as the Anglo-Americans of the Victorian era (Charles Freeman, discussed earlier, is an exception). Nonetheless, the underlying narrative of a Church hostile to scientific investigation remains the same in even the most recent popular histories of science. In 2014 Fox television and the National Geographic channel produced the documentary series *Cosmos*, presented by astrophysicist Neil deGrasse Tyson and itself a remake of Carl Sagan's original series *Cosmos: A Personal Voyage*

(PBS, 1980). Each series incorporated brief accounts of major figures in the history of astronomy and cosmology (primarily from the period of the Scientific Revolution): Ptolemy, Tycho Brahe, Nicolaus Copernicus, Johannes Kepler, and Christian Huygens. But the 2014 series spends an astonishing eleven out of forty-three minutes in its first episode recounting the story of the Dominican friar Giordano Bruno (1548–1600), who was tried for heresy by the Roman Inquisition and burned at the stake in a series of trials from 1593 to 1600. Bruno is famous to this day for supporting Copernicus's heliocentric theory before Galileo, but he was not a practicing astronomer and had no data to back up his ideas. And because he died in such a tragic fashion, he makes a better focus for a television show than Galileo, who (although he was also punished by the Roman Inquisition) died peacefully in advanced old age.

As the historian of science Rebekah Higgitt points out, the new *Cosmos* series turns Bruno into a "scientific hero and martyr" in the face of a darkly oppressive Catholic Church (Higgitt 2014). But however unfair the trial of Bruno, he was actually found guilty of heresy for problematic elements of his theology and mysticism, not for any of his unfounded scientific ideas. Higgitt explains that this rewriting of Bruno's story for educational television only perpetuates "anti-religious propaganda coming from the scientific and media establishment" (Higgitt 2014). And for the popular viewer, who might not understand that the Inquisition of the later sixteenth century was very much a product of its specific time in the Reformation era, it is easy to project this image of a science-suppressing Church far back into the Middle Ages, when it simply was not the case.

PRIMARY DOCUMENTS

TERTULLIAN, *PRESCRIPTION AGAINST HERETICS*
(ca. 200 CE)

Tertullian of Carthage (ca. 155–240 CE) was one of the first formal Christian theologians, who helped define Christian doctrine at a time when the faith was still small and sometimes condemned in the Roman Empire. In defining orthodox Christian beliefs, he also helped define the errors of "heretics," who held incorrect ideas about the faith. In his Prescription against Heretics, *he blames the rise of heresies on the continuing popularity of Greek "pagan" philosophy, which would include Greek science. He calls for Christians to follow only the words of Scripture, and not to try to mix Christian theology with the ideas of Aristotle, Plato, or the Stoics. It is in this context that he uttered his most famous phrase, "What indeed has Athens to do with Jerusalem? What concord is there between the Academy and the Church? what between heretics and Christians?" His statement has been used occasionally for the last 1800 years to support the Christian rejection of science.*

Chapter 1. Introduction: Heresies Must Exist, and Even Abound.

The character of the times in which we live is such as to call forth from us even this admonition, that we ought not to be astonished at the heresies (which abound) neither ought their existence to surprise us, for it was foretold that they should come to pass; nor the fact that they subvert the faith of some, for their final cause is, by affording a trial to faith, to give it also the opportunity of being "approved." Groundless, therefore, and inconsiderate is the offence of the many who are scandalized by the very fact that heresies prevail to such a degree. How great (might their offence have been) if they had not existed. When it has been determined that a thing must by all means be, it receives the (final) cause for which it has its being. This secures the power through which it exists, in such a way that it is impossible for it not to have existence. . . .

Chapter 6. Heretics are Self-Condemned.
Heresy is Self-Will, While Faith is Submission of Our Will to Divine Authority

On this point, however, we dwell no longer, since it is the same Paul who, in his Epistle to the Galatians, counts "heresies" among "the sins of the flesh," who also intimates to Titus, that "a man who is a heretic" must be "rejected after the first admonition," on the ground that "he that is such is perverted, and committeth sin, as a self-condemned man." Indeed, in almost every epistle, when enjoining on us the duty of avoiding false doctrines, he sharply condemns heresies. Of these the practical effects are false doctrines, called in Greek heresies, a word used in the sense of that choice which a man makes when he either teaches them to others or takes up with them for himself. For this reason it is that he calls the heretic condemned, because he has himself chosen that for which he is condemned. We, however, are not permitted to cherish any object after our own will, nor yet to make choice of that which another has introduced of his private fancy. In the Lord's apostles we possess our authority; for even they did not of themselves choose to introduce anything, but faithfully delivered to the nations of mankind the doctrine which they had received from Christ. If, therefore, even "an angel from heaven should preach any other gospel" than theirs, he would be called accursed by us. The Holy Ghost had even then foreseen that there would be in a certain virgin called Philumene an angel of deceit, "transformed into an angel of light," by whose miracles and illusions Apelles was led when he introduced his new heresy.

Chapter 7. Pagan Philosophy the Parent of Heresies. The Connection between Deflections from Christian Faith and the Old Systems of Pagan Philosophy

These are "the doctrines" of men and "of demons" produced for itching ears of the spirit of this world's wisdom: this the Lord called "foolishness," and "chose the foolish things of the world" to confound even philosophy itself. For philosophy it is which is the material of the world's wisdom, the rash interpreter of the nature and the dispensation of God. Indeed heresies are themselves instigated by philosophy. From this source came the Aeons, and I known not what infinite forms, and the trinity of man in the system of Valentinus, who was of Plato's school. From the same source came Marcion's better god, with all his tranquility; he came of the Stoics. Then, again, the opinion that the soul dies is held by the Epicureans; while the denial of the restoration of the body is taken from the aggregate school of all the philosophers; also, when matter is made equal to God, then you have the teaching of Zeno; and when any doctrine is alleged touching a god of fire, then Heraclitus comes in. The same subject-matter is discussed over and over again by the heretics and the philosophers; the same arguments are involved. Whence comes evil? Why is it permitted? What is the origin of man? and in what way does he come? Besides the question which Valentinus has very lately proposed—Whence comes God? Which he settles with the answer: From enthymesis and ectroma. Unhappy Aristotle! who invented for these men dialectics, the art of building up and pulling down; an art so evasive in its propositions, so far-fetched in its conjectures, so harsh, in its arguments, so productive of contentions— embarrassing even to itself, retracting everything, and really treating of nothing! Whence spring those "fables and endless genealogies," and "unprofitable questions," and "words which spread like a cancer?" From all these, when the apostle would restrain us, he expressly names philosophy as that which he would have us be on our guard against. Writing to the Colossians, he says, "See that no one beguile you through philosophy

THE CHURCH SUPPRESSED SCIENCE

and vain deceit, after the tradition of men, and contrary to the wisdom of the Holy Ghost." He had been at Athens, and had in his interviews (with its philosophers) become acquainted with that human wisdom which pretends to know the truth, whilst it only corrupts it, and is itself divided into its own manifold heresies, by the variety of its mutually repugnant sects. What indeed has Athens to do with Jerusalem? What concord is there between the Academy and the Church? what between heretics and Christians? Our instruction comes from "the porch of Solomon," who had himself taught that "the Lord should be sought in simplicity of heart."

Away with all attempts to produce a mottled Christianity of Stoic, Platonic, and dialectic composition! We want no curious disputation after possessing Christ Jesus, no inquisition after enjoying the gospel! With our faith, we desire no further belief. For this is our palmary faith, that there is nothing which we ought to believe besides.

Source: Tertullian. 1885. *Prescription against Heretics.* In *Anti-Nicene Fathers,* vol. 3, edited by Alexander Roberts, James Donaldson, and A. Cleveland Coxe. Buffalo, NY: Christian Literature Publishing Company. Reprinted at http://www.newadvent.org /fathers/0311.htm. Punctuation modified slightly.

EDWARD GIBBON ON THE MURDER OF HYPATIA: *DECLINE AND FALL OF THE ROMAN EMPIRE* (1776–1788)

Edward Gibbon's (1737–1794) History of the Decline and Fall of the Roman Empire is widely considered one of the founding works of modern scholarly history. In six volumes, published over twelve years, Gibbon used primary sources to construct a rational and secular history of the Roman Empire, its fall, and the nature of the following Middle Ages. He was one of the first historians to blame the rise of Christianity and the formation of the Church for the fall of Rome and ensuing "Dark Ages," an idea that was popular among Enlightenment philosophers and the Protestants of Great Britain. His story of the murder of Hypatia is central to his argument about the destructive influence of the Church, and it has been repeated in this form to the present day.

Hypatia, the daughter of Theon the mathematician, was initiated in her father's studies; her learned comments have elucidated the geometry of Apollonius and Diophantus, and she publicly taught, both at Athens and Alexandria, the philosophy of Plato and Aristotle. In the bloom of beauty, and in the maturity of wisdom, the modest maid refused her lovers and instructed her disciples; the persons most illustrious for their rank or merit were impatient to visit the female philosopher; and Cyril beheld, with a jealous eye, the gorgeous train of horses and slaves who crowded the door of her academy. A rumor was spread among the Christians, that the daughter of Theon was the only obstacle to the reconciliation of the praefect and the archbishop; and that obstacle was speedily removed. On a fatal day, in the holy season of Lent, Hypatia was torn from her chariot, stripped naked, dragged to the church, and inhumanly butchered by the hands of Peter the reader, and a troop of savage and merciless fanatics: her flesh was scraped from her bones with sharp oyster shells, and her quivering limbs were delivered to the flames. The just progress of inquiry and punishment was stopped by seasonable gifts; but the murder of Hypatia has imprinted an indelible stain on the character and religion of Cyril of Alexandria.

Source: Gibbon, Edward. 1827. *The History of the Decline and Fall of the Roman Empire.* 12 vols. Oxford: D. A. Talboys, 6:17–18.

JOHN WILLIAM DRAPER, *HISTORY OF THE CONFLICT BETWEEN RELIGION AND SCIENCE* (1875)

John William Draper (1811–1882) is remembered as a pioneer in the fields of chemistry and photography, famed for producing some of the first clear photographs around 1840. But he was also an amateur historian, writing books on the U.S. Civil War and European intellectual history. He was an active promoter of the "conflict thesis" claiming that religion and science are always necessarily in conflict. This thesis is sometimes called the "Draper-White thesis" after him and his contemporary Andrew Dickson White. In this passage Draper paints the Middle Ages not merely as backward and superstitious, but as a period when the Church discouraged medicine and scientific investigation for its own profit. Physicians, Draper claims, would take money away from religious shrines. He blames the medieval popes directly for encouraging fearful superstitions, such as when one pope tried to "exorcise" a comet from the sky.

An illiterate condition everywhere prevailing, gave opportunity for the development of superstition. Europe was full of disgraceful miracles. On all the roads pilgrims were wending their way to the shrines of saints, renowned for the cures they had wrought. It had always been the policy of the Church to discourage the physician and his art; he interfered too much with the gifts and profits of the shrines. Time has brought this once lucrative imposture to its proper value. How many shrines are there now in successful operation in Europe?

For patients too sick to move or be moved, there were no remedies except those of a ghostly kind—the Pater-noster or the Ave [the Our Father and Hail Mary prayers]. For the prevention of disease, prayers were put up in the churches, but no sanitary measures were resorted to. From cities reeking with putrefying filth it was thought that the plague might be stayed by the prayers of the priests, by them rain and dry weather might be secured, and deliverance obtained from the baleful influences of eclipses and comets. But when Halley's comet came, in 1456, so tremendous was its apparition that it was necessary for the pope himself to interfere. He exorcised and expelled it from the skies. It slunk away into the abysses of space, terror-stricken by the maledictions of Calixtus III, and did not venture back for seventy-five years!

The physical value of shrine-cures and ghostly remedies is measured by the death-rate. In those days it was, probably, about one in twenty-three, under the present more material practice it is about one in forty. . . .

To the medical efficacy of shrines must be added that of special relics. These were sometimes of the most extraordinary kind. There were several abbeys that possessed our Savior's crown of thorns. Eleven had the lance that had pierced his side. If any person was adventurous enough to suggest that these could not all be authentic, he would have been denounced as an atheist. During the holy wars the Templar-Knights had driven a profitable commerce by bringing from Jerusalem to the Crusading armies bottles of the milk of the Blessed Virgin, which they sold for enormous sums; these bottles were preserved with pious care in many of the great religious establishments. But perhaps none of these impostures surpassed in audacity that offered by a monastery in Jerusalem, which presented to the beholder one of the fingers of the Holy Ghost! Modern society has silently rendered its verdict on these scandalous objects. Though they once nourished the piety of thousands of earnest people, they are now considered too vile to have a place in any public museum.

How shall we account for the great failure we thus detect in the guardianship of the Church over Europe? This is not the result that must have occurred had there been in Rome an unremitting care for the spiritual and material prosperity of the continent, had the universal pastor, the successor of Peter [i.e., the pope], occupied himself with singleness of purpose for the holiness of his flock.

Source: Draper, John William. 1875. *History of the Conflict between Religion and Science*. New York: D. Appleton and Co., 268–70.

ANDREW DICKSON WHITE, *A HISTORY OF THE WARFARE OF SCIENCE WITH THEOLOGY IN CHRISTENDOM* (1896)

Andrew Dickson White's A History of the Warfare of Science with Theology in Christendom *was the culminating work of decades of conflict and debates between religious and scientific figures in the later nineteenth century, kindled especially by Charles Darwin's publication of* On the Origin of Species *in 1859. White took the side of scientists who demanded that the study of the natural world be entirely separated from religious belief, and to make his point he endeavored to show that religious institutions, especially the Catholic Church, always had and have the goal of suppressing and delegitimizing scientific progress. His book is still widely read over a century after it was published, and continues to perpetuate the fiction that the medieval Church actively kept people in ignorance. He extends his condemnation of Christianity beyond just the Middle Ages, claiming that for twelve hundred years (apparently ca.300–1500) "the physical sciences were thus discouraged or perverted by the dominant orthodoxy" (by which he means Catholicism). Unlike John William Draper (see previous document), who could see no light at all in the Dark Ages, White was a more careful historian who does acknowledge the scientific discoveries of several medieval philosophers, like Albert the Great (1200–1280), but he emphasizes they were constantly hindered by Church authorities.*

This [Greek] legacy of belief in science, of respect for scientific pursuits, and of freedom in scientific research, was especially received by the school of Alexandria, and above all by Archimedes, who began, just before the Christian era, to open new paths through the great field of the inductive sciences by observation, comparison, and experiment.

The establishment of Christianity, beginning a new evolution of theology, arrested the normal development of the physical sciences for over fifteen hundred years. The cause of this arrest was twofold: First, there was created an atmosphere in which the germs of physical science could hardly grow—an atmosphere in which all seeking in Nature for truth as truth was regarded as futile. The general belief derived from the New Testament Scriptures was, that the end of the world was at hand; that the last judgment was approaching; that all existing physical nature was soon to be destroyed: hence, the greatest thinkers in the Church generally poured contempt upon all investigators into a science of Nature, and insisted that everything except the saving of souls was folly.

The belief appears frequently through the entire period of the Middle Ages; but during the first thousand years it is clearly dominant. From

Lactantius and Eusebius, in the third century, pouring contempt, as we have seen, over studies in astronomy, to Peter Damian, the noted chancellor of Pope Gregory VII, in the eleventh century, declaring all worldly sciences to be "absurdities" and "fooleries," it becomes a very important element in the atmosphere of thought.

Then, too, there was established a standard to which all science which did struggle up through this atmosphere must be made to conform—a standard which favoured magic rather than science, for it was a standard of rigid dogmatism obtained from literal readings in the Jewish and Christian Scriptures. The most careful inductions from ascertained facts were regarded as wretchedly fallible when compared with any view of nature whatever given or even hinted at in any poem, chronicle, code, apologue, myth, legend, allegory, letter, or discourse of any sort which had happened to be preserved in the literature which had come to be held sacred.

For twelve centuries, then, the physical sciences were thus discouraged or perverted by the dominant orthodoxy. Whoever studied nature studied it either openly to find illustrations of the sacred text, useful in the "saving of souls," or secretly to gain the aid of occult powers, useful in securing personal advantage. Great men like Bede, Isidore of Seville, and Rabanus Maurus, accepted the scriptural standard of science and used it as a means of Christian edification. . . .

First among these was Albert of Bollstadt, better known as Albert the Great, the most renowned scholar of this time. Fettered though he was by the methods sanctioned in the Church, dark as was all about him, he had conceived better methods and aims; his eye pierced the mists of scholasticism; he saw the light, and sought to draw the world toward it. He stands among the great pioneers of physical and natural science; he aided in giving foundations to botany and chemistry; he rose above his time, and struck a heavy blow at those who opposed the possibility of human life on opposite sides of the earth; he noted the influence of mountains, seas, and forests upon races and products, so that Humboldt justly finds in his works the germs of physical geography as a comprehensive science.

But the old system of deducing scientific truth from scriptural texts was renewed in the development of scholastic theology; and ecclesiastical power, acting through thousands of subtle channels, was made to aid this development. The old ideas of the futility of physical science and of the vast superiority of theology was revived. Though Albert's main effort was to Christianize science, he was dealt with by the authorities of the Dominican order, subjected to suspicion and indignity, and only escaped persecution for sorcery by yielding to the ecclesiastical spirit of the time, and working finally in theological channels by scholastic methods.

Source: White, Andrew Dickson. 1896. *A History of the Warfare of Science with Theology in Christendom.* 2 vols. New York: D. Appleton and Co, 1:375–77.

What Really Happened

The fiction of this chapter, that the medieval Church suppressed science, is closely linked in terms of its sources and arguments with the fiction in chapter 2, that medieval people thought Earth was flat. Both are almost wholly false and are the creations of early modern and modern authors who sought to attack the contemporary Catholic Church by delegitimizing its medieval past. There is no evidence that the medieval Church intentionally suppressed scientific investigation. As shown earlier, the main examples used to support this claim—the murder of Hypatia and the trial of Galileo—do not apply: Hypatia was not killed for religious reasons or for her teaching, and the 1633 trial of Galileo does not belong to the Middle Ages but to the intellectual upheavals of the early modern Counter-Reformation. There were scientific investigations and writings during the Middle Ages, especially after the eleventh century, almost all took place under the protection of the Church and with its encouragement, and they were performed and described by Catholic clerics and monks.

To be clear, medieval science, as far as it existed, was not modern science. Historians usually call the study of nature in the Middle Ages "natural philosophy" because medieval thinkers tended to explain natural phenomena following the rules of logic rather than by systematic observation. In this respect, medieval "scientists" are still far removed from the experiments of Galileo and Isaac Newton. Scientific investigation in the Middle Ages was often inspired by passages from the Bible (but not restricted by the Bible) and subjected to the logical rules and teachings of Plato and Aristotle. Nonetheless, medieval thinkers were exceptionally free in what they imagined to be covered by the Bible. They usually followed the ideas of St. Augustine of Hippo, who argued in his book on how to read and understand the Bible, *De doctrina christiana* ("On Christian Doctrine," written 397–426 CE), that whatever pagans have said or written can and should be appropriated by Christians so long as it supports their faith. Augustine's ideas were second in importance only to the Bible during the Middle Ages, and totally superseded the writings of other theologians like Tertullian (see previous discussion), who had warned against pagan philosophy and science.

The study of nature in the Middle Ages was included under the study of philosophy, and was guided especially by the ideas of Aristotle. These ideas were known only indirectly in the Early Middle Ages, through the works of early medieval Christian authors like Boethius and Cassiodorus, but in the High Middle Ages Europeans read Aristotle's scientific works directly through Latin translations. These works, known in the Middle Ages as the *libri naturales* ("books on nature"), included Aristotle's works on physics, human nature, animal generation and reproduction, the heavens, and meteorology, among others. These were all translated in the twelfth and thirteenth centuries and were not only allowed, but even required, reading at the universities of the later Middle Ages (Black 2016, 84–89). Most medieval schools, including the universities, were under the direct supervision of the bishops and popes of the Catholic Church. The Church did ban the teaching of certain ideas at the universities during the thirteenth century, but the bans usually concerned the nature of angels or of the human soul, and did not limit the investigation of the natural world. Instead, this encouraged theologians and natural philosophers to read the works of Aristotle even more closely and to challenge and rethink his ideas.

The Primary Documents reproduce writings from two medieval philosophers (out of many more who could be named) who were both members of the Church and dedicated to the investigation of nature, physics, and cosmology. Adelard of Bath (ca. 1080–1152) was an English cleric in the service of the bishop of Bath and Wells and Robert Grosseteste, also an Englishman, was none other than the Bishop of Lincoln. Both were active scholars and authors whose works demonstrate a profound interest in scientific subjects during the Middle Ages. Adelard translated or wrote works on astronomy, physics, and mathematics, and stands as one of the earliest and most important introducers of Greek and Arabic science into Europe. In his work *Natural Questions*, he provides an introduction to the "new" science of his day in the form of a dialogue between himself and his nephew. The nephew asks a series of seventy-six questions about subjects as diverse as the shape of Earth, the functions of the eye, body hair, tides and rivers, and eclipses. Every one of Adelard's responses is based on logic and some on direct observation. Even though his answers at times are laughable according to modern science, the point here is that his natural investigations are not banned, suppressed, or censored by a Church that is afraid of science.

Even if we readily acknowledge that there was scientific investigation in the Middle Ages, most people still believe that real "science" began in the Scientific Revolution of the sixteenth and seventeenth centuries. It is at that time philosophers like René Descartes, Galileo, and Isaac Newton finally rejected Aristotle and built a new system of knowledge based on the controlled scientific experiment. While there is much to support that standard narrative of history, some historians of science push the beginnings of modern science back to the medieval universities of the thirteenth century (Crombie 1953; Lindberg 2007; Hannam 2011). It is at that time when learned clerics and monks, like Roger Bacon, Robert Grosseteste, and Albert the Great, began to describe formal experiments to test their theories or hypotheses about the workings of nature.

In the Primary Documents is included an excerpt from one of Grosseteste's works in which he outlines a scientific experiment for testing his hypothesis that a certain plant causes blood to appear in the urine. Historians of science and philosophy still vigorously debate the question of whether Grosseteste should be considered a founder of the modern scientific method, but there is general agreement that he introduced to Western Europe some of the elements of the closely observed, controlled experiment (Lewis 2013, Part 11: "Scientific Method"). Those scholars who insist that the early modern Scientific Revolution was the real start of modern science will be quick to note that these medieval scientists still accepted Aristotle as fact, still tried to align their science with the Bible, and did not leave formal, reproducible accounts of their experiments. This is true, but what matters here is that scientific experiments and advances were made entirely within the culture of the medieval Church and with the approval of Church authorities. Medieval science was seen as a path toward surer knowledge of God and not as a potential enemy of religion.

PRIMARY DOCUMENTS

ADELARD OF BATH, *NATURAL QUESTIONS* (ca. 1130)

See the Primary Documents of chapter 2 for a detailed introduction to Adelard of Bath and his Quaestiones Naturales, *or* Natural Questions, *completed around 1130. The following excerpts include the opening conversation of this work, in which Adelard praises the learning of the "Saracens" (Arab Muslims) when compared to French philosophy and a second passage in which Adelard teaches his nephew to use his reason and not to blindly follow ancient "authority." Also included is a "question" where Adelard explains that a "magic" pitcher which can pour out of different holes depending on where you place your fingers (still a popular science experiment) works not by witchcraft, but through the natural properties of the four elements.*

Here begins Adelard's treatise to his Nephew.

ADELARD: You will remember, Nephew, how seven years ago when you were almost a child in the learning of the French, and I sent you along with the rest of my hearers to study with a man of high reputation, it was agreed between us that I should devote myself to the best of my ability to the study of Arabic, while you on your part were to acquire the inconsistencies of French ideas.

NEPHEW: I remember, and all the more because, when departing, you bound me under a solemn promise to be a diligent student of philosophy. The result was that I applied myself with great diligence to this study. Whether what I have said is correct, the present occasion will give you an opportunity of discovering; since when you have often set them forth, I, as hearer only, have marked the opinions of the Saracens [medieval term for Muslims], and many of them seem to me quite absurd; I shall, therefore, for a time cease to exercise this patience, and when you utter these views, shall attack them where it seems good to me to do so. To me it seems that you go too far in your praise of the Arabs [this applies to Muslim, Christian, and Jewish scholars who wrote in the Arabic language], and show prejudice in your disparagement of the learning of our philosophers. Our reward will be that you will have gained some fruit of your toil; if you give good answers, and I make a good showing as your opponent, you will see that my promise has been well kept.

ADELARD: You perhaps take a little more on you than you ought; but as this arrangement will be profitable not only to you but to many others, I will pardon your forwardness, making however this one stipulation, that when I adduce something unfamiliar, people are to think not that I am putting forward an idea of my own, but am giving the views of the Arabs. If anything I say displeases the less educated, I do not want them to be displeased with me also: I know too well what is the fate which attends upon the teachers of the truth with the common herd, and consequently shall plead the case of the Arabs, not my own.

NEPHEW: Let it be as you will, provided nothing causes you to hold your peace.

ADELARD: I think then that we should begin with lighter matters, and if here I fail to give you a reasonable account, you will know what to expect in more important subjects. Let us begin then at the bottom, and so proceed upwards. . . .

ADELARD: It is a little difficult for you and me to argue about animals. I, with reason for my guide, have learned one thing from my Arab teachers, you, something different; dazzled by the outward show of authority you wear a head-stall. For what else should we call authority but a head-stall [the blinders put on a plow animal to prevent it from seeing to the sides]? Just as brute animals are led by the head-stall where one pleases, without seeing why or where they are being led, and only follow the halter by which they are held, so many of you, bound and fettered as you are by a low credulity, are led into danger by the authority of writers. Hence, certain people arrogating to themselves the title of authorities have employed an unbounded licence in writing, and this to such an extent that they have not hesitated to insinuate into men of low intellect the false instead of the true. Why should you not fill sheets of paper, aye, fill them on both sides, when to-day you can get readers who require no proof of sound judgment from you, and are satisfied merely with the name of a time-worn title? They do not understand that reason has been given to individuals that, with it as chief judge, distinction may be drawn between the true and the false. Unless reason were appointed to be the chief judge, to no purpose would she have been given to us individually: it would have been enough for the writing of laws to have been entrusted to one, or at most to a few, and the rest would have been satisfied with their ordinances and authority. Further, the very people who are called authorities first gained the confidence of their inferiors only because they followed reason; and those who are ignorant of reason, or neglect it, justly desire to be called blind. However, I will not pursue this subject any further, though I regard authority as matter for contempt. This one thing, however, I will say. We must first search after reason, and when it has been found, and not until then, authority if added to it, may be received. Authority by itself can inspire no confidence in the philosopher, nor ought it to be used for such a purpose. Hence logicians have agreed in treating the argument from authority not as necessary, but probable only. If, therefore, you want to bear anything from me, you must both give and take reason. I am not the man whom the semblance of an object can possibly satisfy; and the fact is, that the mere word is a loose wanton abandoning herself now to this man, now to that.

Chapter LVIII. Why, if a vessel be full and its lower part open, water will not flow from it unless the upper lid be first removed.

NEPHEW: There is another point in which I am in doubt about the nature of eater. As you know, some little time past we visited an old witch in order to study magic, and there attracted by her sense, or perhaps her nonsense, we spent some days. In the house was a vessel of remarkable powers, which was brought out at meal-times. Both at top and bottom it was pierced with many holes; and when water for washing the hands had been put into it, so long as the servant kept the upper holes closed by putting his thumb over them, no water came out of the lower holes: but as soon as he removed his thumb, there was at once an abundant flow of water for the benefit of us who were standing round. This seemed to me to be the effect of magic; and I said, "What wonder that the old woman is a sovereign enchantress, when her man-slave can work such wonders!" You, however, though according to your habit you paid great attention to enchantments, refused to regard this as magic. Now tell me what you think about this matter of the water: the lower holes were always open, and yet it was only at the water-carrier's will that water issued from them.

ADELARD: If it was magic, it was nature's rather than the servant's power. The body of this sensible universe is composed of four elements; they are so closely bound together by natural affection, that just as none of them would exist without the other, so no place either is, or could be, empty of them. Hence it happens, that as soon as one of them leaves its position, another immediately takes its place; nor is this again able to leave its position, until another which it regards with special affection is able to succeed it. When, therefore, the entrance is closed to that which is to come in, in vain will the exit be open for the departing element: thanks to this loving waiting, it will be all in vain that you open an exit for the water, unless you give an entrance to the air. These elements, as I have said, are not pure, and are so closely conjoined together, that they neither can nor will exist without one another. Hence it happens that if there be no opening in the upper part of the vessel, and opening be made at the lower end, it is only after an interval, and with a sort of murmuring, that the liquid comes forth. The quantity of air which comes in is equal to that of the water which goes out; and the air finding the water porous, passes through it, thanks to its natural tenuity and lightness, and takes possession of the apparently empty upper part of the vessel.

Source: Adelard of Bath. 1920. *Natural Questions.* Printed with *Dodi Ve-Nechdi (Uncle & Nephew).* In *The work of Berachya Hanakdan,* edited and translated by H. Gollancz. Oxford: Oxford University Press, 92, 98–99, 143–44.

ROBERT GROSSETESTE, COMMENTARY ON ARISTOTLE'S *POSTERIOR ANALYTICS* (ca. 1230)

The following passage comes from Grosseteste's Latin commentary on the Posterior Analytics *of Aristotle, written about 1230, in which he explores how scientific knowledge (here called "universal") can be gathered with the senses as they observe individual things around us. Here he explores the specific question of whether we can gain universal knowledge if one our senses is dulled or lacking. Grosseteste does this by discussing the meaning of Aristotle's statement in* Posterior Analytics *I.18: "It is also clear that the loss of any one of the senses entails the loss of a corresponding portion of knowledge, and that, since we learn either by induction or by demonstration, this knowledge cannot be acquired." He treats the passage first in a purely philosophical manner but then applies his understanding of Christian theology to the question: How do God and the angels understand universal concepts without bodily senses? This religious question, rather than leading him away from science, instead guides him to propose an early form of a controlled experiment for testing the universal truth of observed data. In this case, he explores the effects of the herb scammony on a patient's urine, and makes a hypothesis based on repeated observation under controlled circumstances. He learned this example from the Islamic physician and philosopher Avicenna (980–1037 CE), but adapts it here in a Christian, educational context.*

"It is also clear that if any one sense, etc." After explaining all the ways in which ignorance is said to occur because of an [incorrect] arrangement [of a proposition], Aristotle thereafter explains whence comes the ignorance which is said to be caused by a lack [of information], so that his lecture on the causes by which ignorance arises will be complete. . . . He therefore says that on the occasion of the failure of any one of the senses there is a failure of some part of knowledge, and from this will occur the ignorance which comes from denial. This is proved thus: Since the senses are perceptive of individual things, when any one sense is lacking, the perception of some individual things will be also be lacking. Therefore, since inductive reasoning begins with individual things, when one sense is lacking, the induction based on the individual things (which the deficient sense is supposed to perceive) also fails, and when the induction based on those individual things fails then the universal understanding of those individual things within the mind also fails, because that universal conclusion cannot be accepted except through inductive reasoning. With the failure of a universal conclusion in the mind, demonstration also fails, because demonstration is based on universal conclusions, and when demonstration fails then the knowledge also fails which can be acquired through demonstration alone. Therefore the failure of one part of knowledge [scientia] comes initially from the failure of one of the senses, and this is said to be the ignorance caused by a lack [of information].

Yet I say that some knowledge can exist without the assistance of the senses, for all forms of knowledge exist in the mind of God forever, and not only is the understanding of universal concepts certain in that mind, but also of the understanding of all individual things, even though the divine mind conceives of individual things in a universal manner, because it knows all individual essences in an abstract way. For we [humans] do not comprehend the individual nature of our humanity except insofar as we mix it up with accidental features. But the [mind of God] knows the individual nature of [our humanity] in the purity of its essence, as it can avoid mingling it with our accidental features.

Likewise the Intelligences [i.e., angels] receive illumination from the First Light [i.e., God] and can see in that First Light all knowable things, both universal and individual; and also by reflecting on itself, an Intelligence understands those things which come in the future because it is the cause of those things. Therefore there exist a most complete knowledge [scientia] in those beings [i.e., God and angels] which lack senses. Likewise if the loftiest part of the human soul, which is called the intellectual property and which does not come from the action of any part of the body, nor does it need any bodily function in performing its own work, were not clouded over and aggravated by the burden of a corrupted body, it also could possess a complete knowledge through the illumination receive from the higher Light, without the aid of the senses, just as a soul will possess when freed from its body or just as some people might who are wholly released from the love and dreams of bodily things.

However, because the purity of mind's eye is clouded over and aggravated by our corrupt body, all the powers of the rational soul in a begotten human being are so occupied by the burden of the body that they can hardly act and are, so to speak, stunned. And so when, through the passage of a time, the senses begin to work through the repeated meeting of one of the senses with sense objects, the reason wakes up, mixed together with those senses, and is carried to the sense objects as if in a boat. But the reason, now that is has woken up, begins to distinguish and observe separately those things which had been confused in the senses, for example when sight confused color, size, shape, and mass [of an object], and in its judgment all of these attributes are accepted as one thing. But the awakened reason distinguished color from size, and the shape from the mass, and again the shape and size from the substance of a body, and thus through division and abstraction it reaches an understanding of the substance of a body separate from its size and shape and color. But nevertheless the reason, through this action, will not know the universal essence of a thing except after it has made this abstraction from many individual things and there has occurred to it one and the same judgment, discovered in many individual things.

Therefore this is the path by which we hunt a simple universal truth, derived from individual things through the aid of the senses. And we—having a soiled mind's eye—cannot acquire a complex, experimental universal truth except through the help of the senses. [Such a case is] when the senses repeatedly perceive two sense objects, of which one is the cause of the other, or is in some other way related to it, and the senses cannot perceive the intervening relation. For example, when someone frequently observes the eating of scammony and the accompanying urination of red bile, but does not see that scammony attracts and draws out red bile, by frequently observing these two visible things, he can begin to hypothesize [estimare] a third invisible thing, namely, that scammony is the cause of bringing out red bile. Then reason awakes from this hypothesized connection, kept frequently in the memory, and from the sensibly perceived connections by which the hypothesized connection was made, and once awake it begins to wonder and consider whether the situation holds just as the memorized hypothesis suggests. These two things [i.e., observation and hypothesis] direct the reason to experimentation, namely, that he gives a person scammony to eat under controlled circumstances, with the removal of all other substances which purge red bile. And when scammony is frequently given under these firmly controlled circumstances, removing all other substances which purge red bile, this universal conclusion is formed in the reason: that all scammony purges red bile by its own power. And this is the way to use sense data experimentally to form universal principles.

Source: New translation of Robertus Grosseteste. 1981. *Commentarius in Posteriorum Analyticorum Libros.* Edited by Pietro Rossi. Florence: Leo S. Olschki, 212–15.

Further Reading

Adelard of Bath. 1920. *Natural Questions*. Printed with *Dodi Ve-Nechdi (Uncle & Nephew)*. In *The work of Berachya Hanakdan*, edited and translated by H. Gollancz. Oxford: Oxford University Press.

Black, Winston. 2016. "The Quadrivium and Natural Sciences." In *The Oxford History of Classical Reception in English Literature*. Vol. 1, *800–1558*, edited by Rita Copeland, 77–94. Oxford: Oxford University Press..

Crombie, Alastair. 1953. *Robert Grosseteste and the Origins of Experimental Science, 1100–1700*. Oxford: Clarendon Press.

Draper, John William. 1875. *History of the Conflict between Religion and Science*. New York: D. Appleton and Co.

Finocchiaro, Maurice A. 2009. "Myth 8. That Galileo Was Imprisoned and Tortured for Advocating Copernicanism." In *Galileo Goes to Jail and Other Myths about Science and Religion*, edited by Ronald L. Numbers, 68–78. Cambridge, MA: Harvard University Press.

Freeman, Charles. 2003. *The Closing of the Western Mind: The Rise of Faith and the Fall of Reason*. New York: Alfred A. Knopf.

Gibbon, Edward. 1871. *The History of the Decline and Fall of the Roman Empire*. London: Bell and Daldy.

Gitlin, Marty. 2016. *The Totally Gross History of Medieval Europe*. New York: Rosen Publishing Group.

Hannam, James. 2011. *The Genesis of Science: How the Christian Middle Ages Launched the Scientific Revolution*. Washington, DC: Regnery Publishing.

Higgitt, Rebekah. 2014. "Cosmos and Giordano Bruno: The Problem with Scientific Heroes." *Guardian*, March 14, 2014. https://www.theguardian.com/science/the-h-word/2014/mar/14/cosmos-history-science-giordano-bruno-danger-heroes.

Lewis, Neil. 2013. "Robert Grosseteste." In *Stanford Encyclopedia of Philosophy*, edited by Edward N. Zalta. Summer 2013 ed. https://plato.stanford.edu/archives/sum2013/entries/grosseteste/.

Lindberg, David C. 2007. *The Beginnings of Western Science: The European Scientific Tradition in Philosophical, Religion, and Institutional Context, Prehistory to A.D. 1450*. 2d ed. Chicago: University of Chicago Press.

Lindberg, David C. 2009. "Myth 1. That the Rise of Christianity Was Responsible for the Demise of Ancient Science." In *Galileo Goes to Jail and Other Myths about Science and Religion*, edited by Ronald L. Numbers, 8–18. Cambridge, MA: Harvard University Press.

Tertullian. 1885. *Prescription against Heretics*. In *Anti-Nicene Fathers*. edited by Alexander Roberts, James Donaldson, and A. Cleveland Coxe. Vol. 3. Buffalo, NY: Christian Literature Publishing Company. http://www.newadvent.org/fathers/0311.htm.

White, Andrew Dickson. 1896. *A History of the Warfare of Science with Theology in Christendom*. 2 vols. New York: D. Appleton and Co.

Whitfield, Peter. 1999. *Landmarks in Western Science: From Prehistory to the Atomic Age*. London: British Library.

7

Thousands of Children Died on Crusade in the Year 1212

What People Think Happened

The story of the Children's Crusade is regularly invoked as an example of the essential and painful differences between the Middle Ages and modernity: it highlights the barbaric violence of the period, the corruption of the Catholic Church, the heartlessness of medieval parents, and the disorganization of major military endeavors. How else can we explain the idea of children going on crusade, led to the slaughter in foreign lands by a Church that cared more for its religious agenda than their lives? The event is so absurd and heartbreaking that, in the words of a nineteenth-century popular historian, "It was as if the Church had maliciously gathered and ruthlessly tossed fifty thousand infants from a cliff into the boiling sea, in order to calm its angry waves" (Boyd 1892, 317).

According to medieval and modern accounts of the Children's Crusade, some twenty thousand children (or even fifty to one hundred thousand in other accounts) were inspired in the year 1212 to go on crusade to the Holy Land to rescue Christendom from the infidels. This came after the Egyptian sultan Saladin took back Jerusalem from the Christian Crusaders in 1187. The Third Crusade of 1189–1192, led by King Richard Lionheart of England and Philip II of France, failed to take back the city, and the Fourth Crusade of 1202–1204 never even reached Jerusalem but instead conquered Christian Constantinople. If the knights and kings of Europe could not succeed, perhaps children could.

In some versions of the story these crusader children were inspired on their own by visions of the rescue of Jerusalem, but in others the children are deceived by the clergy of a desperate and wicked Church. The young crusaders followed two charismatic child prophets: twelve-year-old Stephen of Cloyes in France and ten-year-old Nicholas of Cologne in the German lands of the Holy Roman Empire. The French Children's Crusade hired ships in Marseilles to take them to the Holy Land. They were never heard from again, except for rumors that most had drowned in a shipwreck, the remainder being sold into slavery in Egypt. Most of the German children never left Europe, since they found neither papal approval nor enough ships to take them. Some gave up during the journey over the Alps, some remained in Italy, and most returned home after the embarrassed pope told them to come back when they had grown up.

How the Story Became Popular

We have seen in previous chapters how many medieval fictions are entirely modern creations, but the Children's Crusade was discussed widely soon after 1212. This might seem to indicate that the Children's Crusade was real, but we are faced with significant differences among the medieval sources, which do not agree about why this event occurred, who started or went on this "crusade," and what happened to the participants. In the Primary Documents are provided excerpts from eight different histories and chronicles from the thirteenth century, out of a surviving fifty-six Latin sources from the period (Dickson 2008, 9–14). Most of these sources describe the gathering of "boys" (*pueri*) or "children" (*infantes*) in hostile and negative language. This was not a true crusade, but a "heresy," the act of "lunatics," and "the craft of the devil." The age of these "boys" is rarely given, but many chroniclers emphasize that they left their parents or were locked up by their parents to prevent them leaving, which emphasizes their younger age. Sicard of Cremona, author of one of the following passages, says the leader of this crusade seemed to be twelve years old.

Each medieval author focused on a different shocking element of the "crusade," to show how it was improper and ineffective: their leader was taken around in a decorated chariot, naked women ran around the towns at the same time, the children had false visions, they thought they could walk over the Mediterranean Sea as if over land, mothers ate their children in a time of famine, and so on. But none of the medieval sources group together all the key elements of the Children's Crusade as it described earlier, namely, the separate French and German groups of children, egged on by a desperate and wicked Church, who either drown in shipwrecks or were sold into slavery.

This complete story of the Children's Crusade, as it was known throughout the twentieth century, is primarily the invention of one modern author, the Reverend George Zabriskie Gray, a theology professor in Cambridge, Massachusetts, in his 1870 book *The Children's Crusade: An Episode of the Thirteenth Century*. He cobbled together details from all the medieval sources he could find, and made up many of his own, to create a long and detailed narrative that appealed greatly to modern audiences. His book was widely read in the later nineteenth and early twentieth centuries, and was even reprinted without critique or emendation in 1972. Gray read deeply in the primary sources, which was uncommon and difficult for amateur historians of his time, but he took all of them at face value as true representations of the event. He wove his lengthy story of the tragedy of the Children's Crusade out of the details found in dozens of different medieval sources. But his conclusion (see Primary Documents) was entirely his own, in which he argued that the Children's Crusade was not an episode of spontaneous enthusiasm but rather was planned by Pope Innocent III and put into action by his nefarious clergy and monks. This idea is not represented in any of the medieval sources and is instead a product of his own anti-Catholic and antipapal attitudes as a U.S. Episcopalian clergyman. Gray's arguments were streamlined and simplified by later authors, such as James P. Boyd in his 1892 book *Story of the Crusades*, which was illustrated with older engravings by the French artist Gustave Doré (see Primary Documents).

Gray was not alone, however. One of the clearest reasons for the persistence of belief in the Children's Crusade is that Sir Steven Runciman (1903–2000), one of the greatest Crusade historians of the twentieth century, described it as entirely real. He devoted five pages of his monumental, three-volume *History of the Crusades* to the Children's Crusade (Runciman 1951–1954, 3:139–44), and this work is still in print and appears in scholarly bibliographies. Runciman accepted the existence of both Stephen of Cloyes, a "hysterical" shepherd boy, and of the German boy Nicholas, each of whom supposedly led thousands of children on pilgrimage to Jerusalem. Runciman cites only one medieval source for this section and does not seem to have actually read any of the modern scholarship on the subject, which he places in a footnote (Dickson 2008, 188–89). The story of the Children's Crusade, whether fact or fiction, was simply too useful for Runciman as evidence to support his impassioned denunciation of the entire crusading era: "the Crusades were a tragic and destructive episode . . . and the Holy War itself was nothing more than a long act of intolerance in the name of God, which is the sin against the Holy spirit" (Runciman 1951–1954, 3:480).

The Children's Crusade, as depicted by Doré and described by Gray and Runciman, has shaped literature and films in the last half century. Kurt Vonnegut could build on popular knowledge of the Children's Crusade when he gave his novel *Slaughterhouse-Five* (1969) the alternate title *Slaughterhouse-Five, or The Children's Crusade*. The protagonist Billy Pilgrim is an inversion of the armed pilgrims of the medieval Crusades, absolutely refusing to fight and struggling to find meaning in the universe. Similarly, the 1987 movie *Lionheart* (dir. Franklin Schaffner) reinvented the Children's Crusade, retaining the children and the story of slavery, but moving the events to the time of the Third Crusade under King Richard the Lionheart of England. Eric Stoltz plays a knight in exile (young but clearly an adult) who protects a group of orphans from a wicked prince who wants to enslave them. The knight eventually leads the children in the Third Crusade.

Recent children's books on the Middle Ages also repeat, unsurprisingly, Runciman's and Gray's story. The illustrated book *What If You Met a Knight?* includes a dramatic illustration of a young boy wearing a Crusader's red cross on his clothing and holding up a wooden cross. The author describes Stephen of Cloyes and Nicolas of Cologne as real figures and invents a new detail about the crusade: "Disease killed most of the children before they got to the Mediterranean" (Adkins 2006, 29). A recent children's history of the Crusades makes different (and unfounded) claims that fifty thousand children participated in this movement and that most of them died by shipwreck or were sold into slavery to African Muslims (Cartlidge 2002, 29). Similarly, the 2005 book for children *Knights and Chivalry* describes just Stephen but also focuses on the children being sold into slavery (Elgin 2005, 22). These books are intended to shock their modern children readers and elicit sympathy in them for these medieval children who died or were enslaved for a movement, designed by adults, that we can scarcely understand today. These books also continue the theme started by George Zabriskie Gray, albeit more subtly, in condemning the Catholic Church for allowing or even encouraging the death of children.

Elements of the usual story of the Children's Crusade can be found in the medieval sources. These are primarily local histories or chronicles, usually written by monks about current events.

PRIMARY DOCUMENTS

MEDIEVAL CHRONICLERS ON THE CHILDREN'S CRUSADE (THIRTEENTH CENTURY)

The following eight passages all come from historical chronicles written by monks and clerics in the thirteenth century. Note how each author tells a different version of the "crusade" and does not agree on the age or purpose of the crusaders, their plans, or their outcome. The farther removed an author was from these pilgrims, whoever they were, the more elaborate their story. Matthew Paris, a monk at St. Alban's Abbey in England (1200–1259), was only a child during the "crusade" and nowhere near it, but he gives the most details of their wickedness and misguided purpose. Compare the Annals of Genoa, *written by the contemporary eyewitness and civic chronicler Ogerio Pane, who does say the group was led by a boy, but was otherwise made up of men, women, boys, and girls. He says little about their purpose or destination (Dickson 2008, 108–11).*

Matthew Paris, Historia Major

In the course of the same year (1213), in the following summer, there arose in France a certain heresy never before heard of. For a certain boy, instigated by the enemy of mankind [the devil], a boy indeed in years, but most vile in his way of life, went through the cities and towns in the realm of the French, as though sent by the Lord, singing in French measures: "Lord Jesus Christ, give us back the Holy Cross," with many other things added. And when he was seen and heard by other boys of the same age, an infinite number followed him; who, wholly infatuated by the craft of the devil, left their fathers and mothers, their nurses and all their friends, singing in like manner as their master sang. Nor, wonderful to say, could either bolts restrain them, or the persuasion of their parents recall them from following their aforesaid master to the Mediterranean Sea, which crossing, they went on their way singing in orderly procession, and in troops. For now no city could hold them for their multitude. But their master was placed in a chariot adorned with coverings, and was surrounded with guards shouting about him, and armed. But such was their number that they crushed one another through excess of crowding. For he regarded himself blessed who could carry away some threads or hairs from his garments. But at last, by the device of the old impostor Sathanas [Satan], they all perished either on land or in the sea.

Chronicle of Albert of Stade

Assembly of lunatic boys: About that time boys, without a master, without a leader, from all the towns and cities of all countries, ran with eager steps toward the parts beyond the sea, and when it was asked of them whither they were running, they answered: To Jerusalem, to get back the Holy Land. Very many of them were locked up by their parents, but in vain, for, breaking fastenings or walls, they ran out. The Pope, having heard these reports, sighing said: "these boys have laid it to us, that we sleep while they run for the recovery of the Holy Land." To this day it is not known what became of them. But many returned, of whom when the cause of the expedition was asked, they said that they knew not. Naked women also about the same time ran through the towns and cities saying nothing.

Vincent of Beauvais, Speculum Historiale ("Historical Mirror")

Also in the above-mentioned year little boys, to about 20 thousand as it is reckoned, were marked with the cross, and coming in bands to various seaports, in particular, Marseilles and Brindisi, returned famished and stripped. But it was that the Old Man of the Mountain, who had been used to bring up the Arsacidae [an ancient Persian dynasty, but here confused with the Muslims sect called the Assassins] from boyhood, had detained two European clerks in prison, and would never let them go, till he had received a faithful promise from them that they would bring him some boys of the realm of France. By them therefore the aforesaid boys were supposed to have been enticed by some false reports of visions, and by promises to them when they were marked with the cross.

Ogerio Pane, Annals of Genoa (Annales Ianuenses), 1212

But in the month of August, on the Sabbath day, eighth Kalends of September, a certain Teutonic boy, named Nicholas, entered the city of Genoa for purposes of pilgrimage, and with him a great multitude of pilgrims carrying crosses and staves, in the judgment of a working man more than 7000, men and women, boys and girls. And on the Lord's day following they departed from the city; but many men, women, boys, and girls of that number remained at Genoa.

Chronicle of Sicard of Cremona

In the same year, 1212, under the guidance of boys seemingly of twelve years, who said that they had seen a vision, and who took the sign of the cross, in the parts of Cologne, an innumerable multitude of poor people of either sex, and of boys, made pilgrimage through Germany, marked with the cross; and they came into Italy, saying with one heart and one voice, that they would cross the seas dry-shod, and recover the Holy Land of Jerusalem by the power of God. But at the end it all as it were came to nought. In the same year there was so mighty a famine, especially in Apulia and Sicily, that mothers even ate their children.

Chronicle of Lambert of Liège

A wonderful movement of children as well from the Roman as from the Teutonic kingdom, and chiefly of shepherds, both of the male and of the female sex. But they wept most profusely whom their fathers and mothers did not suffer to go. We believe that this was effected by magical arts, because their labour had no results, for at the last they were dispersed, and their journey was brought to nought. But their intention was that they would cross the sea, and, which their fathers and kings had not done, recover the sepulchre of Christ; but because this work was not of God it had no effect.

Chronicle of Godfrey of St. Pantaleon, Cologne

In that same year from all France and Germany boys of diverse ages and ranks, marked with the cross, affirmed that they were commanded by God to proceed to Jerusalem, for the succour of the Holy Land. After the example of whom a multitude of youths and women, marking themselves with the cross, set in order to go with them. To whom also some evil-disposed men joining themselves, nefariously and secretly took from them the things they had brought out, and those which they daily received from the faithful, and went away secretly: one of whom being taken at Cologne ended his life on the gallows. Many also of them perished in the woods and desert places of heat, hunger, and thirst: others, having crossed the Alps, as soon as they entered Italy were spoiled and driven back by the Lombards and returned with disgrace.

Chronicle of St. Medard, Soisson

1209: An innumerable multitude of children and boys from different parts, cities, castles, towns, camps, and farms of France, going out without the permission and assent of their parents, said that they had undertaken to cross the sea in quest of the Holy Cross: but they succeeded not at all.

For all, in different ways, were ruined, died, or returned. They say indeed and affirm for a certainty, that every ten years before that wonder happened, fishes, frogs, butterflies, birds, proceeded in like manner, according to their kind and their season. At that time so great a multitude of fishes was caught that all marvelled greatly. And certain old and decayed men affirm as a certain thing, that from different parts of France an innumerable multitude of dogs gathered together at the town of Champagne which is called Manshymer. But those dogs having divided into two parties, and fighting bravely and bitterly against one another, nearly all slew one another in their mutual slaughter, and very few returned.

Source: Sources are translated and printed in Hecker, J. F. C. 1859. *The Epidemics of the Middle Ages.* Translated by B. G. Babington. 3d ed. London, 354–59.

GEORGE ZABRISKIE GRAY CREATES THE MODERN MYTH OF THE CHILDREN'S CRUSADE (1870)

George Zabriskie Gray (1837–1889) was a U.S. Episcopalian minister who served in New York and New Jersey before becoming head of the Episcopal Theological School in Cambridge, Massachusetts. He is best remembered now as the author of the 1872 book The Children's Crusade: An Episode of the Thirteenth Century, *which has shaped most popular impressions since then of the so-called Children's Crusade. The following passage comes toward the end of the book, where he elaborates his new and unsupported theory that the Children's Crusade was created, or at least encouraged, by the wicked Pope Innocent III.*

We have now traced, from its commencement to its sad termination, a movement which is unique in the varied history of the world, and the wildest delusion of an age of delusions. Sixty thousand families, it is estimated, were by it saddened or bereaved, and, in its mad current, nearly a hundred thousand children were carried away to hardships or to death. Of this number at least a third never saw again the homes whence the songs and banners had lured them. They died by the banks of every stream, and in every valley along the routes of the three armies; some while seeking the distant sea, others while wearily seeking their homes. Others still, as we have seen, sailed from Pisa, Brindisi, and Marseilles to die in shipwreck and in slavery.

And most extraordinary is the briefness of the space of time within which it was all comprehended. Eight short months comprised it, from the call of Stephen among his flocks by Cloyes, to the scene of martyrdom in distant Bagdad. Within this short period, the great throb of child-life rose and ceased, its work complete. We can scarcely believe that all transpired so rapidly, but this rests upon distinct assertions of the authorities.

It was stated that the cruel delusion was the work of the emissaries of Rome, who, despairing of arousing Europe to a new interest in the Crusades, thought such a movement, for which they found the children ready, owing to the arts and appeals to which their elders were accustomed, would conduce to the result which they sought to effect. They succeeded probably better than they had intended, and awoke a spirit which they could not, if they would, suppress. For the deception the Pope had no words of rebuke, for its progress no syllables of prohibition, for the victims no tears of sympathy. He was not a man to be influenced by sentiments of a tender nature, and he saw in this an auxiliary to his great desire. We noticed the cruelty with which he decreed that the children must renew the attempt to rescue Palestine when older, and redeem the vows which they had taken. In keeping with this conduct was a remark which has been preserved, uttered by him when endeavoring to raise a new crusade: "These boys shame us, for, while they rush to the recovery of the Holy Land, we sleep." It resulted then, as we saw, that this fatal and delusive undertaking furnished an argument wherewith to appeal to the adults. And this man's assumed name was Innocent. His original name was Lothario, Count of Segno.

Source: Gray, George Zabriskie. 1872. *The Children's Crusade: An Episode of the Thirteenth Century.* New York: Hurd and Houghton, 220–22.

JAMES P. BOYD, *STORY OF THE CRUSADES* (1892)

James P. Boyd published his Story of the Crusades *in 1892, which was lavishly illustrated with one hundred full-page engravings which Gustave Doré had made for an earlier publication in 1877. His account of the Children's Crusade is a simplified version of George Zabriskie Gray's (see previous document) for a popular audience.*

Amid the encouragement afforded by this victory [at the Battle of Las Navas de Tolosa in Spain, 1212], the Holy See renewed its exhortations to the faithful to enlist for the defence of the Kingdom of Jesus Christ. But still Europe had no ear for the complaints of Jerusalem, and it is said the Pope wept tears of despair at the indifference of the nations of the

West. But while he could not entice Kings, barons or warriors to second a cause he so dearly espoused, the influences he set at work had an effect which, at this age, startles human credulity, and which would have been impossible at any period except one abounding in prodigies. Blinded by a false zeal, yet confident of their power over young and weak imaginations, ecclesiastics had gone through France and Germany exhorting the children to a Crusade in the name and for the sake of Jesus. So much had they imposed on childish emotions, that Europe was presented with the pitiable spectacle of fifty thousand infantile fanatics, braving parental authority, and gathering in villages and cities, bearing the emblems of the Church and singing the song of "Lord Jesus, restore to us our holy Cross." When asked where they were going, the reply was, "We are going to Jerusalem to deliver the Sepulchre of the Savior." While some denounced the folly and danger of such an infatuation, most of the faithful pretended to see in it an inspiration from Heaven, and a show, on the part of Jesus Christ, of his divine power for the purpose of confounding adult leaders and warriors, and reprimanding their pride and indifference, by entrusting his cause to the hands of simple minded and shrinking infancy. . . .

As such an outburst of fanaticism invited, so it was soon crowned by, disasters. The crowds of youthful and deceived enthusiasts were wantonly set upon by depraved men and women, who took advantage of their innocence to plunder them of the money and presents foolishly showered upon them by sympathetic lookers on and designing prompters. Yet, swarms of them drifted over the Alps in search of Italian ports, whence to embark on their insane enterprise. Other swarms from France directed their course to Marseilles. The sea voyage had been robbed of its terrors for them by the clerical leaders, who imposed on them the miraculous revelation that the year (1213) would witness the drying up of the sea and the opening of an easy road to Syria over the bed of the Mediterranean. On their way to the sea coast, many of these infatuated innocents lost their way amid forests and mountains and perished of hunger, exposure, fatigue and wild beasts. Many were cured by hardship of their delusions, and returned home to confess with shame their disobedience and to repent of their imprudence. Among those who embarked, some were shipwrecked, while many fell an early prey to the enemies they had set out to conquer. If any of them ever reached the Holy Land, sight of them must have carried terror to the Christians of the East, rather than to Mussulmen [Muslims]. While the latter would gladly welcome them as inoffensive captives, prepared ready to hand by the inhuman zeal of their religious teachers, the former would stand aghast at the laws, the institutions and the men which encouraged or permitted such a condemnation of helpless innocence to exile and death. It was as if the Church had maliciously gathered and ruthlessly tossed fifty thousand infants from a cliff into the boiling sea, in order to calm its angry waves. Yet, such was the spirit of Europe, at the time, that no authority interposed to check the madness which exposed its innocence to certain destruction. When it was announced to the Pope that the flower of the youth, and the consolation of the age, of France and Germany, had been swept away by cruel and uncompensated death, there came the shockingly indifferent reply, not to say, the cold blooded exposure of design;—"These children reproach us with having fallen asleep, whilst they were flying to the assistance of the Holy Land." Precisely what assistance they could have rendered the cause of Christianity in a land where even the strongest of mailed Knights and the bravest of warriors could not make headway against powerful enemies, must be left to the secret working of ecclesiastical imagination.

Source: Boyd, James P. 1892. *Story of the Crusades.* Philadelphia: P. W. Ziegler and Co., 315, 317.

GUSTAVE DORÉ, "THE CHILDREN'S CRUSADE" (1877)

Gustave Doré (1832–1883) was one of the greatest engravers and book illustrators of the nineteenth century, and his images remain popular to this day. In 1877 he made a lavish series of one hundred illustrations for Jean-François Michaud's Histoire des Croisades, *including this dramatic and idealized vision of the Children's Crusade. These engravings were used in multiple French and English histories of the Crusade, including James P. Boyd's* Story of the Crusades *(see previous document).*

Source: "The Crusade of Children," illustrated by Gustave Doré. In *Story of the Crusades*, by James P. Boyd. Philadelphia: P. W. Ziegler and Co., 1892, plate LXII, 316.

What Really Happened

Unlike other fictions about the Middle Ages, which are exaggerations or distortions of actual events or aspects of medieval culture, the Children's Crusade as described earlier never happened. There is no convincing evidence from 1212 or at any other time in the Middle Ages of a large group of children (which at that time usually meant people under about fourteen years old, the age of puberty) marching to the Holy Land to participate in the crusading movement to recapture Jerusalem and fight against non-Christians. Nor is there any evidence of large numbers of children dying in this attempt, whether on land or by sea, or being captured and sold into slavery. The Crusade historian Thomas Madden sums up this myth neatly: "The Children's Crusade was not an army of children, and it was not a crusade. Indeed, it was not even one thing, but a blanket term used to describe a variety of popular uprisings and processions" (Madden 2013, 129). If the key elements of the Children's Crusade—namely, that it was a genuine crusade composed of actual children—are not true, how do we account for the numerous medieval sources that appear to tell the story of children crusaders coming to a horrible end?

The Children's Crusade is a good example of an event that both medieval and modern people want to have happened, albeit for different reasons. For medieval audiences, the story of thousands of children taking up the cross was an object of awe, a testament to God's power and to the European certainty that Christians would once again hold Jerusalem and hold it forever. The idea of a crusade of children also benefited the Church more than an actual Children's Crusade, because it could be used to shame the growing number of wealthy warrior nobles who could go on crusade but decided not to. For modern audiences, on the other hand, the Children's Crusade serves as an emblem of much that was supposedly wrong about the Catholic Middle Ages: brutal, misguided, unmerciful. Modern authors can also blame both the medieval Catholic clergy and medieval Muslims for this lack of mercy (two groups that have frequently come under attack since the Enlightenment): the Church for sending the children in the first place and the Muslims for supposedly enslaving these defenseless children.

Part of the persistence of the fiction of a Children's Crusade is the fact that there was no one definition of a "crusade," then or now. A crusade is now commonly understood primarily as large-scale warfare between Christians and Muslims in the medieval Near East, and the crusaders as the professional warriors engaged in those battles. That definition is certainly true of some medieval crusaders, but others were unarmed pilgrims, some were servants and wives of the warriors, some went to places far distant from Jerusalem (like Islamic Spain or pagan Lithuania), and some fought enemies of the Church who were not Muslims, including Christians in several cases like the Albigensian Crusade and the Fourth Crusade. So, depending on how you spin the meaning of a crusade, there is some truth to the existence of children's crusades in the thirteenth century.

To understand the extent of that truth, we need to explore what actually happened in the year 1212. By 1212, Christian warriors of Europe had been fighting battles that we now call "crusades" for over a century. In that period, crusading against Muslims and other stated enemies of the Church had become an integral part of the fabric of European culture. Historians count four major crusades before 1212: the First Crusade of 1095–1099, the Second of 1147–1149, the Third of 1189–1192, and the Fourth in 1202–1204. This neat division, however, is a modern construction, and Europeans throughout the twelfth century took crusading vows to go to Jerusalem or fight Muslims wherever they could find them.

Crusading saw dramatic changes during the pontificate of Pope Innocent III (r. 1198–1216), who was pressed to turn the tide of crusading after the devastating loss of Christian Jerusalem in 1187 to the Muslim sultan Saladin and the failure of the Third Crusade to recover it. Innocent called multiple crusades against different enemies and locations: the Fourth Crusade (1202–1204), which ended up killing Byzantine Greek Christians and taking the city of Constantinople, rather than fighting Muslims and reclaiming the city of Jerusalem; the Albigensian Crusade (1209–1229), in southern France, aimed at rooting out Christian heretics known as Cathars; smaller "crusades" against political enemies in Europe; and he arranged for the Fifth Crusade in Egypt (1217–1221) but did not live to see it.

In the midst of this dramatic redefinition of crusading, with papally-approved crusaders fighting through Europe, North Africa, and the Near East, it is highly likely that individuals and groups not trained for crusading warfare were motivated to take the pilgrimage to Jerusalem. This is the context for what seems to have been an actual event in the year 1212. Far too many chronicles record an unexpected expedition or pilgrimage in that year for it to be a complete fiction. But the story we are concerned with here is not simply that there was a popular pilgrimage or criticism of crusading at that time, but that the pilgrims and their leaders were all young children and that they died or suffered horribly during their "crusade." If we read the thirteenth-century evidence more carefully than George Zabriskie Gray or Steven Runciman, we are led to doubt both the age of the pilgrims and the outcome of their journeys.

One of the earliest accounts of this "crusade" comes from the anonymous "Marbach Annalist," a monk and chronicler at the Augustinian Abbey of Marbach, who around the year 1212 recorded a large and disorganized pilgrimage movement in Germany and France (see Primary Documents). The group was made of adults and children, men and women, as well as the very old. There is no indication of children as leaders or of children in any significant numbers. The clergy and the papacy, rather than encouraging this movement (as Gray and others argue), were disturbed by it and ordered the pilgrims back home. The church leaders revoked the crusading vows of the children and the elderly, who were not fit to go to Jerusalem or on any other crusade. There is no tale of children enslaved or dying in shipwrecks, although some of the young women pilgrims were raped on the way home. This tale is tragic, if true, but it in no way supports the usual stories of the Children's Crusade.

Another chronicler, Jacobus de Varagine, wrote much later in the thirteenth century about the "crusade," but his work is considered dependable for the city of Genoa, where the events he describes took place and where he served as archbishop. He actually names the pilgrim leader Nicholas from Germany, but does not describe him as a child. Jacobus notes that "even children" were among the pilgrims, but this does not indicate they were the leaders or in the majority. Like the Marbach Annalist, Jacobus heaps scorn on the whole affair and says that it came to nothing. Even the Primary Documents given as examples of the "fiction" show the wide diversity among the medieval chroniclers. Very few give a specific age, so we cannot make assumptions about how old the "boys" (*pueri*) actually were. In the medieval period a *puer* could be a teenager or an unmarried adult child, and the same goes for the feminine *puella*. Historians of medieval childhood and of the Children's Crusade in particular continue to argue whether *puer* can indicate a specific age, a stage in life, or even a stage in social integration. But Gary Dickson, in his comprehensive study of the Children's Crusade, its history and myths, shows that the *pueri* have gotten gradually younger in the sources over the last eight centuries (Dickson 2008, 33–35), transforming from youthful shepherds who should not be going on crusade (probably closer to the reality of this "crusade") to mere infants ripped from their mothers' arms to be used as bait by a corrupt Church. It seems likely there were some genuine children in this movement, which struck contemporary observers as worth remarking on, but the idea of entire crusade organized and led by children is a later invention.

PRIMARY DOCUMENTS

MARBACH ANNALIST (AFTER 1212)

The earliest record of the so-called Children's Crusade comes from the anonymous "Marbach Annalist," a monk and chronicler at the Augustinian Abbey of Marbach in Germany, who around the year 1212 recorded this account of passing pilgrims.

At that time there was a foolish expedition, young and silly persons taking the mark of the cross without any discretion, rather for curiosity than for their salvation. Persons of both sexes, boys and girls, not under age only, but also grown up, married women with virgins, set out, going with empty purses not only through all Germany, but also through parts of Gaul and Burgundy; neither could they by any means be restrained by their parents and friends, but used all efforts to join that expedition, so that everywhere in the towns and in the country they left their tools and whatever they had in hand at the time, and joined the bands as they passed by. And as for such novelties we are often a folk of easy faith, many thought that this came to pass not through lightness of mind, but by a divine inspiration and a kind of piety. For which reason they also succoured them in their expenses, furnishing food and other necessary things.

But when the clergy and some others of sounder mind spoke against it, and judged that expedition vain and useless, the laics [lay people] vehemently cavilled, saying, that the clerks were unbelievers, and that they opposed this thing for envy and covetousness, rather than for truth and righteousness. But forasmuch as no affair that is commenced without the balancing of reason and without vigour of counsel, attains to a good conclusion; after this foolish multitude arrived at the parts of Italy, they were separated and scattered through the cities and towns, and many were kept by the inhabitants of the land as servants and handmaids. Others are said to have reached the sea, who were taken prisoners by the sailors and mariners, and carried to other distant parts of the earth. But the rest coming to Rome, when they saw that they could go no further, not being sustained with any authority, at last became aware that their labour was frivolous and empty: and yet they were by no means absolved from the vow of the cross, except the boys under the age of discretion, and those who were oppressed with old age. therefore, thus deceived and perplexed, they began to return; and they who formerly used to pass through the countries in parties and troops, and never without the song of encouragement, now returning, singly and in silence, barefooted and famished, were a scoffing to all men: also many virgins were ravished, and lost the flower of their chastity.

Source: Marbach Annalist. 1212. Printed in J. F. C. Hecker. In *The Epidemics of the Middle Ages*, translated by B. G. Babington. 3d ed. London, 1859, 357.

JACOBUS DA VARAGINE, *CHRONICLE OF THE CITY OF GENOA* (ca. 1290)

Later in the thirteenth century, perhaps around 1290, the famed religious author and archbishop of Genoa Jacobus da Varagine (1230–1298) wrote a chronicle of his city, the Chronicon Januense. *He records the arrival of the pilgrim Nicholas in Genoa, but he is not described as a child, and the pilgrims seem mostly to be adults, with only some young children with them. Like the Marbach Annalist (see previous document), Jacobus scathingly condemns this misguided pilgrimage and says they never actually went on Crusade.*

In the year of the Lord 1222 [perhaps an error for 1212?] in the month of August, there came to Genoa a certain Theuton [German] named Nicholas, in the habit of a pilgrim, and there followed him a great multitude of pilgrims both great and small, even young children, and all had pilgrims' coats marked with crosses, and pilgrims' staves, and pilgrims' wallets, saying that the sea would be dried up at Genoa, and thus they must go to Jerusalem.

But many of them were sons of nobles, whom their fathers had provided with harlots. But the Genoese agreed that they must withdraw from the city, partly because they thought they were prompted by levity more than by necessity; partly because they feared lest they should bring dearth into the city; partly because they apprehended danger to the city from so great a multitude; chiefly because the Emperor was then in rebellion with the Church, and the Genoese clave to the Church against the Emperor. After a short time all that thing came to nothing, because it was founded upon nothing.

Source: *Chronicle of the City of Genoa.* Printed in J. F. C. Hecker. In *The Epidemics of the Middle Ages*, translated by B. G. Babington, 3d ed. London, 1859, 357–58.

Further Reading

Adkins, Jan. 2006. *What If You Met a Knight?* New Milford, CT: Roaring Brook Press.

Boyd, James P. 1892. *Story of the Crusades.* Philadelphia: P.W. Ziegler and Co.

Cartlidge, Cherese. 2002. *The Crusades: Failed Holy Wars.* San Diego, CA: Lucent Books.

Dickson, Gary. 2008. *The Children's Crusade: Medieval History, Modern Mythistory.* New York: Palgrave Macmillan.

Elgin, Kathy. 2005. *Knights and Chivalry*. Mankato, MN: Smart Apple Media.

Gray, George Zabriskie. 1872. *The Children's Crusade: An Episode of the Thirteenth Century*. New York: Hurd and Houghton.

Gray, George Zabriskie. 1972. *The Children's Crusade*. Foreword by Thomas Powers. New York: William Morrow and Co.

Hecker, J. F. C. 1859. *The Epidemics of the Middle Ages*. Translated by B. G. Babington. 3d ed. London: Trübner and Co.

Madden, Thomas F. 2013. *The Concise History of the Crusades*. 3d ed. Lanham, MD: Rowman and Littlefield.

Runciman, Steven. 1951–1954. *A History of the Crusades*. 3 vols. Cambridge: Cambridge University Press.

8

There Was a Female Pope Named Joan

What People Think Happened

The Roman Catholic Church was arguably the most powerful institution of the Middle Ages in terms of its influence on the lives and beliefs of all Europeans from peasants to the Holy Roman Emperor, as well as in terms of its financial and landholdings. Like any powerful institution, the Church came (and still comes) under scrutiny and serious criticism. Criticisms began during the Middle Ages, well before the Protestant reformers of the sixteenth century, like Martin Luther and John Calvin, directly attacked central aspects of Catholicism like the papacy. Medieval bishops and monks did not blindly follow the popes, but often criticized them for failing to uphold the dignity and holiness of their office, and these critics of the papacy held up certain stories as key examples of the problems of the papacy.

One of the most pervasive stories about the medieval papacy, which persists to this day, tells of a medieval pope who was actually a woman in disguise. The story about this female pope, or "popess" as she is also called (DiMarco 2008), has been discussed seriously in books, pamphlets, and documentaries for the last 750 years, but is also treated as fiction in numerous novels, plays, and even operettas. These works tell of a woman who rose through the ranks of the Catholic clergy to become Pope "John," sometimes through her own ambition, sometimes inspired by the devil. She is usually named Joan (*Joanna* in Latin) but the Italian author Giovanni Boccaccio called her Giliberta, and the Bohemian theologian and heretic John Huss named her Agnes (Boureau 2001, 138, 210; see Primary Documents). Medieval chroniclers variously claim that she came to the papacy in the year 855, or 896, or 1099, and reigned only briefly, or for up to a highly specific period of two years, seven months, and four days (according to Martin of Poland; see Primary Documents).

There are many variations on the story of the popess, but the version that some people still believe runs as follows: Joan (*Joanna*) was an English peasant girl with a thirst for knowledge, but she was not allowed to go to school. Her parents, however, supported her desire to learn and disguised her as a boy named John (*Johannes Anglicus*, "John the Englishman") and she was then able to go to school and excel at her studies in both religious and secular topics. Joan kept her true identity hidden for years from everyone except her secret lover; in some versions of the story, she is German and her lover is actually the Englishman, and thus her title *Anglicus* comes from him. Thanks to her learning, she-disguised-as-he became a renowned teacher and then a priest. She went to Rome, as many ambitious clerics did in the Middles Ages, and rapidly ascended the Roman ecclesiastical hierarchy. She was widely admired in Rome for her holiness and learning and easily ascended to the papacy when there was a vacancy. Her identity was revealed in a shocking manner when she became pregnant by her lover and prematurely gave birth in public when she was trying to get on a horse. The people and clergy of Rome were horrified by this deception and sacrilege. They tied her legs to a horse, dragged her through the streets, and beat her until she died. Presumably her newborn baby died as well, but most medieval documents do not mention the fate of her child.

According to supporters of this story, there were two long-term consequences of Joan's brief and shocking papacy. First, when later popes proceeded through the city of Rome, they turned off on a side street at the point where Joan gave birth, as a way of publicly condemning her dishonesty and stressing the infamy she brought to the papacy and the city of Rome (this outcome is emphasized by Giovanni Boccaccio). Second, every succeeding pope-elect, before he can be confirmed officially as pope, must lift up his robes and sit on a special stone chair with a hole in the seat. One of the Roman clergy (a younger cardinal, according to the medieval chronicler Adam of Usk) must then reach under the chair and check that the pope-elect has a penis and testicles and is therefore a genuine man eligible to be pope (Boureau 2001, 12–14).

How the Story Became Popular

The tale of Pope Joan has vanished from every recent history book, but many people still believe it, in most of its particulars, and their opinions are mostly to be found on Facebook and the comments sections of other sites on the internet. But these believers are in good company, for some older historical books vigorously defended the reality of Pope Joan. The Greek author Emmanuel Rhoides (1840–1904, also spelled Rhoïdis) wrote a novel about Pope Joan in 1866, which is still widely available in multiple translations into French and English, including one by the famous twentieth-century British author Lawrence Durrell. Rhoides's novel is presented as a fiction but he provides a scholarly introduction and notes, implying that the work is based on real events.

One of those translators was Charles Hastings Colette, who in 1886 translated only Rhoides's historical introduction and wrote his own lengthy preface to the work in which he condemns those who deny the historicity of Joan: "The reality of the existence and reign, as head of the Roman Church, of a female Pope, has been chronicled and maintained by a phalanx of Papal champions, cardinals, bishops, priests, historians, and even by officials in the Papal Court, and accepted even in histories dedicated to Popes" (Rhoides 1886, 7–8). Colette then proceeds to list dozens of medieval sources mentioning Joan, which he assumed to be truthful representatives of the medieval past. He makes the forceful argument that the story must be true, because most of the sources are by medieval Catholics, and not later Protestant Reformers: Why would Catholics invent and repeat such a potentially embarrassing story?

Rhoides and Colette introduce an important question about historical sources in general: How do we gauge their truth value? In the case of Pope Joan, this question especially concerns medieval chroniclers. Could they make up stories about the papacy or be critical of the Catholic Church? In this section, and then again under "What Really Happened," we will examine some of the medieval sources for Pope Joan, their historical context, and potential biases, to evaluate their accuracy.

Most of the elements of Joan's story can be found together in sources from the later Middle Ages, such as in the writings of John Huss in 1413 (see Primary Documents). The earliest verifiable reference to the story, however, comes from about 1250, a date nowhere near any of the years Joan is supposed to have lived and died (855, 896, 1099). Jean de Mailly was a Dominican friar in Metz who prepared, around 1250, a calendar of historical events and people known as the *Chronica universalis Mettensis*

("Universal Chronicle of Metz"; see the Primary Documents). He recorded not only all the popes known to him, but also religiously significant events like the First Crusade and the capture of Jerusalem in 1099. Under the year 1099 Jean made a note that someone should investigate (*Require* in the Latin) the truth of a female pope (he does not give her name), who gave birth and then was stoned to death.

Jean also adds a curious element not found in many later accounts of the popess: her tomb is marked with the Latin inscription *Petre, Pater Patrum, Papisse Prodito Partum* ("Peter, Father of the Fathers, Make Known the Childbirth of a Popess"). Peter is Saint Peter, the first pope according to Catholic tradition and the founder of the Church, according to Jesus Christ's statement in the Gospel of Matthew (16:18), "Thou art Peter, and upon this rock I will build my church." All later popes, at least since the fifth century, were said to be the "heirs of Saint Peter" and to represent and support Christ's church just as Peter did. Therefore this legendary inscription is addressed to all popes, each of whom represents Saint Peter and is obligated to make known (and presumably condemn) this scandalous episode in which a woman was made pope and then gave birth.

Within a few decades of Jean's *Chronicle* there would appear many more adaptations of Joan's story, most of which move her back in time to the less-well-documented ninth century. Not only did they move her back in time, but they also turned her story into powerful *exempla*, or brief moralizing narratives, designed for inclusion in sermons and religious books. Most of these new authors, like Jean de Mailly himself, were Dominican friars, who were frequently employed as professional preachers and composers of sermons. Friars (from the Latin *fratres* for "brothers") were like monks in that they took lifelong vows of chastity, poverty, and obedience, but they were not confined to secluded monasteries. Rather, they were expected to beg, preach, and teach in urban areas and to move widely around Europe and beyond to strengthen and spread the faith. The Dominican friars, officially known as the "Order of Preachers" (*Ordo Fratrum Praedicatorum*), and the Franciscan friars ("Order of Friars Minor," *Ordo Fratrum Minorum*) were a new kind of religious figure in the thirteenth century. They are named after their founders Saint Dominic, a Spanish priest, and Saint Francis of Assisi. They were established, respectively, in 1216 and 1209, with full support of the papacy.

The Dominican preachers are central to understanding the spread of the Pope Joan story, for they were the ones to elaborate and formalize her story in sermons and books during the later thirteenth century. Two such

Dominicans were Stephen of Bourbon (ca. 1180–1261) and Martin of Poland (d. 1278). Stephen wrote a lengthy and rigorously organized treatise to help his fellow Dominican preachers, called the *Tractatus de diversis materiis praedicabilibus* ("Treatise on Diverse Materials Suitable for Sermons"). Stephen tells much the same story as Jean de Mailly, placing it at the same time, but he provides it as a preachable example of criminal deception rather than just a curious episode in papal history (Boureau 2001, 118–19). He does not give the popess a name, and he emphasizes that she was audacious, insane, and aided by the devil in her rise through the male clergy. Stephen explains that her audacity in stepping outside the strict bounds of medieval womanhood and daring to enter the highest ranks of the Catholic clergy led inevitably to her violent death.

Martin of Poland wrote his *Chronicle of Popes and Emperors* around 1268 (see Primary Documents), a work much more like Jean de Mailly's chronicle than like Stephen's moralized sermon. According to medieval religious historian Alain Boureau, it was Martin's version that fixed the key elements of Joan's story for the rest of the Middle Ages (Boureau 2001, 124). Martin also may be the first to name her as John or Joan and the first to place her in the year 855 after Pope Leo IV. He creates a believable narrative including her childhood, her lover, her rise to fame, and the reasons for her papal election. He also uses her story to provide a historical explanation for why the popes of his time take a certain processional route through Rome. He likewise ventures to explain why she does not appear in the usual catalogue of the popes: she was never actually pope because her female sex invalidated her election.

The inscription described by Jean de Mailly orders the pope not to cover up this story, but to "make it known," presumably to prevent it from happening again. Nonetheless, the Catholic Church has firmly denied the truth of this story since the sixteenth century, as have most historians of the Middle Ages and of Catholicism. Some people, however, who are inclined to believe conspiracy theories, claim that the Church is actually covering up a genuine, shameful event. They are supported by movies and stage plays that, although presented as fiction, nonetheless suggest that Pope Joan herself was real. These include a 1982 play *Top Girls* by Caryll Churchill, in which Joan is one of five of the titular "girls," and the 1972 movie *Pope Joan*, where Liv Ullmann plays a modern evangelical preacher who believes she is Pope Joan reincarnated (New 1993, 110). The movie was reissued in 2009 with the provocative title *She . . . Who Would Be Pope*.

The Catholic conspiracy to hide Pope Joan is more explicit in the 2009 German film *Die Päpstin* ("The Popess"; *Pope Joan* in English-language theaters). In its English-language trailer, the filmmakers claim to be telling an "astonishing true story" which had been erased from history, even though the film is based on the 1996 novel, *Pope Joan*, by Donna Woolfolk Cross, which was distributed as fiction. One need only look at the public comments on YouTube, where the trailer is still posted (as of October 2018), to see evidence of the many people who take the novel and film as truth. The commenters argue that corrupt popes and priests have covered up the real event, while others point out that there are numerous written accounts and images of this female pope, and therefore she must have existed ("Pope Joan—movie trailer [2009]"). In either case, they believe in the reality of Pope Joan. Stories of Pope Joan lead us to investigate the state of the historical record and the supposed deceptions of the Catholic Church.

Artistic representations of the popess provide some of the favorite evidence for those who would believe in her existence. Most of these date from the fifteenth and sixteenth centuries. In the early fifteenth century, a series of historical popes were represented as busts in the cathedral of Siena, and among them was included Pope "Agnes." There are many surviving early printed images of the female pope. For example, she is portrayed clearly as a female pope (Johannes der Sibend, "John the Seventh") holding her child (see Primary Documents). But some images of the popess come from German Protestant contexts, where the female pope is shown as a force for evil, and associated with the devil or the Antichrist. In books written by the reformers Martin Luther in 1522 and Martin Schrott in 1550, the popess is shown riding the horrific beast with seven heads, described in the apocalyptic Book of Revelation in the Christian New Testament (Boureau 2001, 106 and 220). These women could be taken at first simply as personifications of the Catholic Church as the "Whore of Babylon," a technique common in early modern Protestant art, but in each illustration she is given one of the traditional names for the popess: John and Agnes, respectively.

The popess also appears in tarot decks, which were invented or introduced to Europe around 1375. Most modern tarot decks (originally just used for card games but adapted for fortune-telling in the eighteenth century) are based on those painted for the dukes of Milan in the middle of the fifteenth century. These so-called Visconti-Sforza decks, which include the popess, were popular and copied throughout Renaissance Italy; fifteen different partial decks still survive today. The popess is not given a name in the decks, but she is presented as an obviously female pope, wearing the papal tiara and holding a long cross and a book (Boureau 2001, frontispiece and 167–71). Tarot decks also include a series of unique cards showing people or events, called triumphs, tarots, or arcanes, several of which feature medieval people of great authority: the emperor, empress, pope, and popess. The female pope, whether or not she existed, provides a pair for the pope, just as the empress does for the emperor.

The story of Pope Joan has remained popular with different groups and for different reasons for nearly eight centuries. We can examine only a few examples of her legend here, but entire books have been dedicated to the constant reinvention of Joan (Boureau 2001; Pardoe and Pardoe 1988): from medieval clerics who wanted to improve the papacy through criticism of its failures, to Protestants who used it to show the inherent corruption of Catholicism and of the papacy in particular, to modern feminists who see her as an early example of a woman breaking the rules of her society to rise in power, and to other modern people who simply appreciate a titillating rumor about the distant past. These last two inspirations can be found, for example, in the children's book *Rejected Princesses: Tales of History's Boldest Heroines, Hellions, and Heretics*, which presents Joan as a genuine figure in ninth-century Rome and an inspiration for girls today (Porath 2016, 117–20). Pope Joan made headlines again in May 2018 after the musician Rihanna wore a white mitre (the official papal headgear) to the annual Costume Institute Ball at the New York Metropolitan Museum of Art, inspiring popular audiences either to react angrily or to think seriously about the mythical history of a female pope (Hudson 2018).

PRIMARY DOCUMENTS

JEAN DE MAILLY, *UNIVERSAL CHRONICLE OF METZ* (ca. 1255)

This brief passage, our earliest evidence of the Pope Joan story, comes from Jean de Mailly's Universal Chronicle of Metz, *written around 1255. Under the year 1099, after a description of the conquest of Jerusalem in the First Crusade, Jean adds the following:*

Verify the truth of a certain pope, or rather a popess, because she was a woman. She pretended that she was a man, became a notary of the papal curia because of the trustworthiness of her intelligence, then a cardinal, and at last the pope. One day, when she was getting on a horse, she gave birth to a child, and immediately the Roman authorities bound her feet together. She was dragged by the tale of a horse and stoned by the people over the distance of half a league. She was buried right where she died and at that place was inscribed: *Petre, Pater Patrum, Papisse Prodito Partum* ["Peter, Father of the Fathers, Make Known the Birth of a Popess"]. Under this pope was established the Fast of Four Times, which is also called the Fast of the Pope.

Source: New translation of Jean de Mailly. 1879. *Chronica universalis Mettensis.* In *Monumenta Germaniae Historica Scriptorum* 24. Hanover, 514.

MARTIN OF POLAND: A FEMALE POPE NAMED JOHN (ca. 1260)

Martin of Opava, also known as Martin of Poland (d. 1278), was a Dominican friar and the author of the Chronicon pontificum et imperatorum, "Chronicle of Popes and Emperors." *He places the female pope Johannes Anglicus directly after Pope Leo IV in the year 855. The second paragraph here comes from one manuscript of the* Chronicon, *which tells a different version of the story, similar in its essentials but adding more positive details to the popess's story.*

After Leo, Johannes Anglicus, a native of Mainz, sat as pope for two years, seven months, four days, and died in Rome. After this the papacy was empty for one month. He, as some claim, was a woman. When she was a girl she had been taken to Athens in men's clothing by her sweetheart, and there she progressed so far in diverse sciences that no one could be found to equal her. She excelled so much that afterwards, she taught the trivium [grammatical arts] in Rome, where she had great masters among her disciples and students. And when a high opinion of her life and knowledge developed in that city, she was elected as pope by the consent of all. But during her papacy she became pregnant by her boyfriend. She was ignorant, however, of the time of birth, and while she was travelling from Saint Peter's toward the Lateran Palace, she gave birth in a narrow way between the Colisseum and the church of Saint Clement. Afterwards she died and, as it is said, was buried on that very spot. Because the lord pope always turns away from that street, many people believe that he does this on account of his hatred of that event. She is not placed in the catalogue of holy popes on account of the nonconformity of the female sex in this matter.

[*From another manuscript:*] But in the study of the quadrivium [mathematical sciences] she demonstrated her excellence not only in her lectures but also through the performance of many marvellous things, for it was through her skill and counsel that there occurred many marvels in Rome. . . . She is remembered to this day, sculpted in stone, and that neighborhood is called Vicus Papisse [Popess-Town]. But she moved to a convent, took on the habit of religion [i.e., became a nun], and lived for such a long time in a state of penitence, that her son became the Bishop of Ostia. When she saw in her final days that she was about to die, she ordered that she be buried in that place where she had given birth, but because her son could not accept that, he brought her body to Ostia and buried it honorably in a major church. And by her good deeds God works many miracles to this very day.

Source: Martinus Polonus. 1879. *Chronicon pontificum et imperatorum.* In *Monumenta Germaniae Historica Scriptorum* 24. New translation. Hanover, 428–29.

JOHN HUSS, *ON THE CHURCH* (1413)

John Huss (or Jan Hus, 1369–1415) was a priest and professor of theology from Prague in Bohemia (now the Czech Republic). He was a vigorous critic of some aspects of the Catholic Church, especially of the abuses and moral failings of the popes and other clergy. He wrote numerous books on theology and the Church, but his most famous is called simply On the Church (De Ecclesia) *from 1413. The following passage comes from this work, in which he describes cases of women and illiterate men becoming popes, for the purpose of discrediting the institution as a whole. Huss was condemned as a heretic by a Catholic church court at the Council of Constance in 1415 and then burned at the stake.*

I assume that the pope stands for that spiritual bishop who, in the highest way and in the most similar way, occupies the place of Christ, just as Peter did after the ascension. But if any person whatsoever is to be called pope—whom the Western church accepts as Roman bishop—appointed to decide as the final court ecclesiastical cases and to teach the faithful whatever he wishes, then there is an abuse of the term, because according to this view, it would be necessary in cases to concede that the most unlettered layman or a female, or a heretic and antichrist, may be pope. This is plain, for Constantine II, an unlettered layman, was suddenly ordained a priest and through ambition made pope and then was deposed and all the things which he ordained were declared invalid, about A.D. 707 [Constantine II was actually pope 767–768]. And the same is plain from the case of Gregory [possibly Pope Gregory VI, 1045–1046], who was unlettered and consecrated another in addition to himself. And as the people were displeased with the act, a third pope was superinduced. Then these quarreling among themselves, the emperor came to Rome and elected another as sole pope.

As for a female, it is plain in the case of Agnes, who was called John Anglicus, and of her Castrensis, 5:3 [John's name for the chronicler Ranulph of Higden, from Chester, England], writes: "A certain woman sat in the papal chair two years and five months, following Leo. She is said to have been a girl, called Agnes, of the nation of Mainz, was led about by her paramour in a man's dress in Athens and named John Anglicus. She made such progress in different studies that, coming to Rome, she read the trivium to an audience of great teachers. Finally, elected pope, she was with child by her paramour, and, as she was proceeding from St. Peter's to the Lateran, she had the pains of labor in a narrow street between the Colosseum and St. Clement's and gave birth to a child. Shortly afterward she died there and was buried. For this reason it is said that all the popes avoid this street. Therefore, she is not put down in the catalogue of popes."

Source: John Huss. 1915. *The Church*, edited and translated by David S. Schaff. New York: Scribner's, 126–27.

PLATINA, *LIVES OF THE POPES* (1479)

Bartolomeo (or Baptista) Platina (1421–1481) was the librarian to the Vatican under Pope Sixtus IV and wrote his Lives of the Popes *for him in 1479. Like many later medieval chroniclers, he includes the female pope and places her in 855 after Leo IV. He draws on the work of Martin of Poland, and even names him, but he elaborates further on her supposed wickedness and the impact of her story on the selection of popes. Even though Platina does seem to believe in the existence of the female pope, he expresses serious doubt that she is the reason behind the so-called* Sedes Stercoraria *(usually translated as "Posterior Chair" but it really means the "Toilet Chair"), an idea which he attributes to vulgar and obscure authors.*

John, of English extraction, was born at Mentz [i.e. Mainz] and is said to have arrived at Popedom by evil arts; for disguising herself like a man, whereas she was a woman, she went when young with her paramour, a learned man, to Athens, and made such progress in learning under the professors there that, coming to Rome, she met with few that could equal, much less go beyond her, even in the knowledge of the Scriptures; and by her learned and ingenious readings and disputations, she acquired so great respect and authority that upon the death of Leo (as Martin says), by common consent she was chosen Pope in his room. As she was going to the Lateran Church, between the Colossean Theatre (so called from Nero's Colossus) and St. Clement's, her travail came upon her, and she died upon the place, having sat two years, one month, and four days, and was buried there without any pomp. Some say, the Pope for shame of the thing does purposely decline going through that street when he goes to the Lateran, and that to avoid the like Error, when any Pope is first placed in the Porphyry Chair, which has a hole made for the purpose, his Genitals are handled by the youngest Deacon. As for the first I deny it not; but for the second, I take the reason of it to be, that he who is placed in so great authority may be minded that he is not a God but a man, and obnoxious to necessities of Nature, as of easing his body, whence that Seat hath the name of *Sedes stercoraria*. This story is vulgarly told, but by very uncertain and obscure authors, and therefore I have related it barely and in short, lest I should seem obstinate and pertinacious if I had admitted what is so generally talked; I had better mistake with the rest of the world; though it be certain, that what I have related may be thought not altogether incredible.

Source: Baptista Platina. 1685. *The Lives of the Popes from the Time of Our Saviour Jesus Christ to the Reign of Sixtus IV*, translated Paul Rycaut. London, 165.

IMAGE OF POPE JOAN FROM THE
NUREMBERG CHRONICLE (1493)

This early printed image shows the popess holding her child and names her as "John VII." It comes from the Nuremberg Chronicle *of 1493, written by Hartmann Schedel in Latin and then translated by Georg Alt into German. It is one of the most famous books from the early decades of printing. The* Chronicle *is an illustrated paraphrase of the Bible, which combines biblical stories with secular history and contemporary events. Many copies were beautifully colored by hand in imitation of contemporary illuminated manuscripts.*

Source: "Johannes der Sibend," from the *Nuremberg Chronicle*, 1493, Brussel and Brussel, page CLXX.

What Really Happened

The story of the "popess" has taken on many layers over the centuries, to include not only Joan herself, but also myths about testing the pope's genitalia, the movement of his parade route, and a conspiracy on the part of an embarrassed Catholic Church to cover up Joan's memory. Historians now agree that Pope Joan and these other elements related to her story are entirely fictional. So how did her story come about and manage to persist for so long? If there were indeed a cover-up, then it clearly failed, for there are a large number of medieval works that record the story of the popess. The French historian Alain Boureau has identified nearly one hundred different sources from the period 1250 to 1500 and many more from the centuries after that, but not a single dependable reference to her before 1250 (Boureau 2001, 315–32). She is not mentioned during or soon after any of those years when she is usually claimed to have been pope (855, 896, 1099). This is a bizarre omission from the historical record for an event that was supposed to have shocked all the people and clergy of Rome itself, but modern believers can simply invoke the myth of the "Dark Ages" and claim that much of the evidence from this time has been lost.

To an uncritical historian, it might appear that there really is evidence of a Pope Joan from those early dates. She is apparently mentioned in medieval manuscripts of a list of popes by the ninth-century official librarian of Rome, Anastatius Bibliothecarius (d. 886). She is likewise named as pope in the year 854 by the chronicler Marianus Scotus (d. 1086), and his near contemporary Sigebert of Gembloux (d. 1112) said, "It is reported that this John was a female, and that she conceived by one of her servants. The Pope, becoming pregnant, gave birth to a child, wherefore some do not number her among the Pontiffs [popes]." (Baring-Gould 1877, 172) These and other sources used to be taken as genuine and early evidence of Pope Joan. However, more careful historians, from as early as the seventeenth century and up to the recent works of the Pardoes and Alain Boureau, have carefully studied the actual manuscripts of these earlier medieval authors and proven that every instance of a female pope mentioned in their works does not occur in the original and was added by scribes who copied their works in the fourteenth and fifteenth centuries. By that time, Pope Joan was well known and taken as a significant historical figure, and it seems that later medieval scribes could not imagine a list of earlier popes that did not include her.

There is also the basic problem of fitting Joan into the known lists of popes from around the years 855, 896, and 1099. The later medieval authors who describe Pope Joan did not have the centuries of detailed historical research describing the papacy that are now readily accessible. It was easy for them, writing in the thirteenth or fourteenth century, to insert a brief papacy for Joan during the distant ninth century. Some sources claim that Joan was elected pope between Leo IV (r. 847–855) and Benedict III (r. 855–858), but there is no contemporary record of her, and documents show that Benedict III was elected pope almost immediately after Leo IV's death in July 855.

The year 896 is a more plausible time for finding upheavals in the papacy and inserting a shadowy female popess, for by the end of the ninth century, the papacy had become a fully politicized office that was fought over by the powerful families in and around Rome. Pope Formosus (r. 891–896) was a widely disliked pope, who was embroiled in imperial scandals and in conflicts with the Byzantine Empire. There were riots in Rome following his death, which saw the election and then ejection of Pope Boniface VI over a period of just sixteen days in April 896, before he died under clearly suspicious circumstances. Most notoriously, Boniface VI's successor, Stephen VI (r. 896–897) oversaw the so-called Cadaver Synod in 897. He ordered the body of Formosus to be exhumed and put it on trial for crimes during life. He was found guilty (of course), his body mutilated, reburied, then re-exhumed and thrown into the Tiber River. No contemporary documents mention a female pope during the upheavals of 896, but to later medieval historians it seemed plausible that she could have become pope during such a low point for the papacy.

The date of 1099 is the most problematic and is found only in the chronicle of Jean de Mailly. This was a hugely important year in the history of the Church and Christianity, because of the crusader conquest of Jerusalem on July 14, 1099. The pope who had called the crusade, Urban II, died soon after on July 29, without getting to hear the news of this victory. His successor, Pope Paschal II, became pope just two weeks later on August 13. The careers of these two prominent popes were well known throughout the rest of the Middle Ages and to this day, so there was no simple way to insert a shadowy popess between them. However, Jean de Mailly may have been thinking not of the actual popes in Rome but of so-called antipopes: these were clerics, often promoted by the Holy Roman Emperor in Germany, who claimed the title of pope but were not recognized by most medieval Catholics or modern historians as genuine popes. The antipope Clement III was supported by Emperor Henry IV and claimed this title for the years 1084–1100. Even though he had immediate successors as imperially sponsored antipopes (Theodoric in 1100–1101 and Adalbert in 1101–1102), it would be easy for a scholar many years later, like Jean de Mailly, to imagine another pope or antipope in this line.

But what do we make of that tantalizing claim in Jean de Mailly's account that there is a statue of Joan with the inscription *Petre, Pater Patrum, Papisse Prodito Partum* ("Peter, Father of the Fathers, Make Known the Childbirth of a Popess")? Jean was apparently doing his best to interpret the meaning of an inscribed statue that stood near the Lateran in Rome until at least the fifteenth century before being destroyed by the papacy. The statue was of a pagan goddess and inscribed with the letters *P.P.P.P.P.* (with five rather than six *P*s). Roman historians have proposed that these letters, typical of ancient statues, meant something like *Pater Patrum Propria Pecunia Posuit* ("The father of fathers erected [this statute] at his own expense") (Conway 1914, 793–795). This "father of fathers," who could be understood as the pope in a medieval context, was probably a priest of the god Mithras, when understood in the original Roman context. Various other statues supposedly of Joan are mentioned by later medieval authors, and these may be complete fabrications or again misunderstood classical images of the goddess Juno nursing the infant Hercules (DiMarco 2008, 63–64). Whatever the case, this series of six *P*s became central to the Joan legend and later authors would reinterpret it to suit their theology and politics (Boureau 2011, 140–41, 148).

Pope Joan was perhaps the invention of confused Romans who misunderstood a pagan statue as representing a female pope. She may also simply have been the product of confusing the masculine *Johannes* for the feminine *Johanna* in a Latin text. Others have proposed that she was invented to satirize the powerful women of the Theophylact family of Rome, who supposedly controlled the papacy during the tenth century, especially the countesses of Tusculum, Theodora and her daughter Marozia (Boureau 2001, 306). But if any of these explanations is true, why did the story not appear until the thirteenth century and usually in the works of the friars? Alain Boureau has tentatively suggested that the story of Joan took off in this period as a criticism of papal politics at a time (the 1250s) when the papacy was similarly critical of the growth and ambitions of the mendicant Dominican and Franciscan orders (2001, 145–51). Most explanations for Joan look to the written and artistic sources of the later Middle Ages, but in one recent case Joan is explained as a possible medieval confusion over a female pseudohermaphrodite with 21-hydroxylase deficiency. A woman with this syndrome can appear to have male genitalia but still become pregnant and give birth. This astonishing argument was made by Dr. Maria New, a pediatrician at Cornell University. New does not propose that Pope Joan actually existed but that stories about her may have been inspired by genuine, historical hermaphrodites (New 1993).

Whether Joan served as a warning, a parable, a legal precedent, or a scandal, every medieval author who mentions her seems to have believed in her historical reality. But while the story of Pope Joan is a very real and important element of medieval history, Pope Joan herself was not.

Further Reading

Baring-Gould, Sabine. 1877. "Antichrist and Pope Joan." In *Curious Myths of the Middle Ages*, 161–89. Oxford: Rivingtons.

Boureau, Alain. 2001. *The Myth of Pope Joan*. Translated by Lydia G. Cochrane. Chicago: University of Chicago Press. Originally published as *La papesse Jeanne*. Paris: Aubier, 1988.

Conway, Bertrand L. 1914. "The Legend of Pope Joan." *Catholic World* 99. April–September 1914, 792–98.

DiMarco, Vincent. 2008. "The Medieval Popess." In *Misconceptions about the Middle Ages*, edited by Stephen J. Harris and Bryon L. Grigsby. New York: Routledge.

Hudson, Alison. 2018. "The Female Pope." *British Library Medieval Manuscripts Blog*, May 12, 2018. http://blogs.bl.uk/digitisedmanu scripts/2018/05/the-one-and-only-female-pope.html.

Huss, John. 1915. *The Church*. Edited and translated by David S. Schaff. New York: Scribner's.

Jean de Mailly. 1879. *Chronica universalis Mettensis*. In *Monumenta Germaniae Historica Scriptorum* 24, 502–26. Hanover: Impensis Bibliopolii Hahniani.

New, Maria I. 1993. "Pope Joan: A Recognizable Syndrome." *Transactions of the American Clinical and Climatological Association* 104:96–119.

Pardoe, Rosemary, and Darroll Pardoe. 1988. *The Female Pope*. Wellingborough, UK: Aquarian.

Platina, Baptista. 1685. *The Lives of the Popes from the Time of Our Saviour Jesus Christ to the Reign of Sixtus IV*. Translated by Paul Rycaut. London: Christopher Wilkinson.

"Pope Joan—movie trailer (2009)," *YouTube*. https://www.youtube.com /watch?v=AKF4Lmt3NsM.

Porath, Jason. 2016. *Rejected Princesses. Tales of History's Boldest Heroines, Hellions, and Heretics*. New York: Dey Street Books.

Rhoïdis, Emmanuel. 1886. *Pope Joan. A Historical Study*. Translated by Charles Hastings Colette. London: George Redway.

9

Medieval Medicine Was
Nothing but Superstition

What People Think Happened

Medicine, perhaps more than any other human activity, has improved since the Middle Ages. While modern people sometimes look back fondly and with admiration on medieval religion, literature, art, or community and family structures, no one could possibly now say, "I wish we could revive medieval medicine!" In the Middle Ages, doctors did not know about germs (bacteria or viruses) and thus had a poor understanding of infection and contagion. They were incapable of preventing or curing infectious diseases and did not fully understand how to keep wounds clean to prevent further injury from infection. Modern medicine, on the other hand, has in just the last century vastly improved your likelihood of surviving a disease or a grievous injury, and medical scientists have helped transform the world by extending lifespans and even eradicating some diseases, like smallpox. But just because modern medicine is undoubtedly more effective in preventing and curing disease than premodern medicine, this does not mean that we should dismiss one thousand and more years of medical history as mere nonsense.

Sadly, this is exactly what happens in popular depictions of medieval medicine and even in some supposedly scholarly works on the history of medicine. Past medicine is viewed through the lens of "progress": if a historical physician did not make a noticeable contribution to the medicine we use today, then he or she is seen as unimportant or even retrogressive in the history of medicine. Medieval medicine, in particular, is often treated not simply as different from, but as the very opposite of, modern medical practice. If modern medicine is supposed to be progressive, effective, rational, natural, and sanitary, then medieval medicine must necessarily (by this logic) be backward, ineffective, irrational, superstitious, and revolting. But even though medieval medicine was often not "right" according to the standards of modern medical theory, neither was it wholly superstitious: at most times and places in the Middle Ages it was a rational and complex system of medical theory based on natural laws and evidence from the body. In this chapter we will explore common misconceptions about medieval medicine, their sources, and the realities of what went on in the practice of healing during the Middle Ages.

Describing European medieval medicine simply as superstition is a mistake also made by popular educators who want to praise another aspect of the medieval past. For example, the organizers of the internationally renowned traveling exhibit *1001 Inventions* and the authors of its multiple companion books claim that medieval Islamic thinkers laid the groundwork for innumerable modern scientific and medical ideas and advances, including a correct understanding of the human cardiovascular system. As the authors of the collection cheekily titled *1001 Distortions* make clear, this and nearly every claim made in *1001 Inventions* is false or taken out of context (Brömer 2016). But whether modern audiences want to imagine that Islamic doctors were ahead of their time, or that European doctors were woefully backward, both approaches suffer from judging sciences in the past through this presentist, progressivist lens.

How the Story Became Popular

You will regularly hear that medieval people thought diseases were caused by elves or goblins. This fits in with our popular image of the Middle Ages as wholly different from now, a disturbing world of fantasy serving as a dark mirror of our time. For example, a recent study of the efficacy of folk remedies by John Mann, a professor of organic chemistry, makes the following claim about early medieval medicine: "Meanwhile, during the Dark Ages in Europe, pharmacy, superstition, and magic became inextricably intertwined. A number of 'leechbooks' . . . were compiled, containing some recognizable drugs, but mostly fanciful brews for fending off elves and goblins" (John Mann, cited in Van Arsdall 2002, 91). Mann referred to no scholar of medieval medicine for these ideas but relied instead on popular opinion about the backwardness of medieval medicine. He also makes the common mistake (discussed more later) of treating the rare examples of Anglo-Saxon leechbooks as representative of all medieval medicine.

In a similar fashion, some historians deny that medicine or doctors even existed during the Middle Ages. The famous nineteenth-century French author Jules Michelet, whose dramatic writings about the Middle Ages still inform some popular accounts, claimed that medieval people could turn only to witches for healing: "The only physician of the people for a thousand years was the Witch. The emperors, kings, popes, and richer barons had indeed their doctors of Salerno, their Moors and Jews; but the bulk of people in every state, the world as it might well be called, consulted none but the *Saga*, or wise-woman" (Michelet 1863, 4). He says the situation was even worse for sick women during the Middle Ages seeking healing: "for never in those days was a male physician admitted to the woman's side, to win her trust in him, to listen to her secrets. The witches alone attended her, and became, especially for women, the chief and only physician" (Michelet 1863, 121). But at another point, Michelet also claims that healing only came from the Church: "Barring the well-paid doctors, Jew or Arab, of the kings, the art of medicine was practised only with holy water at the church door. Thither on Sundays, after the service, would come a crowd of sick" (Michelet 1863, 117). Whether they went to witches or priests, medieval people are portrayed as blindly superstitious and the Middle Ages as wholly without any natural or learned medicine.

A typical portrait of a medieval medical encounter goes something like this: a filthy peasant has a pain in her side (see chapter 3 for myths about dirt and bathing in the Middle Ages). She worries it might be a punishment from God or caused by the neighborhood witch. She visits a physician called a "leech," supposedly named for the leeches prescribed to suck out her bad blood, to hire him to drive out the demons inside her body. He uses every superstitious tool at hand, casting a magic spell, consulting the stars, brewing a noxious herbal potion, and draining some of her blood. Later, when her priest finds out about her visit to the leech, he condemns her for putting her hope in physical medicine instead of prayer alone. The higher authorities of the Catholic Church support this condemnation and seek to identify and punish heretical physicians who promote natural remedies. This is a view of medieval medicine promoted in modern comedy, like Steve Martin's character Theoderic of York, medieval barber, from *Saturday Night Live* (1978), or in serious films like *The Physician* (dir. Philip Stölzl, 2013), based on the 1986 novel by Noah Gordon. *The Physician* is especially representative of popular ideas about medieval medicine, for it represents the European medicine of "Dark Age" England in the eleventh century as woefully backward and superstitious in comparison with the enlightened, rational medicine of the Islamic world (represented by the Persian Muslim scholar Ibn Sina, also known as Avicenna).

Even though these examples are fictional, they draw directly on popular and scholarly representations of medieval European medicine as backward in every way and even as inherently antimedical, leading only to the harm of a patient. In modern works like *The Physician*, the only medical practitioners in Europe are poorly trained "barber surgeons," who are punished by the church for "witchcraft." This fictional portrait is based on a misunderstanding of actual medieval sources and on exaggerations of statements made by historians of medicine and of medieval culture. Throughout the last century, numerous histories of medicine were published that, if they gave any space to the Middle Ages at all, described it in purely negative terms, as the most backward and superstitious of eras. Most of these histories are intended for popular audiences and written by medical doctors, who tend to look only for what they know in the distant past; if it is not there, the past is a failure.

For example, Dr. Howard W. Haggard (1891–1959), a professor of physiology at Yale in the 1930s, wrote the revealingly titled *Mystery, Magic, and Medicine: The Rise of Medicine from Superstition to Science*. He depicts a Middle Ages without creativity or intelligence, a time of "unquestioning submission to Church and Feudal Lord," a time when "Potential genius was suppressed or directed into channels barren of practical results." The few advances made in medicine during the Middle Ages are said to be due to influence from Arabic Muslims, because "the people of Western Europe are living in their walled cities, filthy, undrained, pestilential, while they are suffering from frightful epidemics of disease, while infant mortality rises and length of life declines" (Haggard 1933, 40). If any intelligent form of medicine reached Europe, whether from Galen or Arabic authors, Dr. Haggard informs us that medieval people "venerated" it rather than understood it. In every paragraph we learn more of the medieval failure to "progress" toward modern medicine than of what medieval medical practice was actually like.

But surely this sort of attitude was just a holdover from the nineteenth century, burdened by its obsession with "progress"? No, for the same attitude persists to this day in popular books on medicine. Yet another physician, Richard Gordon, the pen name of the English surgeon Gordon Stanley Ostler (1921–2018), wrote dozens of novels featuring doctors as well as multiple books about the history of doctors and medicine. His

1993 book *The Alarming History of Medicine* obviously is not meant to be a serious work of scholarship, but it is exactly the sort of book to perpetuate myths about the Middle Ages most successfully. He treats the period with even more scorn than Dr. Haggard did. In the Middle Ages, we are told, "Anatomy was dead, and medicine was stillborn. Religion is of course a Good Thing. . . . But it scuppered healing for fifteen centuries" (Gordon 1993, 7). This is because "The early Christian Church resented doctors. They interfered in the death business. . . . The saints ran the body" (Gordon 1993, 6). For Dr. Gordon, any period when religion is dominant cannot possibly see any intelligence or advance in medicine. The same attitude, in a far less flippant tone, pervades Charles Freeman's *The Closing of the Western Mind: The Rise of Faith and the Fall of Reason*. The rise of Christianity, according to Freeman, led to "the rejection of a scientific approach to medicine" which he claims existed under Galen in the second century CE, and that any medieval attempts at medical care were selfishly guided by the caretaker's desire for salvation (Freeman 2003, 320), As we have seen throughout this book, any failures of the Middle Ages to be just like today are blamed on supernatural beliefs, either from ignorance that was supposedly enforced by the Catholic Church or from pagan beliefs that led medieval people astray.

One of those "pagan beliefs" that has especially caught popular attention is the idea that medieval people thought tiny or invisible "elves" caused disease. This is a genuine medieval belief, but it is another case of one rare example being applied to an entire aspect of medieval society. One of the reasons for this is the consistent problem in medieval history and the history of medicine with Anglocentrism, that is, the belief that the England had the most important culture in Europe, if not the world, and therefore that English cultural products can be treated as representative for the entire European Middle Ages. Much of the popular history of medieval medicine is based just on English medieval books, and only on a few of the oldest and least representative examples. The English are proud of the fact that their medieval kingdom produced the first extensive medical writings in the vernacular, that is, in their native tongue (Old English) rather than in classical languages of learning (Latin or Greek). Anglo-Saxon physicians wrote several medical manuals in Old English during the ninth through eleventh centuries, several hundred years before any other nations in Europe started writing medicine down in their own language. These medical books are known as the *Old English Herbarium*, the *Leechbook of Bald*, and *Lacnunga* ("Remedies").

In the years 1864–1866, an English cleric and philologist named Oswald Cockayne (1807–1873) wrote the first modern book to present medieval medicine to a wide audience. He called his book *Leechdoms, Wortcunning and Starcraft of Early England* and included in it editions and translations of the aforementioned Old English medical texts. But Cockayne was not interested in making medieval medicine accessible or historically accurate (Van Arsdall 2008). Instead, he made his translations intentionally fantastic and antiquated, using them to represent the Anglo-Saxons as a nearly pagan group of barbarians, when in fact the Anglo-Saxons of the ninth century were among the most Christian and literate people in Western Europe. The very title of his book helped twist perceptions of medieval medicine to this day. For example, "leechdom" is not a word in modern English, but Cockayne's rendering of the Old English *laecedom*, which simply means "medicine." "Leech" (*laece*) was the word for a physician in Old English not because they used leeches, but the other way around: the parasite is named after the physician, because both draw blood. Likewise, Cockayne invented the word "wortcunning," which reinforced Victorian ideas of medieval witchcraft and superstition, instead of using the phrase "knowledge of medical plants," which more accurately represents medieval medical practice.

Cockayne's skewed presentation of the Anglo-Saxons and of medieval medicine resonated with his audience. His Victorian readers were most interested in those cures that supported their ideas about medieval barbarism and superstition. They were especially drawn to cures that mentioned "elves" as the cause of disease, like that printed in the Primary Documents from the *Lacnunga*, a treatment for a "sudden stitch" (a pain in the side, possibly from rheumatism). These elves are not the tall and beautiful humanoids from the worlds of Middle Earth or *Dungeons & Dragons*, but small and nasty spirits who cause illness with their arrows. In some cases, a sick person is said to be "elf-shot." To be sure, this and other cures in the *Lacnunga* do mention elves and witches, but Cockayne went out of his way to turn the Old English texts into works of fantasy. He used words in his translation that were no longer or never used in nineteenth-century England, such as *lew* and *nithling*. Where the original Old English text simply describes "wives" (*wif*), Cockayne translated it as "witch wives." He added superstition to these texts when it wasn't actually there.

Multiple recent scholars have newly edited and translated this and other Old English medical texts to fix the damage done by Cockayne (Hall 2007, 109–10; Pollington 2000, 228–29). Nonetheless, this cure and the entire *Lacnunga* have been debated hotly by scholars for the last century: Did Anglo-Saxons really believe in elves and witches? Is this passage just a metaphor for the pain of a stitch in the side? Was "elf" just their name for a physical ailment or did they actually believe in this supernatural being? Whatever the case, we need to realize that the *Lacnunga* and its "elves" are almost unique in medieval medicine. Thousands of medical texts survive from the entire Middle Ages, usually in Latin, and most of them avoid any explanation of illness using elves or supernatural creatures. The misconceptions about medieval medicine came primarily from English and U.S. scholars in the century after Cockayne published his book who believed that the *Lacnunga* was typical of the Middle Ages. For example, J. H. G. Grattan was a scholar of Germanic philology, who wrote a book called *Anglo-Saxon Magic and Medicine* in 1952 and used mostly the *Lacnunga* for evidence. He repeats Cockayne's unhistorical use of the word *leechdoms* and considers them a "mass of folly and credulity," in which there is nothing rational, nothing based on the experience of the senses (Grattan and Singer 1952, 92). Similar statements, dismissing medieval medicine as irrational, were made by Charles Singer in *A Short History of Medicine* (Singer 1962, a revision of his 1928 book of the same title) and Stanley Rubin in *Medieval English Medicine* (Rubin 1974).

Even when these authors are careful to state that they are talking only about one aspect of early medieval medicine in England, their ideas are easily taken out of context and applied to all of Europe and for all of the Middle Ages. This is especially true with history books intended for children which (as we have seen in other chapters) retain fictions about the Middle Ages much longer than books intended for college students or adult audiences. In *A Totally Gross History of Medieval Europe*, we are told that medieval Christians attributed all sickness and disease to God, witchcraft, or demons. They did not use medicine but put all their hope in prayer (Gitlin 2016, 24). A book about the history of plague states that before the Black Death of 1348, "Most people's beliefs about illness were based on myths and superstitions. . . . People thought that they were being punished because of sin or bad deeds" (Cefrey 2001, 9–10). These authors fall into the trap of believing that healing must be either religious or natural, but not both, when medieval people were perfectly comfortable attributing the cause of a disease to God's anger at sin while still seeking treatment from a human doctor with natural remedies.

A British website sponsored by the BBC and intended for students preparing for their GCSE (General Certificate of Secondary Education) in history pushes the myth of a Middle Ages without medicine even farther. According to this study guide, the Middle Ages was a period of complete stagnation in medicine, which had lost all medical knowledge from the ancient world. Paradoxically, the study guide also claims that the Church forced Christians to agree with the medical writings of the ancient physician Galen. The Church likewise is said to have forbidden dissection and encouraged people to rely on prayer, saints, and superstition alone for their cures ("Medical Stagnation in the Middle Ages," *BBC–GCSE Bitesize*). Every one of these statements is false.

PRIMARY DOCUMENTS

"FOR A SUDDEN STITCH" (*WIð FÆRSTICE*) AND OTHER REMEDIES, FROM THE *LACNUNGA* (ca. 1000)

The Lacnunga *("Remedies") is a collection of herbal and magical medicine written in Anglo-Saxon England around the year 1000. It is one of several Anglo-Saxon medical texts from the period ca. 900–1050, which include the* Old English Herbarium *and* Bald's Leechbook. *They are written primarily in Old English, with some Latin, and short phrases from Greek and Hebrew. Most Anglo-Saxon medicine, as is the case with medieval medical texts from the continent, is natural and based mostly on herbal remedies. But the* Lacnunga *is famous (or infamous) for including numerous pagan and Christian rituals, magical spells and charms, and references to elves and witches. The following selections are some of the most "superstitious" remedies in the* Lacnunga *including #75–76, "For a sudden stitch," discussed earlier. The reader should understand that the editor and translator of these recipes, Thomas Oswald Cockayne, made them sound intentionally archaic to reinforce how foreign and different they were from nineteenth-century learned medicine. More recent translations are easier to understand for the modern reader.*

75. For a sudden stitch, feverfue and the red nettle which waxeth about a dwelling, and waybread, boil them in butter.
76. Loud were they, lo! loud
  When over the lew they rode:
  They were of stout mood
  When over the lew they rode.
  Shield thee now; thou mayst save this nithling
  Out little spear; if herein it be.

He stood under the linden broad
under a light shield,
Where the mighty witch wives
Their main strength proved.
And yelling they sent darts.
I again will send them another
Flying feathered bolt from the front against them.
Out little spear; if herein it be.
Sat the smith; he sledged a sword.
Little iron, wound sharp.
Out little spear; if herein it be.
Six smiths sat,
Slaughter spears they wrought.
Out spear; not, in spear,
If herein there be, of iron a bit,
A witches work,
It shall melt.
If thou wert on fell shotten,
Or wert on flesh shotten,
Or wert on blood shotten,
Or wert on limb shotten,
Never let be thy life a teased;
If it were an Æsir shot,
Or if it were an elfin shot,
Or if it were a witches shot,
Now will I help thee.
Here's this to boot of Æsir shot
Here's this to boot of elfin shot
Here's this to boot of witches shot
I will help thee.
Fled Thor to the mountain.
Hallows he had two.
May the Lord help thee!
Then take the knife and put it into liquid.

78. If cattle are dying, put into holy water groundsel and springwort and the netherward part of attorlothe and clivers, pour it into the mouth, soon they will be better.

95. For ch-urnel.

Nine were Noðes sisters, then the nine came to be eight, and the eight seven, and the seven six, and the six five, and the five four, and the four three, and the three two, and the two one, and the one none. This may be medicine for thee from churnel and from scrofula and from worm, and from every mischief. Sing also the *Benedicite* nine times.

103. Let the woman who cannot bring her child to maturity go to the barrow of a deceased man, and step thrice over the barrow, and then thrice say these words:

May this be my boot
Of the loathsome late birth.
May this be my boot
Of the heavy swart birth.
May this be my boot
Of the loathsome lame birth.

And when the woman is with child and she goeth to her lord to bed, then let her say:

Up I go,
Over thee I step,
With quick child,
Not with a dying one,
With one to be full born,
Not with a fay one.

And when the mother feeleth that the bairn is quick within her, then let her go church, and when she cometh before the altar, then let her say, to Christ I have said, this is declared. Let the woman who cannot being up her bairn to maturity, let he, herself, take part of her own child's barrow, then afterwards wrap it up in black wool, and sell it to chapmen, and then say:

I it sell,
Or it have sold,
This swarthy wool
And grains of sorrow.

Source: Cockayne, T. O. 1864–1866. *Leechdoms Wortcunning, and Starcraft of Early England Being a Collection of Documents, for the Most Part Never Before Printed Illustrating the History of Science in this Country Before the Norman Conquest.* 3 vols. Rolls Series, 35 i–iii. London: Rerum Britannicarum Medii Aevi Scriptores, 3:53, 55, 63, 67, 69.

What Really Happened

Presenting the "facts" of medieval medicine is difficult, because there was no single system of medieval medicine during the millennium of the Middle Ages. There is a huge gulf between healing in the early and central Middle Ages (ca. 500–1100 CE), when there were few professional physicians and no formal medical training, and healing in the later Middle Ages (ca. 1100–1500 CE), when medical education was formalized and became an official faculty at some universities. These faculties trained and credentialed professional physicians, much like today, although learned physicians with degrees still formed only a small minority of later medieval healers, who also included herbalists, wise women, and midwives, with significant practical experience but little book learning. There could also be great differences between the theoretical medicine of the highly learned scholars of Latin, Arabic, and Greek cultures, and the home remedies of the typically uneducated peasants. Furthermore, medieval people (whether Christian, Muslim, or Jewish) recognized a connection between sinful behavior and some diseases, especially bubonic plague and leprosy (Grigsby 2008, 145–46). Nonetheless, a few basic statements about medieval medicine can be made, which contradict the fictions outlined earlier.

We first need to dismiss those mythmakers who claim that medieval people resorted only to prayer and magic to treat disease. Medieval medicine recognized most diseases as having natural causes, treatable by natural remedies, which could be understood and prepared by men or women, the learned or the uneducated. Even though medieval people had no understanding of viruses and bacteria, they recognized (as we do today) that some diseases spread from person to person by contagion, that certain lifestyles lead to bad health, and that certain people are simply more disposed to get ill than others. Furthermore, modern audiences tend to misunderstand the medieval connection between sin and disease. Rather than attributing a specific disease to a specific sin (which did happen, albeit rarely), medieval people tended to attribute the general presence of illness to the fallen state of humanity in their view of the Christian universe (Amundsen 1996, 187–88). Yes, sin was the cause of disease in a universal sense, but their explanations for how disease affected the body were natural, as were most recommendations for treating disease.

Health and disease were usually explained in terms of bodily harmony or balance: when the body is out of balance, diseases occur. The goal of medicine is to bring the body back into balance. There were a variety of theories developed to explain this system of balance, which focused variously on ideas of tightness and looseness, emptiness and filling, heating and cooling, or the movement of liquids. The most popular theory by far was humoral theory, which was established by the ancient Greek doctor Hippocrates (ca. 460–370 BCE) and his followers. According to humoral theory, health and sickness are determined by the state of four essential substances or "humors" in the body: blood, phlegm, yellow/red bile, and black bile. If one of these humors grows in excess or becomes corrupted from too much or too little food, drink, exercise, or sexual activity, then the humors are considered out of balance and a specific disease could form within the body. Different humors caused different types of disease: phlegm caused colds, red bile caused cholera, black bile caused plague and severe depression.

Diseases were usually understood as products of our own bodies, not of external pathogens, and therefore treatments were directed at modifying the body itself rather than identifying and removing a microscopic pathogen. Those treatments were less invasive than those in modern medicine and were usually accomplished through the moderation of diet and exercise (what they called *regimen*). Less often, a physician would prescribe bloodletting or purgatives, which caused vomiting, urination, or sweating, to force the body to get rid of excess or corrupt humors.

Humoral theory was refined and vigorously promoted by the Greco-Roman physician Galen of Pergamon (ca. 130–210 CE), who wrote hundreds of books on medicine and other topics. The ideas and writings of Hippocrates and Galen, among other ancient physicians, were adopted in the Middle Ages and translated into Arabic (especially in the ninth and tenth centuries) and Latin (mostly during the eleventh and twelfth centuries). Medieval Christians and Muslims shared a similar medical culture and looked back to the same ancient Greek physicians. This shared culture can be seen in the Primary Documents, in a selection from one of the most popular introductory medical textbooks of the Middle Ages. Hunayn ibn Ishaq (809–873 CE), known as Johannitius in Latin Europe, was an Arab Christian working in ninth-century Baghdad as a physician and translator of Greek texts.

Johanittius wrote a brief summary of Galenic medicine called "Questions on Medicine," but known in Europe as the *Isagoge* (Greek for "introduction"). He outlines the "naturals" (defining aspects of the human body including the humors and elements), "non-naturals" (external influences that affect health such as exercise, baths, food, drink, sleep, sexual activity, and emotions), and "contra-naturals" (diseases and aging). As should be clear from the following excerpt, the *Isagoge* is highly rational and organized, and based on natural observation and explanations, even if we now consider those explanations incorrect. A North African Christian monk named Constantine the African, working in Italy at the abbey of Monte Cassino during the 1070s and 1080s, translated the Arabic *Isagoge* into Latin, after which it became the foundation of all serious medical education in Europe for the next five hundred years. Formal medical education in Europe was open only to Christian men, but nearly anyone could practice basic medicine, as medical licensing did not exist in most cities or nations. The *Isagoge* was read by medical students before they progressed to the more ancient and difficult works of Hippocrates and Galen, as well as of some medieval Arabic physicians. The presence of learned Christian physicians and translators like Johanittius and Constantine in the Islamic world also proves false the popular belief that medieval Muslims did not allow Christians in their schools or society (an idea repeated in the novel and movie of *The Physician*).

Medical textbooks like the *Isagoge* taught medieval people the basics of medical theory, but any real physician needed to know medical practice. This was learned through apprenticeship and observation, just like today, but there were also a wide range of practical medical handbooks prepared in both Arabic and Latin. In Latin Europe these books were often called simply *Practica*, and a popular example was the *Practica* of Platearius, an Italian physician from the twelfth century. In the Primary Documents is an excerpt from Platearius's *Practica* concerning the treatment for a common medical complaint, the head cold, known as a catarrh in the Middle Ages and up until the early twentieth century. Platearius explain the possible causes of catarrh using humoral theory and provides detailed remedies also based on the modification of the humors. He even provides an experiment for testing the specific cause of a patient's catarrh (although the method and conclusions of this experiment are unclear).

Myths about medieval medicine are like many others in this book: they come from a tendency to reduce a complex phenomenon to a single example. In this case, modern audiences focus on just the rare instances of some early medieval people attributing disease to "elves" and ignore the vastly more common medieval medical systems that were based on rational theories, the observation of bodily symptoms, and the prescription of natural remedies. Yes, medieval medicine was essentially "wrong" in its understanding of disease causation when compared to modern germ theory, but it laid the foundation for much of what we still consider "right" in modern medical practice: close observation of a patient's symptoms, listening to their narrative of illness, investigating their diet and lifestyle, searching out new remedies in plants and minerals, and debating the nature of the body and its place in the wider world. All of these approaches to healing were established in the ancient Mediterranean, inherited and elaborated by medieval Arabic and Latin cultures, and passed on to the modern world.

PRIMARY DOCUMENTS

A SCHOLARLY INTRODUCTION TO MEDICINE, THE *ISAGOGE* OF JOHANNITIUS (TENTH CENTURY IN ARABIC, ELEVENTH CENTURY IN LATIN)

Hunayn ibn Ishaq (809–873 CE), called Johannitius in Latin Europe, was an Arab Christian who worked in Baghdad as a physician and translator of Greek texts on medicine, science, and philosophy. His Isagoge *(Greek for "introduction") was one of his best-known works in both Arabic and Latin medical education. It provides a brief but detailed introduction to the medical theory associated with Hippocrates and Galen, which focused on identifying the causes of diseases and treating them through the theory of the four humors (blood, phlegm, red or yellow bile, and black bile).*

The Beginning of the Introduction of Johannitius to Medicine

Medicine is divided into two parts, namely theoretical and practical. And of these two the theoretical is further divided into three, that is to say, the consideration of the naturals, the non-naturals, and the contra-naturals. From the consideration of these arises the knowledge of sickness, of health, and of the mean state, and their causes and significations; of when the four humors increase in an abnormal manner, or of what may be the cause or significance of sickness.

Of the Naturals. The naturals are seven in number: elements, qualities, humors, members, energies, operations, and spirits. But some add to these four others: namely, age, color, figure, and the distinction between male and female.

The Elements. There are four elements: fire, air, water, and earth. Fire is hot and dry; air is hot and moist; water is cold and moist; earth is cold and dry.

The Qualities. There are nine qualities, eight unequal and one equal. Of the unequal, four are simple: namely, hot, cold, moist, and dry. From these arise four compound qualities: hot and moist, hot and dry, cold and moist, cold and dry. The equal is when the body is so disposed that it is in good condition and in a mean state, when it has a proper amount of all four.

Of the Humors. The humors are four in number: namely, blood, phlegm, reddish bile, and black bile. Blood is hot and moist, phlegm is cold and moist, reddish bile is hot and dry, black bile is cold and dry.

Of phlegm. There are five varieties of phlegm. There is the salt phlegm, which is hotter and drier than the rest and is tinged with the biliary humor. There is the sweet phlegm belonging to hotness and dampness, which is tinged with the sanguine humor. There is the acrid phlegm belonging to coldness and dryness, which is tinged with the melancholic humor. There is the glassy phlegm, which arises from great coldness and coagulation such as occurs in old people who are destitute of natural warmth. And there is another which is cold and moist; it has no odor, but retains its own coldness and moistness.

Of reddish bile. Reddish bile exists in five different fashions. There is reddish bile which is clear or pure and hot, both by nature and substance, of which the origin is from the liver. There is another which is straw-colored, from which the origin is from the watery humor of phlegm, and pure reddish bile, and therefore it is less hot. Another is vitelline. It is similar to the yolk of an egg, and it has its origin from a mixture of coagulated phlegm and clear red bile, like the green of a leek, and it arises generally from the stomach or the liver; and there is another which is green like verdigris, and which burns after the fashion of a poison, and its origin is from too much *adustio* [overheating of the *humors*], and it possesses its own proper color and its own energies, both good and evil.

Of black bile. Black bile exists in two different fashions. In one way it may be said to be natural to the dregs of blood and any disturbance of the same, and it can be known from its black color whether it flows out of the body from below or above, and its property is cold and dry. The other kind is altogether outside the course of nature, and its origin is from the *adustio* of the choleric quality, and so it is rightly called black, and it is hotter and lighter, and having in itself a most deadly quality and a pernicious character. . . .

Of the Qualities of the Body. The qualities of the body are five in number: namely, excess or grossness; thinness or tenuity; wasting, squalidity, and the mean state. There are two kinds of grossness, the one consisting in excess of flesh, and the other in fat. Excess of flesh arises from excess of heat and humors; but fatness from cold and intense humidity; loss of fat or thinness arises from heat and intense dryness. Wasting arises from cold and intense humidity, or from an intensity of both together. And the mean state arises from a proper proportion of the humors. These are the appearances of the body.

Of the Difference between Male and Female. The male differs from the female in that he is hotter and more dry; she, on the contrary, is colder and more moist.

The Beginning of the Treatise on the Non-naturals

And first of the Changes of the air. Changes of the air come about in five different ways; from the seasons, from the rising and setting of the stars, from the winds, and from the different countries and their exhalations.

Of the seasons. There are four seasons; namely, Spring, which is hot and moist; Summer, which is hot and dry; Autumn, which is cold and dry; Winter, which is cold and moist. The nature of the air is also changed by the stars, for when the sun approaches a star or a star the sun, the air becomes hotter. But when they separate, the coldness of the air is altered, namely, either increased or diminished.

Of the Number and Properties of the Winds. There are four winds; the East, the West, the North, and the South. And of these the nature of one is cold and dry and of another hot and moist. The two others are of an equal nature, for the East is hot and dry and the West is cold and moist. The South is slightly hotter and moister and the North colder and dryer.

Of Varieties of Places and their Qualities. There four varieties of places; namely, height, depth, nearness to mountains or to the sea, and those particular qualities in which one district differs from another. Height produces cold and depth the contrary. The relation to mountains is as follows: if the mountains are to the south, the locality will be the cooler, for the mountains keep off the hot winds, and so the north winds seek it out with their cool breath. But if the mountains are to the north of the locality the reverse is the case. As regards relation to the sea: if the sea is on the south the locality will be hot and dry, if to the north it will be cold and dry. Soils differ among themselves. Stony land is cold and dry; fat and heavy land is hot and moist; clay lands are cold and moist. Exhalations from marshy land or other places where decay is going on also change the air and give rise to disease and pestilence. . . .

Of the Contra-naturals

There are three contra-naturals; namely, disease, the cause of disease, and the concomitants or sequel of disease. Disease is that which primarily injures the body, without the aid of any intermediary, as, for instance, heat in continuous fever.

Of Fevers. Fever is an unnatural heat, i.e. heat which overpasses normal course of nature. And it proceeds from the heart into the arteries, and is harmful by its own effects. And of it there are three kinds: the first in the spirit, which is called ephemeral; the second arises from the humors which putrefy, and which is therefore called putrid; and the third affects for ill the solid portions of the body, and this is called hectic. Of these three the ephemeral variety arises from non-essential causes.

Putrid fever arises from putrid matters, and these are simple and uncombined, and they are four in number. The first is that which arises from putridity of the blood and burns up both the interior and exterior of the body; such, for instance, is continuous fever. The second is that which arises from putridity of reddish bile; such, for instance, is tertian fever. The third arises from putridity of phlegm; such, for instance, is quotidian fever. And the fourth arises from putridity of black bile; this attacks the sick man after an interval of two days, and it is called quartan.

In addition there are three kinds of fevers occurring from putridity. First there is the fever which lessens day by day; such, for instance, as that called *peraugmasticus*, i.e. decreasing. Secondly, that which increases until it departs; such as that called *augmasticus*. Thirdly, that which neither decreases not increases until it again departs; such, for instance, as that called *homothenus*.

Continued fever arising from putridity in the veins begins to decline by departing from out the veins into other parts of the body. Goose-skin or shivering occurs in fevers from an infusion of putrid matter in to the sensitive members, which gnaws and makes them cold. And, therefore, goose-skin occurs in these fevers which are characterized by remissions or variations, for the putrid matters are outside the veins. . . .

Of the Qualities of the Body. The qualities of the body are three in number: namely, health, sickness, and the mean state. Health is that condition in which the temperament of the body and the seven naturals are working according to the course of nature. Sickness is defect in temperament outside the course of nature, and injuring nature, whence arises an effect of harm which may be felt. The mean state is that which is neither health nor disease. And there are three kinds of this mean state: (*a*) when health and disease co-exist in the same body; which may happen in different members, as in the blind or the lame; (*b*) in the bodies of the aged, in whom no one member remains that is not in evil case or suffers; (*c*) in those who are well at one season and sick at another. For instance, persons of a cold nature are sick in the winter and well in the summer; and those of a moist nature are sick in childhood, but well in youth and old age. Those of a dry nature are well in childhood, but sick in youth and old age.

Health, sickness, and the mean state are evident in three ways; (1) in the body in which any one of them occurs; (2) in the cause which produces, which governs, and which preserves them; (3) in their indicating signs.

Source: Johanittius. 1912. *Isagoge*. Printed in *John of Gaddesden and the Rosa Medicinae*, translated by H. P. Cholmeley. Oxford, 136–66.

PLATEARIUS, *PRACTICA*: EXPLANATION AND TREATMENT FOR A HEAD COLD (ca. 1150)

Platearius was a twelfth-century physician and author most likely from Salerno in southern Italy. He is one of numerous authors with the name "Platearius," which probably represents a family dynasty of physicians. The port city of Salerno was famous at least since the tenth century for the knowledge of its doctors, who were influenced by medical knowledge from the nearby Greek and Islamic cultures. So many doctors taught and wrote around Salerno between the tenth and thirteenth centuries that historians often speak of the "Salernitan school" of medicine, even though there probably was no organized school until the foundation of the University of Salerno in 1231. "Salernitan" medicine can be recognized by its focus on strengthening or balancing the patient's four humors through a combination of herbal remedies, bloodletting, and dietary regimen. This medical system is applied in this excerpt, in which Platearius explains the causes and cures for head colds (catarrh).

Concerning Catarrh. Catarrh [head cold] is the flowing of humors from the head. It comes about from internal and external causes: from external such as from hot air, from the cold and from humidity; from internal such as from the ingestion of food and drunk, and from the qualities of the humors and the body parts.

Catarrh happens principally in five ways: from an excess of humors caused by the weakness of the flowing mechanisms; from heat which dissolves and causes [humors] to flow; from a cold which constrains or expresses them or from a lubricating humidity; from the liquidity or fluidity of those humors; from the weakness of the retentive virtue.

The diversity of these causes is distinguished by the proper signs, so that the manner of curing is varied according to the variety of causes. [*Platearius proceeds to define the five causes of catarrh in greater detail.*]

The Cure. A catarrh made from the excess of humors is cured properly and principally through the evacuation of the superfluous humors. Therefore if blood is in excess, there should be a bloodletting from the cephalic vein, providing that the body is sanguineous and its powers and age permit, and especially if the humors flow to the spiritual members [the lungs and the region of the thorax]. But if the humors should flow down elsewhere and there persists an excess of other humors, a laxative medicine should be given in a solid substance, such as in golden pills [a popular and expensive remedy in the High Middle Ages], or pills made from the five kinds of myrobolans [small plums from Asia often used in medicine]. After the third day of purgation, give red madder. If the infirmity should not be relieved in this fashion, apply constrictives for the cure of the catarrh coming from cold, which I treat below. Have the patient inhale hot water through nose, apply an ointment to the forehead and temples of oil of roses or violets or another substance of a cold nature. If the catarrh doesn't stop like this, give the strongest opiate which can be found with the water from the decoction of violets and roses, such as the [compounds known as] *Sleep* or *Rose Madder. . . .*

A common experiment for a catarrh due to cold, to lubricating humidity, or to the weakness of the retentive virtue: the patient swallows three grains of pure frankincense the size of a bean without any liquid in the afternoon.

Keep in mind that these remedies should be repeated often, if applied once without the desired effect.

Source: Platearius. 2016. *La Practica de Plateario,* edited by Victoria Recio Muñoz. Florence: SISMEL, 234–45. New translation.

Further Reading

Amundsen, Darrel W. 1996. *Medicine, Society, and Faith in the Ancient and Medieval Worlds.* Baltimore: Johns Hopkins University Press.

Brömer, Rainer. 2016. "Only What Goes around Comes Around: A Case Study on Revisionist Priority Disputes—Circulation of the Blood." In *1001 Distortions: How (Not) to Narrate History of Science, Medicine, and Technology in Non-Western Cultures,* edited by Sonja Brentjes, Taner Edis, and Lutz Richter-Bernburg, 201–12. Würzburg: Ergon Verlag.

Cefrey, Holly. 2001. *The Plague.* New York: Rosen Publishing Group.

Cholmeley, H. P. 1912. *John of Gaddesden and the Rosa Medicinae.* Oxford: Clarendon Press.

Cockayne, T. O. 1864–1866. *Leechdoms, Wortcunning, and Starcraft of Early England Being a Collection of Documents, for the Most Part Never Before Printed Illustrating the History of Science in this Country Before the Norman Conquest.* 3 vols. Rolls Series 35 i–iii. London: Rerum Britannicarum Medii Aevi Scriptores.

Conrad, Lawrence I., Michael Neve, Vivian Nutton, Roy Porter, Andrew Wear. 1995. *The Western Medical Tradition, 800 BC to AD 1800.* Cambridge: Cambridge University Press.

Demaitre, Luke. 2013. *Medieval Medicine: The Art of Healing, from Head to Toe.* Santa Barbara, CA: Praeger.

Freeman, Charles. 2003. *The Closing of the Western Mind: The Rise of Faith and the Fall of Reason.* New York: Alfred A. Knopf.

Gitlin, Marty. 2016. *The Totally Gross History of Medieval Europe.* New York: Rosen Publishing Group.

Gordon, Richard. 1993. *The Alarming History of Medicine.* New York: St. Martin's Press.

Grattan, J. H. G., and Charles Singer. 1952. *Anglo-Saxon Magic and Medicine Illustrated Specially from the Semi-pagan Text 'Lacnunga.'* Oxford: Oxford University Press.

Grigsby, Bryon. 2008. "Medieval Misconceptions." In *Misconceptions about the Middle Ages*, edited by Stephen J. Harris and Bryon L. Grigsby, 142–50. New York: Routledge.

Haggard, Howard W. 1933. *Mystery, Magic, and Medicine: The Rise of Medicine from Superstition to Science.* New York: Doubleday, Doran and Co.

Hall, Alaric. 2007. *Elves in Anglo-Saxon England: Matters of Belief, Health, Gender, and Identity.* Anglo-Saxon Studies 8. Woodbridge, Suffolk, UK: Boydell Press.

Jolly, Karen Louise. 1996. *Popular Religion in Late Saxon England: Elf Charms in Context.* Chapel Hill, NC: University of North Carolina Press.

"Medical Stagnation in the Middle Ages." 2014. *BBC – GCSE Bitesize.* http://www.bbc.co.uk/schools/gcsebitesize/history/shp/middleages /medievalcivilisationrev3.shtml.

Michelet, Jules. 1863. *La sorcière: The Witch of the Middle Ages.* Translated by L. J. Trotter. London: Simpkin, Marshall, and Co.

Pollington, Stephen. 2000. *Leechcraft. Early English Charms, Plantlore, and Healing.* Little Downham, Ely, UK: Anglo-Saxon Books.

Rawcliffe, Carole. 1999. *Medicine and Society in Later Medieval England.* London: Sandpiper Books.

Rubin, Stanley. 1974. *Medieval English Medicine*. New York: Barnes and Noble Books.

Singer, Charles, and E. Ashworth Underwood. 1962. *A Short History of Medicine*. 2d ed. Oxford: Oxford University Press.

Siraisi, Nancy G. 1990. *Medieval and Early Renaissance Medicine: An Introduction to Knowledge and Practice*. Chicago: University of Chicago Press.

Van Arsdall, Anne. 2002. *Medieval Herbal Remedies: The Old English Herbarium and Anglo-Saxon Medicine*. New York: Routledge.

Van Arsdall, Anne. 2008. "Rehabilitating Medieval Medicine." In *Misconceptions about the Middle Ages,* edited by Stephen J. Harris and Bryon L. Grigsby, 135–41. New York: Routledge.

10

Medieval People Believed in Witches and Burned Them at the Stake

What People Think Happened

You know what a witch is, of course: pointed hat, black cat, ugly face and long nose, flies on a broom? This is the witch from the fairy tales of *Snow White* and *Hansel and Gretel*, the Wicked Witch of the West from *The Wizard of Oz* book and film (1900, 1939), or—in her more positive manifestations—Professor McGonagall in the *Harry Potter* books and movies (1997–) and Kiki in Hayao Miyazaki's *Kiki's Delivery Service* (1989). Accounts of frightening women practicing magic, especially hostile magic, go back at least to the ancient Greeks, as seen with the characters of Circe and Hecate in the poems of Homer and Hesiod. Yet these "witches" are not human, but rather a titan and a goddess. The stereotypical female, human witch is instead a product of the last five centuries in European culture and has remained remarkably stable in that time.

If you dig a bit deeper, the stereotype gets darker. She is a practitioner of black magic, in league with the devil. She celebrates dark rites in covens and orgies, where she murders and eats children. Witches, who are almost always women except for the rare male "warlock," gather in demonic "Sabbaths" to celebrate the "Black Mass," an evil inversion of the Catholic Mass. Under the influence of psychotropic herbs like belladonna, these wizened crones reject Christ, worship Satan in the form of a cat or a goat, perform horrific dances, and behead poisonous toads (these elements come from Michelet 1863, 150–56). Such demonic rituals gave witches the power to perform a wide variety of magic, but especially spells for kindling lust or causing pain and death. We meet these more frightening figures as the Weird Sisters in Shakespeare's *Macbeth* (1606), the many portrayals of Morgan Le Fay in modern Arthurian stories, in Roald Dahl's *The Witches* (1983, filmed in 1990), or in *The Blair Witch Project* (1999), and Robert Eggers's *The Witch: A New England Folktale* (2016).

Most of these witches, whether good or evil, demonic or simply nasty, are treated as relics from the past. Their appearance, speech, home, and magic all seem drawn from the Middle Ages. This connection of demonic, female witches with the Middle Ages is made explicit in a series of movies that place witches (genuine or falsely accused) in the context of the medieval crusades and Black Death. These include the comedy *Monty Python and the Holy Grail* (1975), the Swedish classic *The Seventh Seal* (1957), as well as the medieval thrillers *Black Death* (2010) and *Season of the Witch* (2011, loosely based on *The Seventh Seal*). Witches are situated naturally in these "medieval" fantasies, which anachronistically combine crusaders, plague, tales of King Arthur, and papal inquisition.

Stories like this about magic-using women have a long pedigree, but are not nearly as old as many people believe. The Middle Ages is frequently depicted as a time of widespread superstition and belief in all forms of magic, including witchcraft. They are consequently also imagined to be a time when innocent women were tortured and killed—often by burning at the stake—after accusations of witchcraft. The medieval Church is claimed to have organized and led massive witch-hunts across Europe, which continued into the early modern period and across the Atlantic Ocean, culminating with the infamous witch trials of Salem, Massachusetts, in 1692.

According to the popular fiction, millions of women were killed in "medieval" witch-hunts, as professional witch hunters destroyed entire villages, murdering anyone under the slightest suspicion of witchcraft. The "Burning Times," as some label this period, thus amounted to what has been called "gendercide," the alleged attempt by male churchmen to eradicate all women, who were believed to be innately in league with the devil. Popular beliefs about witches can be summed up by one line from Dan Brown's novel *The Da Vinci Code*, which has revived this fiction for countless readers in a new generation: "During three hundred years of witch hunts, the Church burned at the stake an astounding five *million* women" (Brown 2003, 125, emphasis in original).

How the Story Became Popular

The popular belief in medieval witches represents one of the clearest examples of the tendency of modern audiences to impose later historical developments on the medieval period. Because the Middle Ages are frequently depicted as a superstitious, cruel, and sexually repressive era, it seems a logical step to associate female witches and their persecution with the medieval period. However, as we shall soon see, for much of the Middle Ages, it was belief in witches that was condemned as a baseless superstition, and not witchcraft itself. It is only at the very end of the Middle Ages that the Catholic Church dramatically changed its position, arguing that witches did exist and should be punished as devil-worshipping heretics. While some of the actual period of belief in and prosecution of witchcraft (ca. 1430–1680) could rightly be seen as occurring at the very end of the Middle Ages, popular audiences regularly assume that these late medieval and early modern witch hunts are a continuation of beliefs and practices throughout the entire medieval period of 500–1500 CE.

Some modern historians have strengthened the fiction of the "medieval" witch who, even when they describe primarily the sixteenth and seventeenth centuries, call that period "medieval." This can be seen in the classic short history of witchcraft by Pennethorne Hughes, in which most of the chapters fall under a section called "Medieval Witchcraft," even though the author looks primarily at the seventeenth century, a period that has never been considered "medieval" (Hughes 1965). William Manchester, an author wholly hostile to the medieval period in his popular history *A World Lit Only by Fire*, attributes widespread belief in witchcraft to the Middle Ages, even though his only examples are Desiderius Erasmus and Thomas More, two of the central figures of the English Renaissance in the sixteenth century (Manchester 1992, 62).

One of the greatest difficulties for historians of witchcraft throughout the last two centuries is distinguishing the early modern witches from earlier forms of magic. There is frequently a tendency to assume that any medieval reference to magic or a magicuser (often *maleficia* and *maleficus* in medieval Latin) is describing our stereotypical female witch. However, the majority of medieval *malefici* or *magi* are men, especially when they are described as necromancers (*nigromantici*) who summon spirits of the dead to serve them (Kieckhefer 2000, 151–56). Harmful magic in the Middle Ages was a learned art, available only to male clerics (priests and monks). Yet the desire to erase the medieval male magicusers and replace them with female witches is common among nineteenth-century authors on magic from Germany, France, and England, whose ideas are still influential today. (Tuczay 2007, 52–53) These include Georg Conrad Horst's (1769–1832) *Dämonologie, oder Geschichte des Glaubens an Zauberei und dämonische Wunder* (*Demonology, or The History of the Belief in Sorcery and Demonic Magic*, 1818) and Jules Garinet's (1797–1877) *Histoire de la Magie en France* (*History of Magic in France*, 1818). While Horst carefully used archival sources to describe the witchcraft persecutions of the sixteenth through eighteenth centuries, Garinet rooted the witch trials of his native France in a one-thousand-year history of French witchcraft. All instances of medieval magic are treated as precursors to the early modern witch trials, and he modifies or ignores those instances in the Middle Ages when belief in witches was condemned. Garinet's ideas found a broader audience through Charles Mackay in his influential 1841 work *Memoirs of Extraordinary Popular Delusions*, in which Mackay translates with approval long sections of Garinet's book (Mackay 1852, "The Witch Mania," 101–91).

One of the most influential works in pushing early modern witch hysteria back to the Middle Ages was *La Sorcière*, by Jules Michelet (1862), whom we have met in several other chapters of this book as one of the great purveyors of medieval fictions. Michelet's book was translated the very next year into English by L. J. Trotter as *The Witch of the Middle Ages*, further spreading the concept of medieval witches. This work was reprinted many times, and later under the title *Satanism and Witchcraft*. Michelet is remarkable among nineteenth-century authors for showing great sympathy for women and peasants during the Middle Ages, whom he sees as innocent victims of the medieval Church's witch-hunts. However, because he makes the Church into the antagonist for his book, he stretches his history of witches, based mostly after the fifteenth century, throughout the entire medieval period without evidence. In his desire to link the history of medieval Catholicism to the development of witchcraft, Michelet leaps from the story of Saint Martin of Tours in the fourth century to the foundation of the Abbey of Cluny in the tenth century, to tales of witches' covens at the very end of the Middle Ages.

When Michelet is more chronologically precise, he dates the rise of witches to the thirteenth century, claiming it was at that time that medieval people turned away from the Church and toward witchcraft. They did this, Michelet claims, either to heal their leprosy, which he assumes incorrectly to have struck millions of people in this period (see chapter 3 for more on this passage), or to increase their sexual pleasure, which he claims the medieval Church condemned as sinful for all humanity. Medieval people, Michelet argues, could not seek religious healing for their leprosy because that disease was widely believed to be a corporeal sign of excessive sin and to be spread through sexual contact. He argued that "witches," actually sympathetic women healers, appeared at this time to fill the needs of desperate people seeking cures for leprosy. This claim, it should be made clear, is ridiculous: huge numbers of leper hospitals (*leprosaria*) were founded across Europe in the twelfth and thirteenth centuries, all of them religious institutions supported and funded by the Catholic Church. Even though medieval people had no actual cure for leprosy, they cared deeply for those with disease and even admired them as people who would go straight to heaven, since they believed to be atoning for their sins in this life.

Michelet's *La Sorcière* spawned many imitators, most of whom were obsessed with this vision of a violently sexual Middle Ages. One of the most notorious propagators of this fiction was the 1922 Swedish silent film *Häxan* ("The Witches," known also as *Witchcraft through the Ages*). The film, written and directed by the Danish actor Benjamin Christensen (1879–1959), claims to be a serious documentary, comparing the medieval persecution of witches and other episodes of medieval superstition to contemporary psychiatric treatments for the insane (Aberth 2003, 240). Despite its claims to historical objectivity, *Häxan* depends mostly on fictional vignettes in an undated "medieval" past, filled with scenes of sexuality and violence that shocked audiences throughout the twentieth century. The film ends with a dramatic scene of an accused witch being burned at the stake in an unspecific "medieval" scene, which is strikingly similar to the burning of Joan of Arc in the contemporary silent film *Passion of Joan of Arc* (dir. Carl Theodor Dreyer, 1928). Such images have come to represent the Middle Ages in a nutshell for modern audiences: medieval people were blindly superstitious, believing in witches and murdering innocent women in the name of that belief.

PRIMARY DOCUMENTS

MANUSCRIPT ILLUMINATION OF WOMEN ON BROOMSTICKS (1451)

Perhaps the earliest European depiction of stereotypical female "witches" on broomsticks comes from the very end of the Middle Ages, in a manuscript from 1451 of Martin LeFranc's verse compilation Le champion des dames *("The Champion of Women"), first written about 1440. Most of his work praises great women but he also describes some corrupt and sinful ladies, such as these "witches." They are not called witches but rather "Des Vaudoises," that is, "Waldensians," a heretical group that arose in the twelfth century and followed the teachings of a French merchant named Peter Waldo or Valdès. By the end of the Middle Ages the term "Vaudoise" could be used to apply to any heretic (Feminae 2014). Apart from the magical broomsticks, there is nothing else about these women that links them to stereotypical "witches."*

Source: Earliest image of women on broomsticks, possibly by Barthélemy Poignare, in a 1451 manuscript of Martin Le Franc, *Le champion des dames*, Paris.

ALBRECHT DÜRER, *WITCH RIDING BACKWARDS ON A GOAT* (1500)

The depiction of a witch as sexualized, demonic, and flying is primarily a Renaissance creation, and not medieval. One of the more influential images in shaping our modern stereotypes of witches is Albrecht Dürer's engraving of a witch riding backward on a goat (rather than a broomstick, which was already commonly asserted at this time). Dürer also made another engraving of four witches in 1497, and the two images reflect contemporary German interests in female witchcraft. Compare the following engraving with Dürer's contemporary woodcut of a men's bathhouse in chapter 3.

Source: Albrecht Dürer. 1500. "Witch Riding Backwards on a Goat." Image from Museum of New Zealand.

JULES MICHELET, *LA SORCIÈRE: THE WITCH OF THE MIDDLE AGES* (1862)

Jules Michelet (1798–1874) was one of the greatest historians of nineteenth-century France, and is best known for his monumental Histoire de France *(1855). Equally influential was his shorter work,* La Sorcière *("The Witch"), from 1862. It is a bizarre work and totally lacking in any sources, notes, or dates, even by nineteenth-century standards. Michelet details for several hundred pages his view of the history of magic and witchcraft in Europe from antiquity to the Enlightenment, focusing on the witches who supposedly influenced every walk of medieval life. He paints vivid pictures of "witches" acting as doctors, making love potions, advising and tricking kings and queens, lords and ladies, and supplanting the religious authority of priests and bishops. Even though most of his evidence comes from the fifteenth and sixteenth centuries—a point he occasionally admits—Michelet describes demonic witches as a broadly medieval phenomenon. In the chapter excerpted here, Michelet continues his lengthy discourse on the rise and fall of "Sabbaths" or witches' gatherings in the Middle Ages, which he sees as already in decline by the time they were actively persecuted in the fifteenth century.*

Let no one hastily conclude from the foregoing chapter that I attempt to whiten, to acquit entirely, the dismal bride of the Devil. If she often did good, she could also do no small amount of ill. There is no great power which is not abused. And this one had three centuries of actual reigning, in the interlude between two worlds, the older dying and the new struggling painfully to begin. The Church, which in the quarrels of the sixteenth century will regain some of her strength, at least for fighting, in the fourteenth is down in the mire. Look at the truthful picture drawn by Clémangis. The nobles, so proudly arrayed in their new armour, fall all the more heavily at Crécy, Poitiers, Agincourt. All who survive end by being prisoners in England. What a theme for ridicule! The citizens, the very peasants make merry and shrug their shoulders. This general absence of the lords gave, I fancy, no small encouragement to the Sabbath gatherings which had always taken place, but at this time might first have grown into vast popular festivals.

How mighty the power thus wielded by Satan's sweetheart, who cures, foretells, divines, calls up the souls of the dead; who can throw a spell upon you, turn you into a hare or wolf, enable you to find a treasure, and, best of all, ensure your being beloved! It is an awful power which combines all others. How could a stormy soul, a soul most commonly gangrened, and sometimes grown utterly wayward, have helped employing it to wreak her hate and revenge; sometimes even out of a mere delight in malice and uncleanness?

All that once was told the confessor, is now imparted to her: not only the sins already done, but those also which folk purpose doing. She holds each by her shameful secret, by the avowal of her uncleanest desires. To her they entrust both their bodily and mental ills; the lustful heats of a blood inflamed and soured; the ceaseless prickings of some sharp, urgent, furious desire.

To her they all come: with her there is no shame. In plain blunt words they beseech her for life, for death, for remedies, for poisons. Thither comes a young woman, to ask through her teats for the means of saving her from the fruits of her sin. Thither comes the step-mother—a common theme in the Middle Ages—to say that the child of a former marriage eats well and lives long. Thither comes the sorrowing wife whose children year by year are born only to die. And now, on the other hand, comes a youth to buy at any cost the burning draught that shall trouble the heart of some haughty dame, until, forgetful of the distance between them, she has stooped to look upon her little page. . . .

We must now speak of the *Sabbaths*; a word which at different times clearly meant quite different things. Unhappily, we have no detailed accounts of these gatherings earlier than the reign of Henry IV [of France, r. 1589–1610]. By that time they were nothing more than a great lewd farce carried on under the cloak of witchcraft. But these very descriptions of a thing so greatly corrupted are marked by certain antique touches that tell of the successive periods and the different forms through which it had passed.

We may set out with this firm idea that, for many centuries, the serf led the life of a wolf or a fox; that he was *an animal of the night*, moving about, I may say, as little as possible in the daytime, and truly living in the night alone.

Still, up to the year 1000, so long as the people made their own saints and legends, their daily life was not to them uninteresting. Their nightly Sabbaths were only a slight relic of paganism. They held in fear and honour the Moon, so powerful over the good things of earth. Her chief worshippers, the old women, burn small candles to *Dianom*—the Diana of yore, whose other names were Luna and Hecate. The Lupercal (or wolf-man) is always following the women and children, disguised indeed under the dark face of ghost Hallequin (Harlequin). The Vigil of Venus was kept as a holiday precisely on the first of May. On Midsummer Day they kept the Sabaza by sacrificing the he-goat of Bacchus Sabasius. In all this there was no mockery; nothing but a harmless carnival of serfs.

But about the year 1000 the church is wellnigh shut against the peasant through the difference between his language and hers. By 1100 her services became quite unintelligible. Of the mysteries played at the church-doors [i.e ., religious plays], he has retained chiefly the comic side, the ox and the ass, etc. On these he makes Christmas carols, which grow ever more and more burlesque, forming a true Sabbatic literature.

Are we to suppose that the great and fearful rising of the twelfth century had no influence on these mysteries, on this night-life of the *wolf*, the *game bird*, the *wild quarry*. The great sacraments of rebellion among the serfs, when they drank of each other's blood, or ate of the ground by way of solemn pledge, may have been celebrated at the Sabbaths. The "Marseillaise" of that time, sung by night rather than day, was perhaps a Sabbatic chant:—"Nous sommes hommes commes ils sont! Tout aussi grand coeur nous avons! tout autant souffrir nous pouvons!" ["We are fashioned of one clay: big as theirs our hearts are aye: We can bear as much as they."]

. . . Of such a nature were the Sabbaths before 1300. Before they could take the startling form of open warfare against the God of those days, much more was needed still, and especially these two things: not only a descending into the very depths of despair, but also *an utter losing of respect for anything*.

To this pass they do not come until the fourteenth century, under the Avignon popes, and during the Great Schism; when the Church with two heads seems no longer a church; when the king and all his nobles, being in shameful captivity to the English, are extorting the means of ransom from their oppressed and outraged people. Then do the Sabbaths take the grand and horrible form of the *Black Mass*, of a ritual upside down, in which Jesus is defied and bidden to thudder on the people if He can. In the thirteenth century this devilish drama was still impossible, through the horror it would have caused. And later again, in the fifteenth, when everything, even suffering itself, had become exhausted, so fierce an outburst could not have issued forth; so monstrous an invention no one would have essayed. It could only have belonged to the age of Dante.

Source: Michelet, Jules. 1863. *La sorcière: The Witch of the Middle Ages*. Translated by L. J. Trotter. London: Simpkin, Marshall, and Co., 131–33, 143–46. Italics are in the original.

What Really Happened

Medieval people did believe in magic. The fiction we are concerned with in this chapter is the idea that medieval people believed in sexualized and demonic female "witches" and violently persecuted innocent women accused of witchcraft. This complex of ideas and actions began to take hold only during the fifteenth century and was most prominent during the sixteenth and seventeenth centuries. Only one woman was executed for witchcraft in the Middle Ages before the fifteenth century: Petronilla of Meath, a barmaid in Kilkenny, Ireland, was accused in 1324 by her employer Dame Alice Kyteler of sacrificing to demons, undermining the Church, and brewing poisonous potions. Kyteler herself was accused of sorcery and fled the country, but poor Petronilla was caught, tried, tortured, and burned at the stake. Her trial is often considered the first official witchcraft trial in Europe, but it is worth emphasizing that none had occurred before this and few others would happen for another century.

Serious discussion of the stereotypical female witch began in the 1480s, and the most active period of "witch hysteria" was in the decades 1560–1630. It is telling that Richard Kieckhefer, in his book *Magic in the Middle Ages*, widely considered one of the best surveys of this topic in English, does not discuss the stereotypical female witch at all except for the last few pages, where the rise of the witch trials is treated as an event primarily after the Middle Ages (2000, 194–200). The image of the sexualized, demonic female magic user that lies behind most of our modern conceptions of a "witch" is a creation of the Renaissance and the early modern eras. What is more, most witch-hunts were led by secular leaders in Protestant lands, like Germany and the American colonies, and not by Catholic Church leaders, even though it was Catholic theologians of the fifteenth century who first established the standard definition of the witch. Nonetheless, all of the four major European Christian churches after the Reformation— Catholic, Lutheran, Calvinist, and Anglican—promoted belief in witches and called for their eradication. Tragically, many women (and a few men) were burned as witches, but not during the Middle Ages; rather, most of them were burned in the supposedly enlightened age of Galileo and Isaac Newton in the seventeenth century.

Medieval beliefs in magic before the fifteenth century took a wide variety of forms and can be difficult to define. For example, we find contradictory statements about "witches" in the capitularies (royal ordinances) of Charlemagne. He issued the "Capitulary for Saxony" in 789 to control the pagan Saxons he had been conquering and forcibly converting to Christianity. Many of the rulings in this capitulary condemn beliefs supposedly held by these pagans, including a belief in witches (here called *strigae* in Latin): "If any one deceived by the devil shall have believed, after the manner of the pagans, that any man or woman is a witch and eats men, and on this account shall have burned the person, or shall have given the person's flesh to others to eat, or shall have eaten it himself, let him be punished by a capital sentence" (*Translations and Reprints from the Original Sources of European History* 1900, 2), In this instance, it is the misguided belief in witches and not witchcraft itself that is punishable by death. These *strigae* can be women or men, and bear little resemblance to later descriptions of "witches." Yet a few years later in 802, after he was crowned Roman Emperor, Charlemagne issued his lengthy and important "Capitulary for the Embassy," which includes orders for how the counts in his empire should perform justice. They "will not, under any pretext, induced by reward or flattery, dare to conceal thieves, robbers, or murderers, adulterers, magicians and wizards or witches, or any godless men, but will rather give them up that they may be bettered and chastised by the law: so that, God permitting, all these evils may be removed from the Christian people" (Henderson 1905, 197). Documents from throughout the Early Middle Ages demonstrate this ambivalence, some condemning belief in magic or witchcraft, while others condemning magicusers themselves and implying a belief in the reality of harmful magic.

A good example of genuine medieval attitudes about magic and witchcraft can be gleaned from penitential manuals, books designed to teach priests how to identify and punish a wide range of sins. One of the most influential penitential manuals from the central Middle Ages is the *Corrector, sive Medicus* ("Corrector, or the Physician"), which was written or copied by Burchard, bishop of Worms, around 1020 and included in his *Decretum*, a compilation of canon (church) law. In the excerpt from the *Corrector* in the Primary Documents, Burchard outlines a wide variety of "magical" or superstitious practices. Most of these involve divination of future events (and one even condemns the practice of making New Year's resolutions!), but some were intended to harm people and their animals, change the weather, or cause people to love or hate one another. Burchard does not believe in any of these practices, for the sin that must be punished is the belief that these practices have any effect. Women feature prominently in this and other works as those who commonly believe these superstitions, but they are not described as "witches" or punished by burning.

For the next four centuries after Burchard, most descriptions of "magic" either continue to condemn magical practices as mere superstition or represent it as a learned art, available only to the men (mostly clerics) who attended the cathedral schools and universities of the High Middle Ages. Beginning in the eleventh century, European scholars began to translate a great number of Arabic books into Latin. Many of these were on Greek philosophy, medicine, or mathematics, but they also included the "occult sciences" of magic, alchemy, and astrology (Kieckhefer 2000, 116–50). These works taught learned Europeans (almost entirely men in this case) that magic was real and was a secret and difficult art. The new magicuser of the High Middle Ages had to master knowledge of the stars, the properties of stones, and (in the most insidious cases) the nature of demons. Even though later female witches came to be identified with devil worship, most medieval demonology was practiced by male necromancers. The Church typically condemned this necromancy, even though most of its practitioners were monks and clergy.

It was only in the fifteenth century that Church theologians began to regularly link suspicions of women, the hunting of heretics, and the condemnation of demonology to create the concept of the female witch. While they allowed the possibility of "natural magic," usable for good purposes and available mostly to learned men, the magic of women became inherently demonic, anti-Christian, and punishable as heresy. It was especially the official inquisitors of the Church, most of whom were German Dominican friars, who transformed witchcraft from the early medieval *maleficium*, available to anyone and not necessarily associated with the devil, into its familiar form of female-dominated, demonic sorcery. Notable among these Dominicans are Johannes Nider, who wrote one of the first witchcraft treatises, *Formicarius* ("Anthill") in 1436, and Heinrich Kramer, who write the *Malleus Maleficarum* ("Hammer of Witches") in 1486. This latter work is excerpted in the Primary Documents. These men and other fifteenth-century authors would draw on a thousand and more years of the history of magic and heresy to craft our familiar picture of the witch. Their works provided the evidence and tools necessary for the witch-hunts of the early modern period, not of the Middle Ages.

PRIMARY DOCUMENTS

BURCHARD OF WORMS, "CORRECTOR, OR THE PHYSICIAN," FROM HIS *DECRETUM* (ca. 1020)

Burchard, bishop of Worms (ca. 950–1025) wrote an influential collection of canon (church) law around 1020 known as the Decretum. *The nineteenth of the twenty books in his* Decretum *is known as the* Corrector, sive Medicus *("Corrector, or the Physician"), and takes the form of a "penitential," or a book listing the penances for various sins and crimes. He probably did not write this himself but incorporated a penitential that was already circulating. Such penitentials were composed and copied throughout the early Middle Ages, but this one was read especially widely through its inclusion in the* Decretum. *Among the sins listed in this penitential are those concerning magic, and the sin is not so much the performance of these acts but believing that they have any effect. In this period, there is little evidence that Church authorities believed in magic or witches.*

On the Magic Art

Have you violated a tomb, in such a way I say, that when you saw someone buried, you broke into their tomb at night and stole their clothing? If you have done this, do two years of penance on the required days.

Have you consulted magicians and invited them into your houses for the sake of asking for something by their wicked art, or of avoiding something. Or, following the custom of the pagans who could foretell divinations for you, have you asked about future events from them, as if from a prophet, or have you invited in those people who cast lots or who hope to know future events through those lots, or those who work with auguries and enchantments? If you have done this, do two years of penance on the required days.

Have you observed the pagan traditions, which fathers have always passed on to their sons as if by hereditary right (with the devil's aid) right up into these days: that is, have you worshipped the elements, namely the moon and sun, or the course of the stars, the new moon, or the eclipse, in such a way that you think you can restore its glow by the aid of your shouting? Or do you think that the elements can assist you or you can assist them, or have you observed the new moon for building a house or performing marriages? If you have done this, do two years of penance on the required days, because it is written: "Everything whatsoever that you perform in word or deed, do this in the name of our Lord Jesus Christ."

Have you observed the Kalends of January according to the pagan rituals, so that you do something more than you did previously on account of the new year, or afterwards are accustomed to do, in such a way I say that you prepare the table in your house with stones or sumptuous foods, or you lead singers and dancers through the towns and open places, or you sit on top of the roof of your house, having drawn a circle around yourself with a sword, so that you could see and understand there what will happen to you in the coming year? Or have you sat at the crossroads on a bull's skin so that you could know your future? Or have you cooked bread on the preceding night, marked with your own name, so that if it rises well, and should bake solid and tall, from that you foresee prosperity for your life in the coming year? Therefore, because you have relinquished God your creator, and turned yourself toward idols and those empty things, and have made yourself apostate, do two years of penance on the required days.

Have you made ligatures [magical knots], enchantments, and the other various fascinations which wicked men, swineherds, or cowherds, and hunters sometimes make, while they say diabolical charms over bread or herbs, and over certain wicked knots, and they hide these things either in a tree, or throw them into the crossing of two or three roads, so they might free their animals or dogs from disease or harm, and damage those of another? If you have done this, do two years of penance on the required days. . . .

Have you gathered medicinal herbs with enchantments other than the Symbol and the Lord's Prayer, that is, by singing the *Credo in Deum* and *Pater Noster*? If you have done otherwise, do ten days of penance on bread and water.

Did you go someplace to pray other than to a church or to some other religious place which your bishop or your priest showed to you, that is, either to springs, or to stones, or to trees, or to crossroads, and at that place did you burn a candle or torch in veneration of that place, or did you bring there bread or some other offering, or did you eat there or request in that place some sort of health for your body or soul? If you have done this, or consented to it, do three years of penance on the required days.

Have you cast lots in books or on tables, as many are wont to do, who presume to tell the future in Psalters and in Gospel Books, or in other things of this sort? If you have done this, do ten days of penance on broad and water.

Have you believed in or were a participant in that perfidious act, namely when enchanters and those who call themselves Senders of Storms are able to change the weather or the minds of men through the incantation of demons? If you have believed, or were a participant, do one year of penance on the required days.

Have you believed in or were a participant in that unbelievable act, namely that there exists a woman who can changes the minds of men through certain wicked words and incantations, that is, either from hatred to love, or from love to hatred, or that she can destroy or snatch away the men's goods by her bewitching acts? If you have believed, or were a participant, do one year of penance on the required days.

Have you believed that there is a woman who can do what certain women, deceived by the devil, affirm that they ought to do either by necessity or by command: that is, with a crowd of demons, transformed into the likeness of women, which common foolishness calls "Holda," on specific nights they can ride on beasts and count themselves among this assembly? If you have been a participant in this ridiculous belief, you ought to do penance for one year on the required days.

Source: Burchard of Worms. 1853. *Corrector, sive Medicus.* In *Burchardi Wormaciensis Ecclesiae Episcopi Decretorum Libri Viginti.* In *Patrologia Latina* 140, edited by J.-P. Migne. Paris, cols. 537–1037, at cols. 960–62. New translation.

HEINRICH KRAMER AND JACOB SPRENGER, *MALLEUS MALEFICARUM,* "THE HAMMER OF WITCHES" (1486)

By far the most important book in the history of witchcraft is the witch-hunting manual Malleus Maleficarum, *or "Hammer of Witches." It was written in 1487 by the Dominican inquisitors Heinrich Kramer (also called Heinrich Institoris) and Jacob Sprenger. Kramer is believed to have written the entire work and used Sprenger's name without permission to add greater authority to the book. The* Malleus *formed the foundation for almost all witch trials up through the eighteenth century, among both Catholics and Protestants, and shaped the popular conception of witches to this day. It is a lengthy and detailed treatise, using the format and terminology of later medieval scholastic philosophy to define witches and provide canonical justifications for persecuting them. As the passages here demonstrate, the authors understood witches to worship and copulate with the devil, to murder children, and to be able to fly.*

Part I. Question VI. *Concerning Witches who copulate with Devils.*

Why is it that Women are chiefly addicted to Evil superstitions?

There is also, concerning witches who copulate with devils, much difficulty in considering the methods by which such abominations are consummated. On the part of the devil: first, of what element the body is made that he assumes; secondly, whether the act is always accompanied by the injection of semen received from another; thirdly, as to time and place, whether he commits this act more frequently at one time than at another; fourthly, whether the act is invisible to any who may be standing by. And on the part of the women, it has to be inquired whether only they who were themselves conceived in this filthy manner are often visited by devils; or secondly, whether it is those who were offered to devils by midwives at the time of their birth; and thirdly, whether the actual venereal delectation of such is of a weaker sort. But we cannot here reply to all these questions, both because we are only engaged in a general study, and because in the second part of this work they are all singly explained by their operations, as will appear in the fourth chapter, where mention is made of each separate method. Therefore, let us now chiefly consider women; and first, why this kind of perfidy is found more in so fragile a sex than in men. And our inquiry will first be general, as to the general conditions of women; secondly, particular, as to which sort of women are found to be given to superstition and witchcraft; and thirdly, specifically with regard to midwives, who surpass all others in wickedness. . . .

What sort of Women are found to be above all Others Superstitious and Witches.

As to our second inquiry, what sort of women more than others are found to be superstitious and infected with witchcraft; it must be said, as was shown in the preceding inquiry, that three general vices appear to have special dominion over wicked women, namely, infidelity, ambition, and lust. Therefore they are more than others inclined towards witchcraft, who more than others are given to these vices. Again, since of these vices the last chiefly predominates, women being insatiable, etc., it follows that those among ambitious women are more deeply infected who are more hot to satisfy their filthy lusts; and such are adulteresses, fornicatresses, and the concubines of the Great.

Now there are, as it is said in the Papal Bull, seven methods by which they infect with witchcraft the venereal act and the conception of the womb: First, by inclining the minds of men to inordinate passion; second, by obstructing their generative force; third, by removing the members accommodated to that act; fourth, by changing men into beasts by their magic art; fifth, by destroying the generative force in women; sixth, by procuring abortion; seventh, by offering children to devils, besides other animals and fruits of the earth with which they work much harm. And all these will be considered later; but for present let us give our minds to the injuries towards men.

And first concerning those who are bewitched into an inordinate love or hatred, this is a matter of a sort that it is difficult to discuss before the general intelligence. Yet it must be granted that it is a fact. For S. Thomas (IV, 34) [referring here to Thomas Aquinas's *Summa Theologiae*], treating of obstructions caused by witches, shows that God allows the devil greater power against men's venereal acts than against their other actions; and gives this reason, that this is likely to be so, since those women are chiefly apt to be witches who are most disposed to such acts.

For he says that, since the first corruption of sin by which man became the slave of the devil came to us through the act of generation, therefore greater power is allowed by God to the devil in this act than in all others. Also the power of witches is more apparent in serpents, as it is said, than in other animals, because through the means of a serpent the devil tempted woman. For this reason also, as is shown afterwards, although matrimony is a work of God, as being instituted by Him, yet it is sometimes wrecked by the work of the devil: not indeed through main force, since then he might be though stronger than God, but with the permission of God, by causing some temporary or permanent impediment in the conjugal act.

And touching this we may say what is known by experience; that these women satisfy their filthy lusts not only in themselves, but even in the mighty ones of the age, of whatever state and condition; causing by all sorts of witchcraft the death of their souls through the excessive infatuation of carnal love, in such a way that for no shame or persuasion can they desist from such acts. And through such men, since witches will not permit any harm to come to them either from themselves or from others once they have them in their power, there arises the great danger of the time, namely, the extermination of the Faith. And in this way do witches every day increase.

And would that this were not true according to experience. But indeed such hatred is aroused by witchcraft between those joined in the sacrament of matrimony, and such freezing up of the generative forces, that men are unable to perform the necessary action for begetting offspring. But since love and hate exist in the soul, which even the devil cannot enter, lest these things should seem incredibly to anyone, they must be inquired into; and by meeting argument with argument the matter will be made clear.

Part II, Question I, Chapter III. *How they are Transported from Place to Place*

And now we must consider their ceremonies and in what manner they proceed in their operations, first in respect of their actions towards themselves and in their own persons. And among their chief operations are being bodily transported from place to place, and to practice carnal connexion with Incubus devils, which we shall treat of separately, beginning with their bodily vectification [i.e., travel]. But here it must be noted that this transvection offers a difficulty, which has often been mentioned, arising from one single authority, where it is said: It cannot be admitted as true that certain wicked women, perverted by Satan and seduced by the illusions and phantasms of devils, do actually, as they believe and profess, ride in the night-time on certain beasts with Diana, a goddess of the Pagans, or with Herodias and an innumerable multitude of women, and in the untimely silence of night pass over immense tracts of land, and have to obey her in all things as their Mistress, etc. Wherefore the priest of God ought to preach to the people that this is altogether false, and that such phantasms are sent not by God, but by an evil Spirit to confuse the minds of the faithful. For Satan himself transforms himself into various shapes and forms; and by deluding in dreams the mind which he holds captive, leads it through devious ways, etc. . . .

Now the following is their method of being transported. They take the unguent which, as we have said, they make at the devil's instruction from the limbs of children, particularly of those whom they have killed before baptism, and anoint with it a chair or a broomstick; whereupon they are immediately carried up into the air, either by day or by night, and either visibly or, if they wish, invisibly; for the devil can conceal a body by the interposition of some other substance, as was shown in the First Part of the treatise where we spoke of the glamours and illusions caused by the devil. And although the devil for the most part performs this by means of this unguent, to the end that children should be deprived of the grace of baptism and of salvation, yet he often seems to affect the same transvection without its use. For at times he transports the witches on animals, which are not true animals but devils in that form; and sometimes even without any exterior help they are visibly carried solely by the operation of the devil's power.

Here is an instance of a visible transportation in the daytime. In the town of Waldshut on the Rhine, in the diocese of Constance, there was a certain witch who was so detested by the townsfolk that she was not invited to the celebration of a wedding which, however, nearly all the other townsfolk were present. Being indignant because of this, and wishing to be revenged, she summoned a devil and, telling him the cause of her vexation, asked him to raise a hailstorm and drive all the wedding guests from their dancing; and the devil agreed, and raising her up, carried her through the air to a hill near the town, in the sight of some shepherds. And since, as she afterwards confessed, she had no water to pour into the trench (for this, as we shall show, is the method they use to raise hailstorms), she made a small trench and filled it with her urine instead of water, and stirred it with her finger, after their custom, with the devil standing by. Then the devil suddenly raised that liquid up and sent a violent storm of hailstones which fell only on the dancers and townsfolk. And when they had dispersed and were discussing among themselves the cause of that storm, the witch shortly afterwards entered the town; and this greatly aroused their suspicions. But when the shepherds had told what they had seen, their suspicions became almost a certainty. So she was arrested, and confessed that she had done this thing because she had not been invited to the wedding: and for this, and for many other witchcrafts which she had perpetrated, she was burned.

Source: Heinrich Kramer and Jacob Sprenger. 1928. *Malleus Maleficarum.* Edited and translated by Montague Summers. London. Part I, Question VI; Part II, Question I, Chapter III.

Further Reading

Aberth, John. 2003. *A Knight at the Movies: Medieval History on Film.* New York: Routledge.

Bailey, Michael D. 2007. *Magic and Superstition in Europe: A Concise History from Antiquity to the Present.* Lanham, MD: Rowman & Littlefield.

Baxstrom, Richard, and Todd Meyers. 2015. *Realizing the Witch: Science, Cinema, and the Mastery of the Invisible.* New York: Fordham University Press.

Brown, Dan. 2003. *The Da Vinci Code.* New York: Doubleday.

Feminae: Medieval Women and Gender Index. 2014. "Two Waldensian Witches, from *Le champion des dames.*" https://inpress.lib.uiowa.edu /feminae/DetailsPage.aspx?Feminae_ID=31909.

Garinet, Jules. 1818. *Histoire de la Magie en France depuis le commencement de la Monarchie jusqu'a nos jours.* Paris: Foulon et Compagnie.

Henderson, Ernest F. 1905. *Select Historical Documents of the Middle Ages.* London: George Bell and Sons.

Hughes, Pennethorne. 1965. *Witchcraft.* Baltimore: Penguin Books.

Kieckhefer, Richard. 2000. *Magic in the Middle Ages.* Cambridge: Cambridge University Press.

Levack, Brian P. 2015a. *The Witch-Hunt in Early Modern Europe*. 4th ed. New York: Routledge.

Levack, Brian P. 2015b. *The Witchcraft Sourcebook*. 2d ed. New York: Routledge.

Mackay, Charles. 1852. *Extraordinary Popular Delusions and the Madness of Crowds*. 2d ed. 3 vols. London: Office of the National Illustrated Library.

Manchester, William. 1992. *A World Lit Only by Fire. The Medieval Mind and the Renaissance: Portrait of an Age*. Boston: Little, Brown, and Co.

Michelet, Jules. 1862. *La sorcière*. Paris: E. Dentu.

Michelet, Jules. 1863. *La sorcière: The Witch of the Middle Ages*. Translated by L. J. Trotter. London: Simpkin, Marshall, and Co.

Pavlac, Brian A. 2012. "Ten Common Errors and Myths about the Witch Hunts, Corrected and Commented." *Prof. Pavlac's Women's History Resource Site*. http://departments.kings.edu/womens_history/witch/werror.html

Translations and Reprints from the Original Sources of European History. 1900. Vol. 6, no. 5. Philadelphia: University of Pennsylvania Press.

Tuczay, Christa. 2007. "The Nineteenth Century: Medievalism and Witchcraft." In *Palgrave Advances in Witchcraft Historiography*, edited by Jonathan Barry and Owen Davies, 52–68. Houndsmills, Basingstoke, UK: Palgrave Macmillan.

11

The Black Death Led to Masked Plague Doctors and Ring around the Rosie

What People Think Happened

Many of the most popular subjects from the Middle Ages are appealing to modern audiences and even romantic, such as castles and cathedrals, or knights and ladies. But another popular medieval subject is much darker, and reflects a modern desire to depict the Middle Ages as filthy, frightening, and primitive (see chapter 3 on the topic of filthy peasants). That subject is plague, also known as the Black Death. Plague is an acute infectious disease caused by the bacterium *Yersinia pestis*. Its symptoms, like swollen lymph nodes, bloody coughing, and internal hemorrhaging, are gruesome and painful. The disease is frequently fatal, both in the Middle Ages and today. The swellings are the most notorious sign of the disease and were called *buboes* from the Greek for "groin," a common location for the lymphatic swellings. Thus the disease is often called bubonic plague, even when the swellings do not appear. Even today, when we have antibiotics to treat plague and a vaccine to prevent it, several dozen or hundred people die each year worldwide from the disease, especially in the island nation of Madagascar, the Democratic Republic of the Congo, and the southwestern United States.

Although plague still exists today, it is usually understood as the archetypal medieval disease, and its presence is used as a sign to the reader or viewer that "we're now in the Middle Ages." There is some good reason for

this, as the medieval Black Death killed a larger percentage of the population than any known human disease, around 50 percent of Europe and the
Middle East, though in terms of actual numbers, more people died in the
1918–1919 influenza epidemic and in the current HIV-AIDS epidemic
(Green 2015a, 9). However, some history books and websites go too far in
this association of the plague with the Middle Ages, and paint the entire
medieval era as constantly overwhelmed by the Black Death. William Manchester, for example, claims in his best-selling book *A World Lit Only by
Fire*: "The Dark Ages were stark in every dimension. Famines and plagues,
culminating in the Black Death and its recurring pandemics, repeatedly
thinned the population" (Manchester 1992, 5). Plague likewise serves as
the backdrop for medieval movies, from comedies like *Monty Python and
the Holy Grail* (1975) to thrillers like *The Season of the Witch* (2011) and
classic art films like *The Seventh Seal* (1957). Modern audiences, whether
seeking entertainment or history, constantly return to macabre descriptions
and images of millions of people dying from this gruesome disease, as they
foolishly tried to fight off the unseen killer with herbs, spells, and prayers.

Two images in particular constantly recur in popular descriptions of
the Black Death: plague doctors with beaked, birdlike masks and children
singing and dancing "Ring around the Rosie" as a simplified description of
the plague. Both of these images are usually attributed to the Middle Ages
and are used as examples of the desperation and ignorance of medieval
Europeans in the face of the plague, when they had no understanding of
germ theory or of the plague pathogen *Yersinia pestis*. When these themes
of confusion, desperation, and music during the Black Death are combined, we get scenes like the monks in *Monty Python and the Holy Grail*
who try to fend off the plague by marching through town chanting *Pie
Jesu Domine* ("O Merciful Lord Jesus"), and rhythmically hitting themselves on the head with boards. Even though most people understand this
movie to be a satire on medieval beliefs, and not actually representative of
the Middle Ages, it is nonetheless common for students to take this movie
scene in particular as suggestive of genuine medieval reactions to plague.
We will thus examine in this chapter the history and context of plague
doctor costumes and "Ring around the Rosie" to understand what both
are really about and how neither is actually medieval.

How the Story Became Popular

The image of the beaked plague doctor is truly terrifying, while also
being ridiculous. It serves as a favorite example of how different the

Middle Ages supposedly were in their approaches to medicine and public health. Brief histories of the Black Death, especially those written
for children, claim that plague doctors in the fourteenth century wore
this costume. For example, Gary Jeffrey and Alessandro Poluzzi include
the plague doctor in a book on the medieval *Black Death* (2013, 45),
while Holly Cefrey uses it to represent the Middle Ages in a book on
the entire history of the plague to the modern day (2001, 14). Likewise,
Susan Wise Bauer, author of numerous popular history books for children and adults, includes an image of a "medieval" plague doctor in her
Story of the World (2007, 229).

Images and descriptions of the beaked plague doctor, however, can
only be traced back to the seventeenth century, when a French account
states that in 1619 Charles de Lorme (1584–1678), chief physician to
Louis XIII, recommended the use of such a costume. He describes a suit
made entirely of Moroccan goat leather, including boots, breeches, a long
coat, hat, and gloves. The main feature of the costume is a beaklike mask,
about half a foot long, filled with perfume or aromatic herbs (Tibayrenc
2007, 680). Several museums in Europe have in their collections beaked
plague doctor masks, which they claim to come from genuine, eighteenth-
century plague doctor outfits.

Charles de Lorme's description is clearly matched by the first engraving
in the Primary Documents, perhaps our earliest image of the plague doctor. The German printer Gerhart Altzenbach made this engraving soon
after 1656, the year of a particular bad recurrence of the plague in Italy.
Even though De Lorme's account comes from France, almost all of our
evidence for beaked plague doctors comes from northern Italy, as can
be seen to this day in Venice, where plague doctor masks are a mainstay
of their Carnival festivities and tourist trade. Likewise, another French
account from 1721, a *Traité de la Peste* ("Treatise on the Plague") by one
Dr. Manget, includes an image of the plague doctor and specifies that
this costume, used by doctors during the last plague in Marseille, had its
origin in Italy (Manget 1721, vol. II, frontispiece).

According to the text of the 1656 Altzenbach engraving, which is
repeated in Latin, French, and German, the image shows what doctors
in Rome were supposedly wearing at that time to protect themselves
from breathing in the foul air around plague victims: a suit of thick, oiled
leather covering the entire body, along with a hat; crystal glasses to protect
the eyes; and a beaklike mask filled with aromatic spices. It is not clear
if Altzenbach had actually seen such doctors, or was basing his image off
of descriptions like that attributed to Charles de Lorme. The wand in

his hand is not magical, but is simply a stick either for warding off rats, indicating instructions, or lifting the patient's bedclothes (depending on which modern description you want to believe).

The primary logic behind the costume is that it would protect the doctor from *miasma*, the medieval and early modern term for poisoned or corrupted air, which they believed transmitted plague between people or which corrupted a person's humors and led to contracting the plague. *Miasma* was thought to come from various foul-smelling sources, such as corpses, swamps, and polluted urban areas. While late medieval people did not know about microscopic bacteria and viruses, they nonetheless grasped that something was wrong with the air when large groups of people suddenly got sick and died. *Miasma* theory persisted well into the nineteenth century among trained physicians, and still underlies popular ideas about air and health, such as the erroneous belief that dead bodies outside of coffins will "poison" the air or water supply.

According to popular, modern accounts of the Black Death, medieval doctors wore these costumes as they moved from house to house in a plague-stricken village. The costume was practical but also served to terrify people intentionally and let them know that plague had arrived in their community. Another seventeenth-century version of this image shows a group of children fleeing, apparently, in terror from the beaked plague doctor. This later image was copied directly from Gerhart Altzenbach's 1656 engraving, but its printer, Paul Fürst, added the title *Doctor Schnabel von Rom* ("Doctor Beaky from Rome") and a mocking description in a mix of Latin and German verse:

> You believe it's just a fable, what is written about Doctor Beaky. He flees the contagion and gets his wages from it. He seeks corpses to make a living, like a Crow in a garbage heap. Ah, believe it, and don't look away from here, because the plague rules over Rome. Who wouldn't be terrified of his little rod or stick. He speaks with it as if he were mute and points out his advice. So many people believe, without a doubt, that he is touched by a black devil. His purse is Hell and gold is the soul he fetches. (New translation from the Latin on the second engraving in the Primary Documents)

Clearly, Fürst and his audience considered this sort of plague doctor foreign and very strange. Fürst also added a new visual element: the plague doctor's wand has a winged hourglass at its tip, alluding to the ancient saying "time flies" (*tempus fugit*). This image does not reflect an actual physician's tool, but is a metaphorical emblem of death, making it clear that this doctor has not arrived to heal you. The elements of the image reinforce the moral of the poem: plague doctors are no help and will do nothing for you but take your money and, perhaps, your life.

More creative modern interpretations claim that the beaked mask was made in imitation of the birds that spread plague (they rarely do and were never thought to do so in the medieval or early modern periods), and that using sympathetic magic, the beaked costume could draw the infection out of the patient onto the costume. Likewise, some current descriptions of the plague costume claim that the eyepieces were made of red glass to ward off evil, that the costume came with leather pants to prevent the swelling of buboes in the groin area, or that the wide-brimmed hat was designed to keep off bacteria. There is no evidence of any of these claims from the surviving early modern images and descriptions of the beaked plague doctor costume.

*   *   *

A similar combination of miasma theory and herbal remedies lies behind popular explanations for the children's rhyme "Ring around the Rosie" (or "Ring around a rosy"). This myth is even more pervasive than that of the masked plague doctor. According to most descriptions of this rhyme, the lines are a coded description of the symptoms, treatment, and likely outcome of the bubonic plague:

> *Ring around a Rosie,*
> *A pocket full of posies,*
> *Ashes, ashes,*
> *We all fall down.*

Supposedly, the "rosie" is a red rash on the plague victim, apparently round or circular like a plague bubo. A "posy" is a small bouquet, so "a pocket full of posies" is understood to be a medieval remedy against plague, that is, the flowers and herbs carried by people to fend off infection from *miasma*, just like the herbs in the plague doctor's mask. "Ashes, ashes" is explained variously as a reference to the cremation of plague victims, the ashen color of a plague victim's skin, or as a corruption of "achoo, achoo" or "a-tishoo, a-tishoo," the sneezing of a sick person. "All fall down" is clearly a reference to the massive number of deaths caused by the plague. These interpretations are found in historical books intended for children, such as the aforementioned works by Bauer (2007, 42) and Cefrey (2001, 14) and Marty Gitlin's *The Totally Gross History of Medieval Europe* (2016, 35), as well as books for college students or adult audiences, like James C. Davis's *The Human Story* (2004, 191). Modern commentators on this rhyme claim that it was written in England during the Black Death of 1348 or the Great Plague of London in 1665, but that the "true" meaning was not uncovered until the twentieth century.

PRIMARY DOCUMENTS

GERHART ALTZENBACH, ENGRAVING OF A PLAGUE DOCTOR, 1656

The following engraving is one of the earliest images of the infamous "beaked" plague doctor of Rome, made by Gerhart Altzenbach in 1656. The engraving includes Latin, French, and German descriptions of the plague doctor's protective suit. Altzenbach may not have seen a real plague doctor suit and was instead basing his image on written descriptions by the French doctor Charles de Lorme, who made the earliest reference to the beaked suit in 1619. There is no evidence that such plague outfits existed in the Middle Ages.

Source: Gerhart Altzenbach. "Kleidung widder den Todt Anno 1656." Image from Yale University, Harvey Cushing/John Hay Whitney Medical Library.

PAUL FÜRST, "DER DOCTOR SCHNABEL VON ROM" ("DOCTOR BEAKY FROM ROME"), 1656

This second image is a satirical version of the previous engraving by Gerhart Altzenbach. Within a year of Altzenbach producing his serious engraving, another German printer, Paul Fürst, mocked the appearance and behavior of these beaked plague doctors. Fürst labeled his image "Doctor Schnabel von Rom" (Doctor Beaky from Rome) and criticizes the greed and ineffectiveness of plague doctors currently active in Rome. A translation of the text is given earlier in this chapter, in the section titled "How the Story Became Popular."

Source: Paul Fürst. "Der Doctor Schnabel von Rom." [1656] 1921. In *Die Karikatur und Satire in der Medizin: Medico-Kunsthistorische Studie von Professor Dr. Eugen Holländer*, by Eugen Holländer. 2d ed. Stuttgart: Ferdinand Enke, fig. 79, p. 171.

What Really Happened

Like many of the medieval fictions in this book, these popular ideas about the Black Death have some foundation in historical truth: plague is a real infectious disease, it has killed many millions of people, and it was explained in terms of *miasma* for some five centuries (ca. 1350–1850) until the advent of germ theory and the discovery of the plague bacterium, *Yersinia pestis*, in 1897 (it was called *Pasteurella pestis* after the microbiologist Louis Pasteur [1822–1895] until the 1970s). But to understand why the masked plague doctor and "Ring around the Rosie" are fictions about the Middle Ages, we need to establish some basic facts about the Black Death in the Middle Ages and early modern era.

Plague did kill millions of people in Europe and Asia, but it was not really a feature of the medieval period. For most of what we call the Middle Ages, roughly between 750 and 1350 CE, there was no plague in Europe, or any other significant epidemic diseases. (That isn't to say there weren't dangerous diseases, but rather that there were no widespread, highly contagious, infectious diseases in this period.) Epidemics of plague (also called pandemics, since they covered such a vast area) struck instead at the very beginning and very end of the Middle Ages (Byrne 2004, 5–6). The so-called First Plague Pandemic appeared in the 540s, with repeated outbreaks until the eighth century. The better-known "Black Death," or Second Plague Pandemic, began during the early fourteenth century in Central and East Asia, but is better known from its arrival in Europe and the Near East in the period 1347–1352 (Green 2015b). The Second Pandemic continued for some four centuries in Europe and Asia, returning every ten to twenty years, hitting some regions but not others. The Italian plague of 1656 and the Great Plague of London in 1665, mentioned earlier, are examples of later outbreaks in the Second Plague Pandemic.

The claims that "Ring around the Rosie" is actually a coded description of the plague plays on many modern myths about the Middle Ages, including the assumptions that medieval people were childish, unsophisticated, nearly illiterate, and powerless in the face of any natural disaster. The reality is that by the fourteenth century, Western Europe had a more sophisticated, urban, and educated culture than had existed in many centuries. The arrival of the plague in Europe in 1347 was greeted by the publication of numerous analytical descriptions of the disease, none of which are in code or reflect the childish tone of "Ring around the Rosie." In these treatises, written first in Latin and then in many of the European vernacular languages, physicians and scholars described the potential causes, symptoms, and prognosis of the plague, while also providing detailed instructions for its prevention and cure. Similar patterns can be seen in the Greek-speaking Byzantine Empire and in Arabic-speaking Islamic lands throughout North Africa and the Near East.

Hundreds of these documents, often called "plague tractates," survive from the fourteenth through eighteenth centuries in Europe, and not a single one mentions "Ring around the Rosie" or agrees with modern explanations of the rhyme. Iona and Peter Opie, the foremost experts in the history of children's rhymes, note that the plague explanation for "Ring around the Rosie" doesn't appear before the 1950s (Opie and Opie 1985, 221–22), and the full explanation as given previously appeared only in 1962 in James Leasor's *The Plague and the Fire*, a popular history of the 1665 plague of London (Leasor 1961, 126). Folklorists agree that the plague interpretation of the rhyme is not accurate and instead reflects the modern tendency, especially after World War II, to look for secret codes in curious documents and songs from the past. In most cases, the simplest interpretation of a rhyme like this is the most likely: it is about flowers, dancing, and literally falling down, all in the name of fun.

There are multiple problems with the popular interpretation of the rhyme. The most serious is that no evidence for the rhyme appears before the nineteenth century, and its earliest print appearances are from the 1880s. English literary historians are very familiar with rhymes that go back to the Middle Ages or early modern era, and it is highly unlikely that, if the rhyme were indeed four or six centuries old, no version would survive until the modern era. Moreover, the line "Ring around the Rosie" does not even appear until the twentieth century, and only in U.S. contexts. The oldest versions from the 1880s and 1890s are all from England and give variations on "ring a ring of roses," which would be difficult to interpret as a "rosy" mark on a plague victim's body. Again, it is even more unlikely that the more recent versions of a children's rhyme actually reflect a distant medieval original.

Even if the rhyme were significantly older than the nineteenth century and actually mentioned "ring around the rosie" in early versions (neither of which is true), no medieval account of plague describes plague symptoms in this fashion. Rather, they focus on the painful swellings on the neck, armpits, or groin, which blacken and sometimes burst, or the purple and black bruises (now known as *petechiae*) caused by internal hemorrhaging. Similarly, neither "ashes" nor "achoo" agree with medieval accounts of the plague. Plague victims were almost all buried, even if haphazardly, since that was expected of a proper Christian burial. Cremation was very rare, and plague would not be associated with "ashes." Nor do medieval accounts of plague focus on sneezing as a sign or symptom of the plague, in which case the interpretation of "ashes" as "achoo" does not hold up either.

When we do find rituals and songs actually related to the Black Death, they are clearly Christian in their language and purpose. Medieval people almost universally understood the plague both as a natural event and as God's punishment for their sins (they had no trouble accepting both science and religion). Even while medieval Christians sought natural remedies for the plague, they understood the need to do more and greater penances for sin, both individually and as communities. After 1347, popes and bishops ordered Christians throughout Europe to make religious processions around their villages and cities to ask God's forgiveness for their sins and to lift the plague from Europe.

For an example of a genuinely medieval song from the time of the Black Death, you can read the following translation of a medieval German song written by or for an extreme penitential group known as Flagellants (*flagella* is Latin for "whip"). Flagellants marched from town to town, dramatically whipping themselves until bloody, for the purpose of showing God that they truly repented for their sins and were taking upon themselves the sins of the whole world. They had appeared a few times before the Black Death in reaction to disasters other than the plague, but they became especially prominent in German lands during the year 1348, when numerous chroniclers report on their activities, movements, and songs. The pope condemned these Flagellants in 1349 because they were denying or usurping the sacramental authority of priests, and claiming that they, even though laymen and laywomen, had the power to preach and to perform miracles. Despite this condemnation, the "Ancient Song of the Flagellants," recorded here, is typical of later medieval attitudes toward the plague, and the centrality of religion in their attempts to ward off the disease.

If we are looking for a dance related to the plague, like the one associated with "Ring around the Rosie," we can find it in the fifteenth- and sixteenth-century paintings of the "Dance of Death" or *Danse Macabre*. The *Danse Macabre* was an allegorical poem, often accompanied by painted or printed images, in which men and women of every social class, pope and emperor at the start down to the peasants at the end, are danced off to death by a skeleton as a lesson in humility: everyone dies and you can't take your wealth or worldly status with you to the afterlife. In the following excerpt, translated from a 1460 German "Dance of Death" (*Vierzeiliger oberdeutscher Totentanz*), Death addresses the Holy Roman

Emperor at the start of the dance, and toward the end the Peasant himself speaks about the arrival of death:

Emperor, your sword won't help you out,
Sceptre and crown are worthless here.
I've taken you by the hand,
For you must come to my dance. . . .

I [the Peasant] had to work very much and very hard,
The sweat was running down my skin.
I'd like to escape death nonetheless,
But here I won't have any luck.

None of the later medieval versions of the *Danse Macabre* refers specifically to plague, just as can be seen in the Primary Documents in the case of the "Flagellant Song," but all were created in the context of the Second Pandemic. In every case of genuinely medieval songs, paintings, or dances related the Black Death, we can see that medieval people's reactions were far more sophisticated and more overtly religious than the supposedly medieval rhyme "Ring around the Rosie."

A third primary source is provided that reinforces the idea that medieval people thought deeply about the natural and supernatural causes of the plague and its effects on European society, without resorting to any metaphorical language of ashes and falling down. The Italian author Giovanni Boccaccio (1313–1375) survived the Black Death in Florence, which was hit worse than almost any city in Europe in the years 1347–1348. In the wake of the plague, around 1350, he wrote his famous collection of stories known as the *Decameron*. While most of the stories are humorous and few of them mention the plague, he wrote a serious preface to this work explaining the arrival of the plague in Florence, its symptoms, the attempts to avoid or treat it, and its consequences for Florentine society and faith. The stories of the *Decameron* were written to distract from the horrors of the Black Death.

*   *   *

If the belief that "Ring around the Rosie" is about the plague is a complete fiction, then the beaked plague doctor is at least halfway to the truth. As we saw earlier, there are abundant primary sources and perhaps genuine artifacts attesting to the existence of elaborate plague doctor costumes from at least the seventeenth century. But that period is not medieval.

While there is no official date for when the Middle Ages ended, most historians treat the medieval era as past by the time of Columbus (1492) or Martin Luther (1517). This isn't just a case of pointless arguing about dates: the seventeenth century is a very different time in Europe, politically, socially, and scientifically. The plague doctor costume is a product of this later, early modern culture, which saw the Scientific Revolution, the start of the Enlightenment, and which had already been through some three centuries of plague by the time we meet "Doctor Beaky."

Images of earlier doctors treating plague victims are rare, but they do exist in manuscripts, panel paintings, and printed books. None of them show this plague costume, but instead depict the physician in the typical robes of a late medieval scholar or gentleman, without any sort of mask (Boeckl 2000, 21, 26–29). The concern of most public health authorities in the fourteenth through seventeenth centuries was preventing contagion by keeping the *miasma* out of entire areas, rather than out of a single doctor's face (Hays 2009, 54–55). As late as the outbreak of 1630 in Tuscany, there is no sign of the masked plague doctor, but rather plague controls focus on fumigating houses to destroy *miasma*. This is confirmed in Carlo Cipolla's study of the 1630 plague in the Florentine suburb of Monte Lupo (Cipolla 1979) and in Giulia Calvi's study of plague politics in Florence itself (Calvi 1989, 155–96). Doctors in the later Middle Ages, and all the way until the early seventeenth century, were certainly concerned about pestilential *miasma* but had different ideas about how to protect the body than we find in the mid-seventeenth-century engravings.

Later medieval plague treatises provide all sorts of instructions for the physician or patients to protect themselves, but most of them concerned methods for keeping pestilential miasma out of the body or for keeping the humors balanced and the body strong enough to fight off the disease. (For more on humors and medieval medicine, see chapter 9.) Instead of focusing on the mouth and lungs, as we might do today to prevent the spread of airborne illnesses, the prevailing medical theory of the later fourteenth century focused on the pores, in the belief that miasma could enter the body through them. One of the most popular examples of a plague treatise was attributed to an otherwise unknown physician named John of Burgundy, and is reproduced here. Most of John's advice concerns eating or not eating certain foods to make sure that the pores stay properly closed. Some of his advice is clearly from the same school of thought that produced the later plague masks: make fires to clear the air or inhale strong-smelling substances: "ambergris, musk, rosemary and similar things if you are rich; zedoary, cloves, nutmeg, mace and similar things if you are poor." But instead of smelling these aromatics constantly, as was required by the seventeenth-century plague mask, the medieval reader of this plague manual only needed to smell them in the morning before heading outside. The current medical theory held that the body would remain fortified against plague for the rest of the day.

So what's the problem with the beaked plague doctor? It's not just that this costume first appears three centuries after the Black Death of 1347–1352, but that one image has been allowed to dominate all popular perceptions of the plague, at the expense of a monumental body of other evidence. And this is a problem not just with images of plague doctors, but with almost all images used to represent the Black Death in popular media, history textbooks, and scientific journals. Lori Jones and Richard Nevell have demonstrated that nearly every medieval image used to represent plague in modern publications and websites was not actually made in the first place to represent that disease (Jones and Nevell 2016). This perpetuation of misinformation has repercussions for both our historical and medical knowledge of the plague, because researchers have used those incorrectly labeled medieval images to represent supposedly medieval ideas about the plague.

The same situation has applied to the beaked plague doctor: the image is so omnipresent that it shapes popular and scholarly perceptions of how the Black Death was treated in the Middle Ages. Not only is the image not medieval, but it does not seem to have been common even in its brief heyday of the later seventeenth and early eighteenth centuries. Almost all surviving, genuine images of the beaked plague doctor appear to be imitations of the 1656 engravings discussed earlier. As we have seen, some of these images were not even meant as actual representations of physicians, but more objects of mockery and satire against the corrupt behavior of plague doctors. There is little written evidence suggesting any plague doctor actually wore such a costume, in the Middle Ages or during the Enlightenment, but there is no doubt that pictures of the costume grabbed the popular imagination at the time and have done so to this very day.

PRIMARY DOCUMENTS

THE ANCIENT SONG OF THE FLAGELLANTS (FOURTEENTH CENTURY?)

The following is an English translation of a medieval German Geisserlied, *or "Flagellant Song," apparently sung by roving bands of Flagellants during the*

Black Death. Note that plague is not mentioned explicitly, so the song could be used for any sort of natural or moral disaster, as flagellation and penitential processions were used in the Middle Ages to appease God's anger in any form. The singers variously address Jesus, his mother Mary, the Archangel Michael, each other, and different groups of sinners whom they blame for their current tragedies. All people are encouraged to give up their sins and live holier lives, but the singing Flagellants claim that they in particular, through their shocking penitential processions, will fend off Christ's anger and the potential destruction of the world.

Whoe'er to save his soul is fain,
Must pay and render back again.
His safety so shall he consult:
Help us, good Lord, to this result.
Ye that repent your crimes, draw nigh.
From the burning hell we fly,
From Satan's wicked company.
Whom he leads
With pitch he feeds.
If we be wise we this shall flee.
Maria! Queen! we trust in thee,
To move thy Son to sympathy.
Jesus Christ was captive led,
And to the cross was riveted.
The cross was reddened with his gore
And we his martyrdom deplore.
"Sinner, canst thou to me atone.
Three pointed nails, a thorny crown,
The holy cross, a spear, a wound,
These are the cruel pangs I found.
What wilt thou, sinner, bear for me?"
Lord, with loud voice we answer thee,
Accept our service in return,
And save us lest in hell we burn.
We, though thy death, to thee have sued.
For God in heaven we shed our blood:
This for our sins will work to good.
Blessed Maria! Mother! Queen!
Through thy loved Son's redeeming mean
Be all our wants to thee portrayed.

Aid us, Mother! spotless maid!
Trembles the earth, the rocks are rent,
Fond heart of mine, thou must relent.
Tears from our sorrowing eyes we weep;
Therefore so firm our faith we keep
With all our hearts—with all our senses.
Christ bore his pangs for our offenses.
Ply well the scourge for Jesus' sake,
And God through Christ your sins shall take.
For love of God abandon sin,
To mend your vicious lives begin,
So shall we his mercy win.
Direful was Maria's pain
When she beheld her dear One slain.
Pierced was her soul as with a dart:
Sinner, let this affect thy heart.
The time draws near
When God in anger shall appear.
Jesus was refreshed with gall:
Prostrate crosswise let us fall,
Then with uplifted arms arise,
That God with us may sympathize.
Jesus, by thy titles three,
From our bondage set us free.
Jesus, by the precious blood,
Save us from the fiery flood.
Lord, our helplessness defend,
And to our aid thy Spirit send.
If man and wife their vows should break
God will on such his vengeance wreak.
Brimstone and pitch, and mingled gall,
Satan pours on such sinners all.
Truly, the devil's scorn are they:
Therefore, O Lord, thine aid we pray.
Wedlock's an honourable tie
Which God himself doth sanctify.
By this warning, man, abide,
God shall surely punish pride.
Let your precious soul entreat you,
Lay down pride lest vengeance meet you,

I do beseech ye, pride forsake,
So God on us shall pity take.
Christ in heaven, where he commands,
Thus addressed his angel bands:
"Christendom dishonours me,
Therefore her ruin I decree."
Then Mary thus implored her Son:
"Penance to thee, loved Child, be done;
That she repent be mine the care;
Stay then thy wrath, and hear my prayer."
          Ye liars!
Ye that break your sacrament,
Shrive ye thoroughly and repent.
Your heinous sins sincerely rue,
So shall the Lord your hearts renew.
          Woe! usurer, though thy wealth abound,
For every ounce thou mak'st a pound
Shall sink thee to the hell profound.
Ye murd'rers, and ye robbers all,
The wrath of God on you shall fall.
Mercy ye ne'er to others show,
None shall ye find; but endless woe.
Had it not been for our contrition,
All Christendom had met perdition.
Satan had bound her in his chain;
Mary hath loosed her bonds again.
Glad news I bring thee, sinful mortal,
In heaven Saint Peter keeps his portal,
Apply to him with suppliant mien,
He bringeth thee before thy Queen.
Benignant Michael, blessed saint,
Guardian of souls, receive our plaint.
Through thy Almighty Maker's death,
Preserve us from the hell beneath.

Source: "The Ancient Song of the Flagellants." 1859. In *The Epidemics of the Middle Ages*, by J. F. C. Hecker, translated by B. G. Babington. 3d ed. London: Trübner and Co., 65, 67, 69.

A PLAGUE TREATISE ATTRIBUTED TO JOHN OF BURGUNDY (LATER FOURTEENTH CENTURY)

In the wake of the Black Death of 1347–1352, many physicians and lay-people took advantage of growing literacy rates in Europe by publishing short manuals for preventing and treating the plague. By far the most popular was the plague treatise attributed to one John of Burgundy, written around 1365 but republished frequently for the next three centuries. The following excerpt includes John's brief explanation for the causes of the plague, as well as part of his lengthy section on prevention and cure.

Everything below the moon, the elements and the things compounded of the elements, is ruled by the things above, and the highest bodies are believed to give being, nature, substance, growth and death to everything below their spheres. It was, therefore, by the influence of the heavenly bodies that the air was recently corrupted and made pestilential. I do not mean by this that the air is corrupted in its substance—because it is an uncompounded substance and that would be impossible—but it is corrupted by reason of evil vapours mixed with it. The result was a widespread epidemic, traces of which still remain in several places. Many people have been killed, especially those stuffed full of evil humours, for the cause of the mortality is not only the corruption of the air, but the abundance of corrupt humours within those who die of the disease. For as Galen says in the book of fevers, the body suffers no corruption unless the material of the body has a tendency towards it, and is in some way subject to the corruptive cause; for just as fire only takes hold on combustible material, so pestilential air does no harm to a body unless it finds a blemish where corruption can take hold. As a result, cleansed bodies, where the puration of evil humours has not been neglected, remain healthy. Likewise those whose complexion is contrary to the immutable complexion of air remain healthy. For otherwise everybody would fall ill and die whenever the air is corrupted.

It follows that corrupt air generates different diseases in different people, depending on their different humours, because it always develops according to the predisposition of the matter it has entered. And therefore there are many masters of the art of medicine who are admirable scholars, well-versed in theories and hypotheses, but who are too little experienced in the practicalities and are entirely ignorant of astrology: a science vital to the physician, as Hippocrates testifies in his *Epidemia*, where he says that no one ought to be put under the care of any physician who

is ignorant of astrology. For the arts of medicine and astrology balance
each other, and in many respects one science supports the other in that
one cannot be understood without the other. I am as a result convinced
by practical experience that medicine—however well it has been compounded and chosen according to medical rules—does not work as the
practitioner intends and is of no benefit to the patient if it is given when
the planets are contrary. Thus if medicine is given as a laxative it should
be with reference to the planets if the patient is to empty his bowels successfully, and also if he is not to have an adverse reaction to the medicine.
Accordingly those who have drunk too little of the nectar of astrology
cannot offer a remedy for epidemic diseases. Because they are ignorant of
the cause and quality of the disease they cannot cure it; for as the prince
of doctors says: 'how can you cure, if you are ignorant of the cause?'
And Avicenna in *Concerning the cure of fevers* emphasizes: 'It is impossible
that someone ignorant of the cause should cure the disease'. Averroes also
makes the point, saying: 'It is not to be understood, except by grasping
the immediate and ultimate cause'. Since, therefore, the heavens are the
first cause, that is the cause it is necessary to understand, since ignorance of the highest cause entails ignorance of the subsequent cause, and
also because the primary cause has a greater impact than the secondary
cause. . . .

CONCERNING PREVENTION. First, you should avoid over-
indulgence in food and drink, and also avoid baths and everything which
might rarefy the body and open the pores, for the pores are the doorways
through which poisonous air can enter, piercing the heart and corrupting
the life force. Above all sexual intercourse should be avoided. You should
eat little or no fruit, unless it is sour, and should consume easily-digested
food and spiced wine diluted with water. Avoid mead and everything else
made with honey, and season food with strong vinegar. In cold or rainy
weather you should light fires in your chamber and in foggy or windy
weather you should inhale aromatics every morning before leaving home:
ambergris, musk, rosemary and similar things if you are rich; zedoary,
cloves, nutmeg, mace and similar things if you are poor. Also once or
twice a week you should take a dose of good theriac the size of a bean.
And carry in the hand a ball of ambergris or other suitable aromatic.
Later, on going to be, shut the windows and burn juniper branches, so
that the smoke and scent fills the room. Or put four live coals in an earth-
enware vessel and sprinkle a little of the following powder on them and
inhale the smoke through mouth and nostrils before going to sleep: take

white frankincense, labdanum, storax, calaminth, and wood of aloes and grind them to a very fine powder. And do this as often as a foetid or bad odour can be detected in the air, and especially when the weather is foggy or the air tainted, and it can protect against the epidemic.

If, however, the epidemic occurs during hot weather it becomes necessary to adopt another regimen, and to eat cold things rather than hot and also to eat more sparingly than in cold weather. You should drink more than you eat, and take white wine with water. You should also use large amounts of vinegar and verjuice in preparing food, but be sparing with hot substances such as pepper, galingale or grains of paradise. Before leaving home in the morning smell roses, violets, lilies, white and red sandalwood, musk or camphor if the weather is misty or the air quality bad. Take theriac sparingly in hot weather, and not at all unless you are a phlegmatic or of a cold complexion. Sanguines and cholerics should not take theriac at all in hot weather, but should take pomegranates, oranges, lemons, or quinces, or an electuary made of the three types of sandalwood, or a cold electuary or similar. You should use cucumbers, fennel, borage, bugloss and spinach, and avoid garlic, onions, leeks and everything else which generates excessive heat, such as pepper or grains of paradise, although ginger, cinnamon, saffron, cumin and other temperate substances can be used. And if you should become extremely thirsty because of the hot weather, then drink cold water mixed with vinegar or barleywater regularly, for this is particularly beneficial to people of a cold and dry complexion and to thin people, and thirst should never be tolerated at such times.

If you should feel a motion of the blood like a fluttering or prickling, let blood from the nearest vein on the same side of the body, and the floor of the room in which you are lying should be sprinkled two or three times a day with cold water and vinegar, or with rose water if you can afford it. The pills of Rasis, if taken once a week, are an outstanding preventative and work for all complexions and in all seasons, but Avicenna and others recommend that they be taken on a full stomach. They loosen the bowels a little, but the corrupt humours are expelled gradually. They should be made as follows: take Socotra aloes, saffron, myrrh and blend them in a syrup of fumitory. Anyone who adopts this regimen can be preserved, with God's help, from pestilence caused by corruption of the air.

Source: "The Treatise of John of Burgundy." 1994. In *The Black Death*, edited and translated by Rosemary Horrox. Manchester: Manchester University Press, 184–88.

GIOVANNI BOCCACCIO, *DECAMERON*, INTRODUCTION (1353)

Giovanni Boccaccio (1313–1375) is one of the key authors of the early Italian Renaissance, known especially for his story cycle known as the Decameron, *completed in 1353. Boccaccio's introduction to the "First Day" (the book is divided into ten days of stories) is the most famous literary treatments of the Black Death, and is generally considered to be a faithful representation of the plague in Florence even though it comes at the start of a collection of fictional and humorous tales. Boccaccio provides careful, analytical descriptions of the symptoms of the plague and the scope of the mortality, as well as the social and religious reactions of the desperate Florentine population.*

I say, then, that the years of the beatific incarnation of the Son of God had reached the tale of one thousand three hundred and forty eight, when in the illustrious city of Florence, the fairest of all the cities of Italy, there made its appearance that deadly pestilence, which, whether disseminated by the influence of the celestial bodies, or sent upon us mortals by God in His just wrath by way of retribution for our iniquities, had had its origin some years before in the East, whence, after destroying an innumerable multitude of living beings, it had propagated itself without respite from place to place, and so calamitously, had spread into the West.

In Florence, despite all that human wisdom and forethought could devise to avert it, as the cleansing of the city from many impurities by officials appointed for the purpose, the refusal of entrance to all sick folk, and the adoption of many precautions for the preservation of health; despite also humble supplications addressed to God, and often repeated both in public procession and otherwise by the devout; towards the beginning of the spring of the said year the doleful effects of the pestilence began to be horribly apparent by symptoms that shewed as if miraculous.

Not such were they as in the East, where an issue of blood from the nose was a manifest sign of inevitable death; but in men and women alike it first betrayed itself by the emergence of certain tumors in the groin or the armpits, some of which grew as large as a common apple, others as an egg, some more, some less, which the common folk called *gavoccioli*. From the two said parts of the body this deadly gavocciolo soon began to propagate and spread itself in all directions indifferently; after which the form of the malady began to change, black spots or livid making their appearance in many cases on the arm or the thigh or elsewhere, now few and large, then minute and numerous. And as the gavocciolo had been and still were an infallible token of approaching death, such also were these spots on whomsoever they shewed themselves. Which maladies seemed set entirely at naught both the art of the physician and the virtue of physic; indeed, whether it was that the disorder was of a nature to defy such treatment, or that the physicians were at fault—besides the qualified there was now a multitude both of men and of women who practiced without having received the slightest tincture of medical science—and, being in ignorance of its source, failed to apply the proper remedies; in either case, not merely were those that covered few, but almost all within three days from the appearance of the said symptoms, sooner or later, died, and in most cases without any fever or other attendant malady.

Moreover, the virulence of the pest was the greater by reason the intercourse was apt to convey it from the sick to the whole, just as fire devours things dry or greasy when they are brought close to it, the evil went yet further, for not merely by speech or association with the sick was the malady communicated to the healthy with consequent peril of common death; but any that touched the clothes the sick or aught else that had been touched, or used by these seemed thereby to contract the disease.

So marvelous sounds that which I have now to relate, that, had not many, and I among them, observed it with their own eyes, I had hardly dared to credit it, much less to set it down in writing, though I had had it from the lips of a credible witness.

I say, then, that such was the energy of the contagion of the said pestilence, that it was not merely propagated from man to mail, but, what is much more startling, it was frequently observed, that things which had belonged to one sick or dead of the disease, if touched by some other living creature, not of the human species, were the occasion, not merely of sickening, but of an almost instantaneous death. Whereof my own eyes (as I said a little before) had cognisance, one day among others, by the following experience. The rags of a poor man who had died of the disease being strewn about the open street, two hogs came thither, and after, as is their wont, no little trifling with their snouts, took the rags between their teeth and tossed them to and fro about their chaps; whereupon, almost immediately, they gave a few turns, and fell down dead, as if by poison, upon the rags which in an evil hour they had disturbed.

In which circumstances, not to speak of many others of a similar or even graver complexion, divers apprehensions and imaginations were engendered in the minds of such as were left alive, inclining almost all of them to the same harsh resolution, to wit, to shun and abhor all contact with the sick and all that belonged to them, thinking thereby to make each his own health secure. Among whom there were those who thought that to live temperately and avoid all excess would count for much as a preservative against seizures of this kind. Wherefore they banded together, and dissociating themselves from all others, formed communities in houses where there were no sick, and lived a separate and secluded life, which they regulated with the utmost care, avoiding every kind of luxury, but eating and drinking moderately of the most delicate viands and the finest wines, holding converse with none but one another, lest tidings of sickness or death should reach them, and diverting their minds with music and such other delights as they could devise. Others, the bias of whose minds was in the opposite direction, maintained, that to drink freely, frequent places of public resort, and take their pleasure with song and revel, sparing to satisfy no appetite, and to laugh and mock at no event, was the sovereign remedy for so great an evil: and that which they affirmed they also put in practice, so far as they were able, resorting day and night, now to this tavern, now to that, drinking with an entire disregard of rule or measure, and by preference making the houses of others, as it were, their inns, if they but saw in them aught that was particularly to their taste or liking; which they, were readily able to do, because the owners, seeing death imminent, had become as reckless of their property as of their lives; so that most of the houses were open to all comers, and no distinction was observed between the stranger who presented himself and the rightful lord. Thus, adhering ever to their inhuman determination to shun the sick, as far as possible, they ordered their life. In this extremity of our city's suffering and tribulation the venerable authority of laws, human and divine, was abased and all but totally dissolved for lack of those who should have administered and enforced them, most of whom, like the rest of the citizens, were either dead or sick or so hard bested for servants that they were unable to execute any office; whereby every man was free to do what was right in his own eyes.

Not a few there were who belonged to neither of the two said parties, but kept a middle course between them, neither laying the same restraint upon their diet as the former, nor allowing themselves the same license in drinking and other dissipations as the latter, but living with a degree of freedom sufficient to satisfy their appetite and not as recluses. They therefore walked abroad, carrying in the hands flowers or fragrant herbs or divers sorts of spices, which they frequently raised to their noses, deeming it an excellent thing thus to comfort the brain with such perfumes, because the air seemed be everywhere laden and reeking with the stench emitted by the dead and the dying, and the odours of drugs.

Some again, the most sound, perhaps, in judgment, as they were also the most harsh in temper, of all, affirmed that there was no medicine for the disease superior or equal in efficacy to flight; following which pre-scription a multitude of men and women, negligent of all but themselves, deserted their city, their houses, their estates, their kinsfolk, their goods, and went into voluntary exile, or migrated to the country parts, as if God in visiting men with this pestilence in requital of their iniquities would not pursue them with His wrath wherever they might be, but intended the destruction of such alone as remained within the circuit of the walls of the city; or deeming perchance, that it was now time for all to flee from it, and that its last hour was come.

Of the adherents of these divers opinions not all died, neither did all escape; but rather there were, of each sort and in every place many that sickened, and by those who retained their health were treated after the example which they themselves, while whole, had set, being everywhere left to languish in almost total neglect. Tedious were it to recount, how citizen avoided citizen, how among neighbors was scarce found any that shewed fellow-feeling for another, how kinsfolk held aloof, and never met, or but rarely; enough that this sore affliction entered so deep into the minds of men and women, that in the horror thereof brother was forsaken by brother nephew by uncle, brother by sister, and oftentimes husband by wife: nay, what is more, and scarcely to be believed, fathers and mothers were found to abandon their own children, untended, unvisited, to their fate, as if they had been strangers. Wherefore the sick of both sexes, whose number could not be estimated, were left without resource but in the charity of friends (and few such there were), or the interest of servants, who were hardly to be had at high rates and on unseemly terms, and being, moreover, one and all, men and women of gross understanding, and for the most part unused to such offices, concerned themselves no further than to supply the immediate and expressed wants of the sick, and to watch them die; in which service they themselves not seldom perished with their gains. In consequence of which dearth of servants and dere-liction of the sick by neighbors, kinsfolk and friends, it came to pass—a thing, perhaps, never before heard of—that no woman, however dainty, fair or well-born she might be, shrank, when stricken with the disease, from the ministrations of a man, no matter whether he were young or no, or scrupled to expose to him every part of her body, with no more shame than if he had been a woman, submitting of necessity to that which her malady required; wherefrom, perchance, there resulted in after time some loss of modesty in such as recovered. Besides which many succumbed, who with proper attendance, would, perhaps, have escaped death; so that, what with the virulence of the plague and the lack of due attendance of the sick, the multitude of the deaths, that daily and nightly took place in the city, was such that those who heard the tale—not to say witnessed the fact—were struck dumb with amazement. Whereby, practices contrary to the former habits of the citizens could hardly fail to grow up among the survivors.

It had been, as to-day it still is, the custom for the women that were neighbors and of kin to the deceased to gather in his house with the women that were most closely connected with him, to wail with them in common, while on the other hand his male kinsfolk and neighbors, with not a few of the other citizens, and a due proportion of the clergy according to his quality, assembled without, in front of the house, to receive the corpse; and so the dead man was borne on the shoulders of his peers, with funeral pomp of taper and dirge, to the church selected by him before his death. Which rites, as the pestilence waxed in fury, were either in whole or in great part disused, and gave way to others of a novel order. For not only did no crowd of women surround the bed of the dying, but many passed from this life unregarded, and few indeed were they to whom were accorded the lamentations and bitter tears of sorrowing relations; nay, for the most part, their place was taken by the laugh, the jest, the festal gathering; observances which the women, domestic piety in large measure set aside, had adopted with very great advantage to their health. Few also there were whose bodies were attended to the church by more than ten or twelve of their neighbors, and those not the honorable and respected citizens; but a sort of corpse-carriers drawn from the baser ranks, who called themselves *becchini* and performed such offices for hire, would shoulder the bier, and with hurried steps carry it, not to the church of the dead man's choice, but to that which was nearest at hand, with four or six priests in front and a candle or two, or, perhaps, none; nor did the priests distress themselves with too long and solemn an office, but with the aid of the *becchini* hastily consigned the corpse to the first tomb which they found untenanted. The condition of the lower, and, perhaps, in great measure of the middle ranks, of the people shewed even worse and more deplorable; for, deluded by hope or constrained by poverty, they stayed in their quarters, in their houses where they sickened by thousands a day, and, being without service or help of any kind, were, so to speak, irredeemably devoted to the death which overtook them. Many died daily or nightly in the public streets; of many others, who died at home, the departure was hardly observed by their neighbors, until the stench of their putrefying bodies carried the tidings; and what with their corpses and the corpses of others who died on every hand the whole place was a sepulchre.

It was the common practice of most of the neighbors, moved no less by fear of contamination by the putrefying bodies than by charity towards the deceased, to drag the corpses out of the houses with their own hands, aided, perhaps, by a porter, if a porter was to be had, and to lay them in front of the doors, where anyone who made the round might have seen, especially in the morning, more of them than he could count; afterwards they would have biers brought up or in default, planks, whereon they laid them. Nor was it once twice only that one and the same bier carried two or three corpses at once; but quite a considerable number of such cases occurred, one bier sufficing for husband and wife, two or three brothers, father and son, and so forth. And times without number it happened, that as two priests, bearing the cross, were on their way to perform the last office for some one, three or four biers were brought up by the porters in rear of them, so that, whereas the priests supposed that they had but one corpse to bury, they discovered that there were six or eight, or sometimes more. Nor, for all their number, were their obsequies honored by either tears or lights or crowds of mourners rather, it was come to this, that a dead man was then of no more account than a dead goat would be today.

Source: Boccaccio, Giovanni. 1921. *The Decameron*. Translated by J. M. Rigg. 2 vols. London: David Campbell, 1:5–11.

Further Reading

Aberth, John. 2017. *The Black Death: The Great Mortality of 1348–1350. A Brief History with Documents*. 2d ed. New York: Bedford/St. Martin's.

Bauer, Susan Wise. 2007. *The Story of the World: History for the Classical Child*. Rev. ed. Vol. 2, *The Middle Ages, from the Fall of Rome to the Rise of the Renaissance*. Charles City, VA: Peace Hill Press.

Boccaccio, Giovanni. 1921. *The Decameron*. Translated by J. M. Rigg. 2 vols. London: David Campbell.

Boeckl, Christine M. 2000. *Images of Plague and Pestilence: Iconography and Iconology*. Sixteenth Century Essays & Studies, 53. Kirksville, MO: Truman State University Press.

Byrne, Joseph P. 2004. *The Black Death*. Westport, CT: Greenwood Press.

Calvi, Giulia. 1989. *Histories of a Plague Year: The Social and the Imaginary in Baroque Florence*. Translated by Dario Biocca and Bryant T. Ragan, Jr. Foreword by Randolph Stearn. Berkeley: University of California Press.

Cefrey, Holly. 2001. *The Plague*. New York: Rosen Publishing Group.

Cipolla, Carlo M. 1979. *Faith, Reason, and the Plague in Seventeenth-Century Tuscany*. Translated by Muriel Kittel. New York: W. W. Norton and Co.

Davis, James C. 2004. *The Human Story: Our History, from the Stone Age to Today*. New York: Harper Perennial.

Gitlin, Marty. 2016. *The Totally Gross History of Medieval Europe*. New York: Rosen Publishing Group.

Green, Monica H. 2015a. "Editor's Introduction." In *Pandemic Disease in the Medieval World: Rethinking the Black Death*, edited by Monica H. Green, 9-26. Kalamazoo, MI: ARC Medieval Press. http://scholarworks .wmich.edu/medieval_globe/1/.

Green, Monica H. 2015b. "Taking 'Pandemic' Seriously: Making the Black Death Global." In *Pandemic Disease in the Medieval World: Rethinking the Black Death,* edited by Monica H. Green, 27–61. Kalamazoo, MI: ARC Medieval Press. http://scholarworks.wmich.edu/medieval_globe/1/.

Hays, J. N. 2009. "The Great Plague Pandemic." In *The Burdens of Disease. Epidemics and Human Response in Western History,* 37–61. Rev. ed. New Brunswick, NJ: Rutgers University Press.

Horrox, Rosemary. 1994. *The Black Death*. Manchester Medieval Sources Series. Manchester: Manchester University Press.

Jeffrey, Gary, and Alessandro Poluzzi. 2013. *The Black Death*. New York: Crabtree Publishing Company.

Jones, Lori, and Richard Nevell. 2016. "Plague by Doubt and Viral Misinformation: The Need for Evidence-Based Use of Historical Disease Images." *Lancet Infectious Diseases* 16, no. 10: e235–40. https://doi.org/10.1016/S1473-3099(16)30119-0.

Leasor, James. 1961. *The Plague and the Fire*. New York: McGraw-Hill.

Manchester, William. 1992. *A World Lit Only by Fire: The Medieval Mind and the Renaissance. Portrait of an Age*. Boston: Little, Brown and Co.

Manget, Jean Jacques. 1721. *Traité de la peste*. 2 vols. Geneva: Philippe Planche.

Mikkelson, David. 2000. "Is 'Ring around the Rosie' about the Black Plague?" *Snopes.com.* https://www.snopes.com/language/literary/rosie.asp.

Opie, Iona, and Peter Opie. 1985. *The Singing Game*. Oxford: Oxford University Press.

Tibayrenc, Michel, ed. 2007. *Encyclopedia of Infectious Diseases: Modern Methodologies*. Hoboken, NJ: Wiley-Liss.

Townsend, G. L. 1965. "The Plague Doctor." *Journal of the History of Medicine and Allied Sciences* 20, no. 3:276.

Bibliography

The following bibliography includes recent, readily accessible, English-language books that are related to the topic. It is not meant to be comprehensive, but rather to introduce curious readers to the broader fields of medieval history and medievalism.

Aberth, John. 2003. *A Knight at the Movies: Medieval History on Film.* New York: Routledge.

Alexander, Michael. 2007. *Medievalism: The Middle Ages in Modern England.* New Haven, CT: Yale University Press.

Andrea, Alfred J., and Andrew Holt, eds. 2015. *Seven Myths of the Crusades.* Indianapolis, IN: Hackett Publishing.

Arnold, John H. 2008. *What Is Medieval History?* Cambridge: Polity Press.

Brentjes, Sonja, Taner Edis, and Lutz Richter-Bernburg, eds. 2016. *1001 Distortions: How (Not) to Narrate History of Science, Medicine, and Technology in Non-Western Cultures.* Würzburg: Ergon Verlag.

Bull, Marcus. 2005. *Thinking Medieval: An Introduction to the Study of the Middle Ages.* Houndsmills, Basingstoke, UK: Palgrave Macmillan.

Classen, Albrecht, ed. 2017. *Bodily and Spiritual Hygiene in Medieval and Early Modern Literature: Explorations of Textual Presentations of Filth and Water.* Berlin: De Gruyter.

D'Arcens, Louise, ed. 2016. *The Cambridge Companion to Medievalism.* Cambridge: Cambridge University Press.

Demaitre, Luke. 2013. *Medieval Medicine: The Art of Healing, from Head to Toe.* Santa Barbara, CA: Praeger.

Elliott, Andrew B. R. 2017. *Medievalism, Politics, and Mass Media: Appropriating the Middle Ages in the Twenty-First Century*. Woodbridge, Suffolk, UK: D. S. Brewer.

Gies, Joseph, and Frances Gies. 1990. *Life in a Medieval Village*. New York: Harper and Row.

Harris, Stephen J., and Bryon L. Grigsby, eds. 2007. *Misconceptions about the Middle Ages*. New York: Routledge.

Harty, Kevin J. 1999. *The Reel Middle Ages: American, Western and Eastern European, Middle Eastern and Asian Films about Medieval Europe*. Jefferson, NC: McFarland and Co.

Heng, Geraldine. 2018. *The Invention of Race in the European Middle Ages*. Cambridge: Cambridge University Press.

Kieckhefer, Richard. 2000. *Magic in the Middle Ages*. Cambridge: Cambridge University Press.

Lindberg, David C. 2007. *The Beginnings of Western Science: The European Scientific Tradition in Philosophical, Religious, and Institutional Context, Prehistory to A.D. 1450*. 2d ed. Chicago: University of Chicago Press.

Powell, James M. 1992. *Medieval Studies: An Introduction*. 2d ed. Syracuse, NY: Syracuse University Press.

Riddle, John M., and Winston Black. 2016. *A History of the Middle Ages, 300–1500*. 2d ed. Lanham, MD: Rowman & Littlefield.

Rosenwein, Barbara H. 2018. *A Short History of the Middle Ages*. 5th ed. Toronto: University of Toronto Press.

Wells, Peter S. 2008. *Barbarians to Angels: The Dark Ages Reconsidered*. New York: W. W. Norton.

Wollenberg, Daniel. 2018. *Medieval Imagery in Today's Politics*. Kalamazoo, MI: ARC Humanities Press.

Index

Page numbers in *italics* indicate illustrations.

About the Author

Winston Black is a scholar and professor of medieval history. He specializes in the history of science and medicine in the medieval world, and explores the interactions of medicine and herbalism with the religious cultures of Europe and the Mediterranean. He is the editor and translator of Henry of Huntingdon's *Anglicanus Ortus: A Verse Herbal of the Twelfth Century* (2012), author of *Medicine and Healing in the Premodern West: A History in Documents* (2019), and coauthor with John M. Riddle of *A History of the Middle Ages, 300–1500*, 2d. ed. (2016). He lives in New England with his wife, Emily Reiner (also a medievalist); two boys; and two cats.

Printed in the USA
CPSIA information can be obtained
at www.ICGtesting.com
LVHW012043231223
767103LV00006B/180